Preface

In India, over the past several years food inflation has been a matter of great concern for the economists and policy makers. Several studies have been conducted on food inflation but the results were inadequate to arrive at policy decisions to contain it. The data on Household Monthly Per capita Consumption Expenditure on food provided by National Sample Survey Organization is useful to know the pattern of consumption and changes in the level of consumption. However, the findings of NSS do not reveal any concrete evidence in support of the popular view that the change in the pattern and level of consumption is the outcome of high food inflation in the economy. In order to arrive at more realistic understanding in to the phenomenon we need to determine the relationship between high food inflation and Household Consumption Expenditure on food. This requires a qualitative study of the phenomenon which would uncover the fact that how people manage their household consumption expenditure on food articles along side high food inflation in the economy.

This book is a write up of the doctoral thesis entitled "An analytical study of food inflation and its management by middle class consumers in Thane city, 2006-2011". The book is a guide to social science research. We hope that the book would help the readers, specially, researchers to conduct multidisciplinary research in the area of business management. The book covers theoretical aspect of the research process and the use of statistical software package such as SPSS. It has also given how to conduct statistical test in SPSS and how to interpret results.

We will be grateful to the readers who send their valuable suggestions and comments for enabling us to improve on the book. The suggestions and feedback can be sent on dineshgabhane.phd@gmail.com and s.b.kishor.spc@gmail.com.

DINESH T. GABHANE

DR. S. B. KISHOR

ACKNOWLEDGEMENT

It is a matter of great privilege and sense of achievement that I have completed my Thesis. This would not have been possible without the unrelenting support of whole team of people with whom I interacted during the course of my research work.

I would like to convey my heartiest thanks and gratitude to all of them. Their contribution and support cannot be expressed in words and no amount of repeated thanks can pay it off.

I would like to thank my supervisor **Dr. S. B. Kishor**, under whose guidance this work has been carried out. His constant guidance, effective suggestions, critical appraisals, encouragement, moral support, etc. helped me to complete my thesis.

I would also like to express my sincere thanks to **Dr. Vinayak Deshpande, Head of Research, Department of Business Management, RTMNU, Nagpur,** for sparing his valuable time for going through the progress reports. Without his support the work would have not been completed.

I am thankful to **Dr. Vilas S. Sapkal, Vice Chancellor of Rashtrasant Tukadoji Maharaj Nagpur University** for providing peaceful environment for carrying out research activities. I am also thankful to the various **Departments of the Ministry, Government of India,** whose timely publication of statistical data on their website helped me in my analysis.

I am also thankful to **Dr. Sachin Deshmukh, fellow Professors and Management students** who always stood by my side in all time of need and helped me in completion of my work.

I am highly **indebted to my parents and my wife** who allowed me to continue my educational pursuits without worrying of the household needs.

At last I would like to thank **Almighty Supreme Force of Universe- Lord Ganesha,** who permitted me to concentrate all my energies on the work and ensured timely successful completion of the work.

DINESH T. GABHANE

ABSTRACT

In India, over the last couple of years, food inflation has been a major cause of concern for the common man who spends nearly half of his household income on food. The long-term average trend of primary food articles in WPI shows a shift from an average rate of 2.4 percent in 2001-05 to 9.2 percent in 2006-10, which was above the tolerance limit. The trend continued to remain upward in 2010-11 with an average rate of 15.8 percent and thereafter. Therefore, the years between 2006 and 2011 were very crucial from the study point of view. Several studies have been conducted on food inflation but these were related to the cause, measures, types, effects of food inflation, etc. NSSO conducts household consumption expenditure survey at national level. However, the findings of NSS can be applied to population of the country at large, but may or may not be applied to a specific class of people from the population of a specific city. There is a need to assess the household consumption expenditure of the lower middle class consumers especially how they manage their consumption expenditure on food articles along side high food inflation.

In this study, the attempt has been made to gain better understanding of the facts in to the phenomenon of food inflation and analyze the management of household consumption expenditure of lower middle class consumers on food articles. To conduct the study, the lower middle class households of Thane city were chosen as a target population. Reason behind selecting lower middle class households from Thane city was that, the city has witnessed a large number of middle class people. Since, the cost of living is very high, every rise in the food prices takes a toll on their pocket. To better understand and make it more meaningful, the management of household consumption expenditure on food articles is disaggregated in to management of CE quantity wise or quality wise or frequency wise.

Survey method was adopted and questionnaire with close ended questions were filled up from the respondents of the Thane city drawn through stratified sampling technique with the help of properly administered interview. Survey data were processed on SPSS (statistical package) at 5% level of significance with the help of statistical tools and techniques such as correlation analysis, regression analysis and factor analysis. Also, reliability test has been conducted to measure the consistency of the data collected and reliability of the measures used.

Finally, from the findings of the study, it has been concluded that, due to high food inflation quantity wise consumption of fruits, vegetables is significantly affected; quality wise consumption of food grains, vegetables and tea is significantly affected, and frequency wise consumption of vegetables, fruits, egg, meat & fish gets and tea is significantly affected.

In other words, persistence of high food inflation in the economy is alarming. Government has to take measures suggested in this study just not to make available food but assure food security through proper dissemation of policies. From researchers and academician view point such a study will help in exploring knowledge in this area of learning.

TABLE OF CONTENTS

LIST OF FIGURES

data view)

LIST OF ACRONYMS

AAY	Antyodaya Anna Yojana
AD	Aggregate Demand
AS	Aggregate Supply
APMC	Agricultural Produce Market Committee
BPL	Below Poverty Level
CIP	Central Issue Price
CRR	Cash Reserve Ratio
CSO	Central Statistics Office
CMCR	Centre for Macro Consumer Research
CE	Consumption Expenditure
CES	Consumption Expenditure Survey
CGIAR	Consultative Group on International Agricultural Research
CIF	Cost, Insurance, Freight
CPI	Consumer Price Index
CPI-AL	Consumer Price Index for Agricultural Labourers
CPI-IW	Consumer Price Index for Industrial Workers
CPI-RL	Consumer Price Index for Rural Labourers
CPI-UNME	Consumer Price Index-Urban Non-Manual Employees
ECA	Essential Commodities Act
EDEs	Emerging and Developing Economies
ESR	Environmental Status Report
FA	Food Articles
FAO	Food and Agriculture Organization
FAPI	Food Articles Price Index
FCI	Food Corporation of India
FDI	Foreign Direct Investment
FI	Food Inflation
FOB	Free on Board
FOMC	Federal Open Market Committee

GoI	Government of India
GNP	Gross National Product
HCE	Household Consumption Expenditure
IPI	Implicit Price Index
IT	Inflation Targeting
KMO	Kaiser-Meyer-Olkin
KMS	Kharif Marketing Seasons
LMCHs	Lower Middle Class Households
MEP	Minimum Export Prices
MGI	McKinsey Global Institute
MSA	Measures of Sampling Adequacy
MSP	Minimum Support Price
MoF	Ministry of Finance
MOSPI	Ministry of Statistics & Programme Implementation
MPCE	Monthly Per Capita Consumer Expenditure
NAADS	National Agricultural Advisory Services
NCAER	National Council of Advance Economic Research
NCEUS	National Commission for Enterprises in the Unorganized Sector
NFSM	National Food Security Mission
NHM	National Horticulture Mission
NSS	National Sample Survey
NSSO	National Sample Survey Organization
NDTL	Net Demand & Time Liabilities
OMSS	Open Market Sales Scheme
TFP	Total Factor Productivity
TPDS	Targeted Public Distribution System
PDS	Public Distribution System
PDFS	Public Food Distribution System
PPI	Producer Price Index
PTI	Press Trust of India
RMS	Rabi Marketing Seasons

RKVY	Rashtriya Krishi Vikas Yojana
RBI	Reserve Bank of India
SLR	Statutory Liquidity Ratio
TE	Triennium Ending
TMC	Thane Municipal Corporation
UNHS	Uganda National Household Survey
US	United States
WFPI	Wholesale Food Price Index
WPI	Wholesale Price Index

CHAPTER 1: INTRODUCTION

Chapter Highlights:

1.1 Introduction to the topic

1.2 Rationale of the Study

1.3 Aim & Objectives of the Study

1.4 Hypotheses of the Study

1.5 Significance of the Study

1.6 Scope & Limitations of the Study

1.7 Conceptual Framework of the study

1.1 INTRODUCTION TO THE TOPIC

In recent years, the major economic challenge faced by India has been the persistence rise in food prices. In India, last two decades have recorded substantial economic growth and improvements in livelihood among urban populations. High rate of development and urbanization results in the increase of middle class. Opinion survey in India reveals that inflation is the most important concern of the middle class people badly affects their consumption expenditure (CE) and standard of living. The middle class in low and medium income economies in the world is increasingly demanding high value agricultural produce and due to various constraints the prices of the commodities have gone up. It has necessitated aggressive intervention of the central bank in tightening the monetary policy even at the cost of economic growth. But, the high inflationary pressure especially the double digit food inflation has a bearing on the consumption expenditure of food articles. The fact that people in the lower income quartile, accounting for more than a quarter of the population, spend nearly 65% of their total expenditure on food commodities, adds gravity to the situation[1]. Even though, the government took several measures to curb food inflation, the problem still persists. In the city of Thane, Maharashtra, the population of middle class people close to 30 percent of the total population. They spend about half of their income on basic necessities[2] and rest goes to education, savings and investments. Food articles from the basket of primary articles in WPI (2004-05 series) continued to face an upside risk to prices. Every increase in the price of the agriculture commodity has adverse effect on their consumption expenditure and additional burden to their pockets. This study is an attempt to understand the extent of impact of high food inflation on household consumption expenditure of middle class and how they manage their consumption expenditure on food articles (FA) alongside high

---

[1] Ramesh Chand, P. S. (2011, February). Managing food inflation in India: Reforms and policy options, Policy brief 35. *National Centre for Agricultural Economics and Policy Research, New Delhi* .

[2] Beinhocker, D. F. (2007, May 19). Next big spenders: India's middle class. *Mckinsey Global Institute* .

food inflation. Following options are identified by the researcher that one has to choose in order to hedge against the higher food prices such as either compromising or sacrificing or adjusting on quantity of food items or quality of food items or frequency of consumption of food items. Here, managing consumption expenditure on FA refers to the strategy middle class consumers generally adopt to allocate their household expenditure on various food items so that it should not exceed their household budget.

Why middle class in Thane city?

Thane city is a part of Mumbai metropolitan region. According to reports of Census India, population of Thane in 2011 is 1,818,872. Because of the huge residential boom, the city has witnessed a large number of immigrants from the city of Mumbai as well as from other parts of the state and country. In Thane, the cost of living is very high; people spend a large percentage of their household income on basic needs and the disposable income is very less. Food constitutes part of living cost and a persistent rise in food prices put heavy burden on household consumption expenditure. Thane is a city which is dominated by middle class population and therefore, it is possible to analyze how these people are managing their household consumption expenditure on food articles alongside high food inflation.

Gopal Vittal (2011) in his article in The Economic Times on, "Inflation will crush middle class", explained the relevance of this study on middle class households. According to him, as per NCAER-CMCR, country's population is divided into five income quintiles based on NSSO survey on Household Income and Expenditure. The top 20 percent (about 45 million) households account for 52 percent of aggregate income and 39 percent of consumption. However, these top 20 percent households are called as upper class and account for more than 45 percent of aggregate non-food consumption. Considering that this class of households contributes almost 93 percent of aggregate savings and hence food inflation has no impact on them.

There are bottom 40 percent (about 90 million) households that account for 14 percent of income and 22 percent of consumption. Their share of food and non-food consumption is 26 percent and 17 percent. They spend a bulk of their household income about 63 percent on food and buy the bare necessities in terms of non-food items. Looking in to their massive spend on food, these are households that are being restraint with inflation and even forced to make greater sacrifices than normally they are used to. However, there is no impact on their savings since these households do not save money anyway.

The most vulnerable are the households that fall in the middle 40 percent (about 90 million) households that account for almost 34 percent of aggregate income and 39 percent of aggregate consumption. They spend about 54 percent of their household income on food and about 5-7 percent each on housing, clothing, education, durables, transport, health and other nonfood items. Their spending on food has now increasing up to 65-67 percent of their household income. To cope with this situation, they have to cut down their consumption wherever possible, buy cheaper products, postpone purchases and cut down discretionary spends. With food being bigger part of their household expenditure their saving is likely to disappear.

1.2 RATIONALE OF THE STUDY

In India, over the past couple of years, food inflation has been the matter of great concern not only to the policy makers but also to the common man who spends almost half of the expenditure on food (NSSO, 2011). No wonder, saying high food inflation inflicts hidden tax on common man.

The period between 2000-01 and 2007-08, saw an average WPI rate of 5.2 percent, which, however, escalated to 7.4 percent post-2008 crisis period. The food inflation especially the food articles price index (FAPI), increased at an even faster pace. The WPI Food inflation has averaged 10 percent during FY 2008-09 to December 2012[3].

The Government of India and Reserve Bank of India take several measures to curb inflation but these efforts are not adequate to bring it down to a comfortable level of 4-5 percent. Moreover, increasing CRR, repo rate and reverse repo rate (policy rates) could affect the growth of the economy.

Correct diagnosis about the nature, structure, causes and factors influencing food inflation is difficult to reach at any policy decision to contain it within comfortable levels.

In India, numerous studies have been done on food inflation covering various aspects related to it. There is a need to focus on impact of high food inflation on the consumption expenditure of lower middle class people of urban population where the cost of living is high.

Findings of the previous studies reveal that, with rising incomes, people switch from cereals based diet to protein based diet i.e. the pressure on prices is more on protein foods (pulses, milk and milk products, eggs, meat and fish) as well as on fruits and vegetables rather than on cereals. These findings may be applicable to the entire population of the country but could not hold true for a specific class of population without ascertaining the increase in real income of households.

National Sample Survey Organization (NSSO), an organization of ministry of statistics & programme implementation (MOSPI), government of India, conducts

---

[3] Ashok Gulati, S. J. (2013, February). Farm trade: tapping the hidden potential. *Commission for Agricultural Costs & Prices, Discussion Paper No. 3, Department of Agriculture and Cooperation, Ministry of Agriculture, GoI, New Delhi GOI, , pp. 1-29.*

household consumption expenditure survey countrywide with the aim to estimate the household Monthly Per Capita Consumer Expenditure (MPCE) and the distribution of households and persons over the MPCE range. This survey helps to find out the differences in level of living of different segments of the population; enables the apex planning and decision making process to allocate nation's resources among sectors, regions, and socio-economic groups; survey data is used to study the level of nutrition of different regions and disparities therein, and in studying demand and supply of commodities (NSS 68th round survey). NSSO estimates of the consumption data would be useful in measuring the quantity wise consumption of food item but fails to explain the cause behind the change in their level of consumption whereas, in this study, the researcher attempts to determine the relationship between food inflation and change in their level and pattern of consumption.

The present study largely focused on lower middle class consumers of Thane city covering the issues related to the impact of high food inflation on their household consumption expenditure and how they manage their household expenditure on food items. The researcher acknowledges and extends the work of NSSO. However, this study differs from NSS in many ways. First, the NSS conduct longitudinal studies to find out the changes in household monthly per capita consumption expenditure whereas, in this study, the researcher has conducted cross-sectional study to find out the impact of food inflation on household consumption expenditure. Second, the NSS conducts surveys at national level whereas the present study emphasizes on a specific class of people from the population of a city. Third, the NSS covers broad range of items in the surveys whereas this study is limited to primary food articles from the WPI. Fourth, the NSS MPCE figures are mainly used to study the pattern and level of consumption but, the present study, besides understanding pattern and level of consumption would be useful in analyzing the management of the consumption expenditure and relative importance of the food items in the food basket.

1.3 AIM & OBJECTIVES OF THE STUDY

The *aim* of this research is to obtain new insights into the problem of food inflation and to study the current problems and opportunities for suitable follow-up actions.

The *objectives* of the research are as follows:

1) To get better understanding of the facts into the phenomenon of inflation in general and food inflation in particular.

2) To determine the relationship between impact of high food inflation on household consumption expenditure on food composite and individual food items.

3) To determine the extent of relationship between impact of high food inflation on household consumption expenditure on food composite and individual food items.

4) To explore how lower middle class consumers manage their consumption expenditure on food items along side high food inflation.

5) To analyze the food items from the basket of food articles on which consumption expenditure gets affected significantly in terms of quantity along side high food inflation.

6) To analyze the food items from the basket of food articles on which consumption expenditure gets affected significantly in terms of quality along side high food inflation.

7) To analyze the food items from the basket of food articles on which consumption expenditure gets affected significantly in terms of frequency of consumption along side high food inflation.

1.4 HYPOTHESIS OF THE STUDY

A hypothesis is a supposition or guess put forward to account for certain facts and used as a basis for further investigation by which it may be proved or disproved.

Following are the hypotheses drawn from the research problem. These hypotheses cover second and third objective of the research.

H_{01}: There exists no significant relationship between impact of high food inflation on household consumption expenditure of food composite and individual food items.

H_{a1}: There exists significant relationship between impact of high food inflation on household consumption expenditure of food composite and individual food items.

H_{02}: There exists no significant change in household consumption expenditure on food composite with the corresponding change in individual food items along side high food inflation.

H_{a2}: There exists significant change in household consumption expenditure on food composite with the corresponding change in individual food items along side high food inflation.

Where, H_0: Null Hypothesis & H_a: Alternate Hypothesis.

For objectives fifth, sixth and seventh, no specific hypothesis is formulated.

1.5 SIGNIFICANCE OF THE STUDY

1) It helps to understand the level of nutrition in the lower middle class people of the population.

2) The household consumption expenditure on different food items are generally used as a yardstick for measuring standard of living.

3) It helps to understand the structural shift of consumers from cereals based diet to protein based diet (dietary pattern).

4) It helps to adjust the weights of commodities in CPI based on their relative importance in the food basket.

5) It helps the government in welfare planning for the vulnerable sections of the population, consumer surveys and framing policies.

6) It provides a road map for proper food management especially timely procurement of agricultural produce and open market sale of the same, whenever need arises.

7) It suggests for framing of proper export and import policy, so that, the domestic demand for the food commodities should be fulfilled.

8) It suggests for effective monetary policy in place resulting in high economic growth of the country and moderate inflation rate.

9) It helps to control the prices of the essential commodities by keeping watch on hoarders and restricting the role of middlemen in the wholesale transaction of such commodities.

10) It creates an urgent need among the policy makers to invest in research and development of agriculture, irrigation, agriculture infrastructure and supply chain.

11) Finally, this study enables us to understand the household management of the lower middle class consumers on consumption expenditure of food items especially in a city where the cost of living is too high.

1.6 SCOPE & LIMITATIONS OF THE STUDY

1) This research is conducted in Thane city and can be extended to other parts of the country.

2) This study is focused on only lower middle class consumers and can be extended to other segments of the population.

3) This research has some limitations of resources especially, financial constrains, as the whole research is self-financed which gives rise to scope for further findings.

4) The responses has been collected from the respondents through cross-sectional study when the inflation was well above the comfortable levels, particularly food inflation gives rise to scope for longitudinal study to cover both the situations of high and low inflation.

5) In this study, the factor considered to study the impact on consumption expenditure is mainly food inflation along with demographic factors such as household annual income, profession, family size and place. There is a scope for including other factors.

6) The study may be affected by the condition that, the respondents should belong to the lower middle class and earn the income from service only, as the business income is not perceived to be transparent further gives rise to scope for study inclusive of both service and business income.

7) As food inflation is a persistent rise in food prices over time, substitution effect is not considered due to its temporary nature.

8) Food items which have relevance to the research are selected for study from the basket of primary food articles in WPI which gives rise to scope for consideration of other food and non-food items in future studies.

9) The accuracy of the data depends mainly on the respondent's unbiased response to the questionnaire which in turn depends on their attitude, personal interest, awareness and knowledge about the subject.

10) Because of constraints some topics remain untouched. It is not possible to cover all the aspects. This study can be used to conduct consumer research on different areas such as; to know the economic status, investments preferences and saving

patterns, consumer psychology and behavior etc. of the middle class consumers in any part of the country either rural or urban.

1.7 CONCEPTUAL FRAMEWORK OF THE STUDY

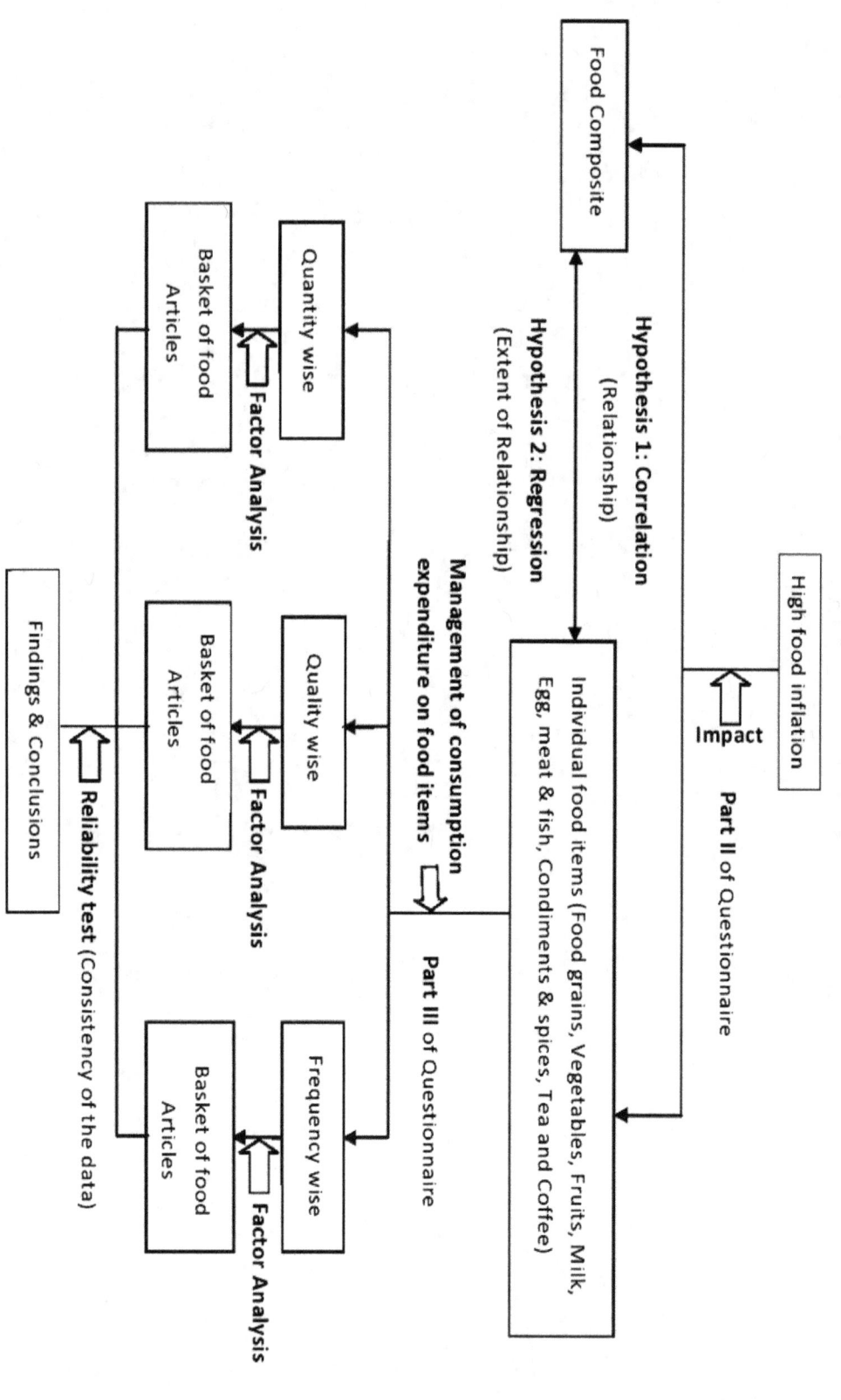

CHAPTER 2: CONCEPTUAL BACKGROUND

Chapter Highlights:

2.1 Inflation in India

2.2 Types of Inflation

2.3 Inflationary Experience of India

2.4 Food Inflation in India

2.5 Nature and Structure of Food Inflation

2.6 High Inflation Episodes in India since 1972

2.7 Food Price: Global versus Developed, Developing and Low Income Countries

2.8 Inflation: India versus World and Emerging & Developing Economies

2.9 Growth of Agriculture Sector in India

2.10 Factors causing Food Inflation

2.11 Inflation in Food Articles: A Commodity wise Analysis of Causal Factors

2.12 Production, Net Exports & Imports and Net Availability of food grains in India

2.13 Declining share of food in consumption basket

2.14 Food grains consumption in urban India: Below the availability

2.15 Food grains availability in urban India: At satisfactory level

2.16 Shift in dietary habits towards protein foods

2.17 Outside food eating in Mumbai: Highest among other cities in India

2.18 Measures of Inflation

2.19 Government measures to curb Inflation

2.20 Other effects of Food Inflation

2.21 Remedies to tackle Food Inflation in India

2.22 Middle class in Indian context

2.23 Profile of Thane city

2.1 INFLATION IN INDIA

Meaning:

In general, inflation is defined as persistence rise in the general price level of goods and services in an economy.

Definitions:

Inflation has been defined in many ways by different economists:

According to:

1) **Silvorman**, "Inflation is the name given to the expansion of the money supplies whether in currency or credit in the excess of the amount justified by government for the trade".

2) **Pigou**, "Inflation exists when income is expanding more than in proportion to the income earning activities".

3) **Hanson**, "Inflation is present when the volume of purchasing power is persistently running ahead of the output of goods and services so that there is a continuous tendency for prices both for commodities and factors of production to rise because the supply of goods and services and FPO's fails to keep pace with demand for them".

4) **Crowther**, "Inflation is a state in which the value of money is falling i.e. the prices are rising".

5) **Coulbourn**, "Inflation is too much of money chasing too few goods".

6) **Laidler and Parkin**, "Inflation is a process of continuously rising prices, or equivalently, of continuously falling value of money".

7) **Ackely**, "A persistent and appreciable rise in the general level or average of prices".

8) **Meyer**, "An increase in the prices that occurs after full employment has been attained".

9) **Milton Friedman**, "Inflation is and can only be produced by increasing the quantity of money faster than the increase in outputs".

10) **Gregory**, "It is an increase in the quantity of purchasing power".

11) **Johnson**, "Inflation is the increase in the quantity of money faster than the national output is expanding".

Terms related to Inflation:

The important terms related to inflation are as follows:

1) **Deflation:** Deflation is a condition of falling prices. It is just opposite of inflation. In deflation, the value of money goes up and prices fall down. Deflation brings a depression phase of business in the economy.

2) **Disinflation:** Disinflation refers to lowering of prices through anti-inflationary measures without causing unemployment and reduction in output.

3) **Reflation:** Reflation is a situation of rising prices intentionally adopted to ease the depression phase of the economy. In reflation along with rising prices, the employment, output and income also increase until the economy reaches the stage of full employment.

4) **Stagflation:** Paul Samuelson describes Stagflation as the paradox of rising prices with increasing rate of unemployment.

5) **Stagnation:** Stagnation is the rate of economic growth which may be a slow or no economic growth at all.

6) **Statflation:** The term' Statflation' was coined by Dr. P. R. Brahmananda to describe the inflationary situation of India. According to Brahmananda, rising prices in the middle of recession is known as Statflation.

2.2 TYPES OF INFLATION

There are different types of inflation, of which, two main types are demand-pull inflation and cost-push inflation.

1) **Demand-Pull Inflation:** It occurs when there is increase in the aggregate demand (AD) faster than the aggregate supply (AS). This increase in aggregate demand is categorized by the four sections of the macro economy: households, businesses, governments and foreign buyers. Demand-pull inflation typically occurs when the economy is growing at a faster rate than the long run trend rate of growth. If demand for goods and services increases, firm will respond by pushing up prices. Figure 1 shows that, due to increase in price from P1 to P2; the aggregate demand curve has shifted from AD1 to AD2.

Figure 1: Shifting of aggregate demand curve from AD1 to AD2

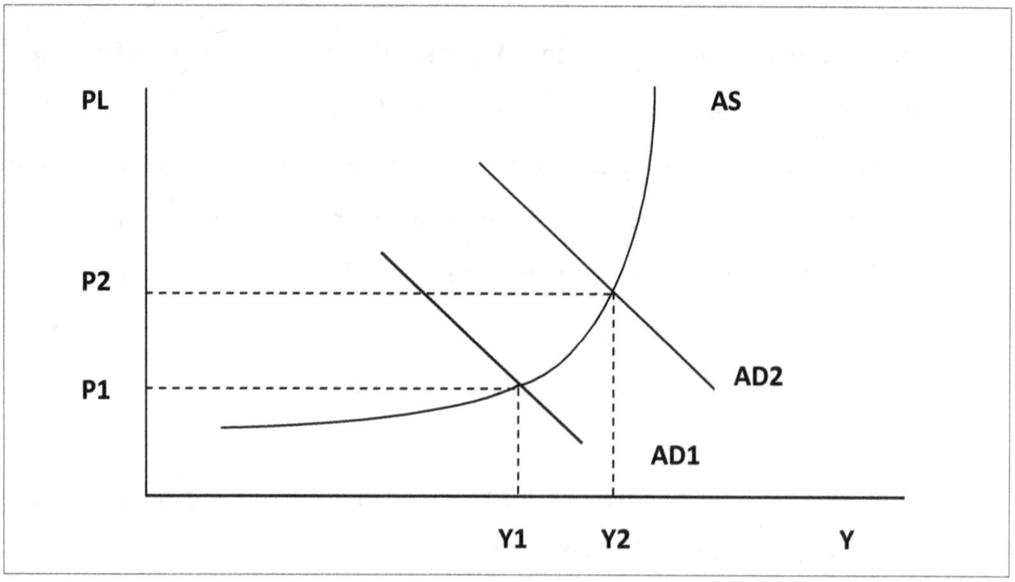

Source: http://www.economicshelp.org

2) **Cost-Push Inflation:** It occurs when there is a rise in prices of raw material, taxes, etc. Cost-push inflation basically means that prices are pushed up by increase in the four factors of production (land, labour, capital or entrepreneurship) when the firms are already running at full production capacity. With higher production cost firms cannot maintain profit margins by producing the same amount of goods and services. As a result, the increase costs are passed on to the consumers which cause a rise in the general price level. Figure 2 shows the shifting of aggregate supply curve from AS1 to AS2 due to increase in cost of production.

Figure 2: Shifting of aggregate supply curve from AS1 to AS2

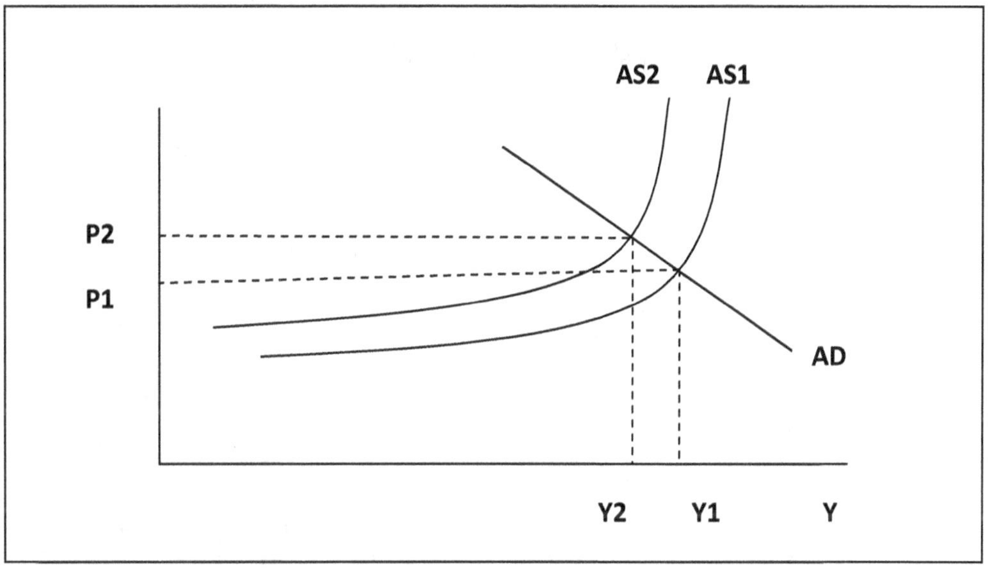

Source: http://www.economicshelp.org

3) **Wage Push Inflation:** Rising wages of people in a firm tends to cause inflation. In effect it is the combination of demand pull inflation and cost push inflation. Rising wages increase cost of production and this cost is passed onto consumers in the form of higher prices. On other hand, rising wage increases consumer's purchasing power and therefore cause increased consumption and aggregate demand.

4) **Imported Inflation:** Depreciation in the exchange rate of currency make imports more expensive and exports more competitive. As a result, there is an increase in

demand causing prices to go up. The increase in prices is solely due to the exchange rate effect.

5) **Temporary Factors:** The inflation rate increases due to the increase in the indirect taxes. For example, if the VAT rate increases all goods coming under VAT will be expensive. This effect is temporary, as the increase in VAT rate is subject to change.

2.3 INFLATIONARY EXPERIENCE OF INDIA

Past inflation trends in India (2000-01 to 2009-10)

The historical average long-term inflation rate was around 7.5 percent. Monthly WPI inflation data suggest that there was a structural break around the mid-2000s with the inflation rate during the latter half being higher (Figure 3).

Figure 3: WPI Inflation shows structural break

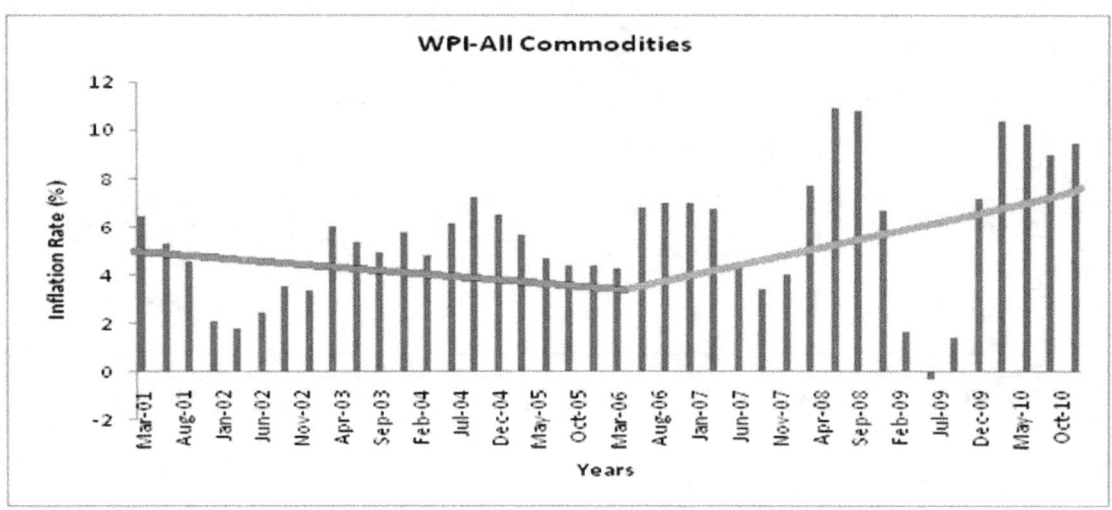

Source: http://www.rbi.org.in

Average WPI inflation increased from 5.2 percent in the first half of 2000s to 5.5 percent in the second half (Table 1). This was largely contributed by primary food inflation. In fact, the core non-food manufactured products inflation moderated from 4.2 percent to 3.9 percent[4].

Table 1: Average WPI Inflation

(In percent)

Group/Sub-group	2001-10	2001-05	2006-10	2010-11	Q1: 2011-12
WPI	5.4	5.2	5.5	9.6	9.4
Primary Food Articles (14.3)	5.8	2.4	9.2	15.8	9.1
Protein (6.4)	6.3	3.5	9.0	20.5	5.9
Milk (3.2)	6.3	4.5	7.9	20.6	7.3
Egg, Meat & Fish (2.4)	5.6	2.3	8.8	26.6	9.0
Industrial Raw Materials (16.2)	7.9	8.4	7.4	17.2	16.5
Non-food manufactured products (55.0)	4.0	4.2	3.9	6.1	7.2

*Figures in the bracket indicate weights in WPI.
Source: Office of Economic Advisors, GoI.

Head line inflation varied from a low of 3.3 percent in 1999-2000 to a high of 7.2 percent in 2000-01.In year 2002-03 inflation remained at a comfortable level of 3.4 percent irrespective of the fact that, the country faced a severe drought situation and simultaneous impact of several others adverse developments such as border tensions and high international crude oil prices. The increased international crude oil prices and domestic food prices as a result of deficient monsoon spurt inflation in India during the first half of 2004-05. Inflation began to ease in the second half of 2004-05 under the impact of a combination of fiscal and monetary measures and weakening of south-west monsoon. In 2005-06, WPI inflation eased to 4.3 percent as compared to 6.5 percent a year earlier[5].

---

[4] Mohanty, D. (2011, August 13). Changing inflation dynamics in India. *Speech delivered at the Motilal Nehru National Institute of Technology (MNNIT), Allahabad, Reserve Bank of India* , pp. 3-4.

[5] GoI. (2011-12). *Economic survey 2011-12*. Retrieved from Ministry of Finance, Governemnt of India: http://indiabudget.nic.in/es2011-12/estat1.pdf

The ten year average headline WPI inflation was around 5.4 percent from 2000-01 to 2009-10 (Table 1).In this decade, year 2000-01, 2003-04, 2004-05, 2006- 07, and 2008-09 had higher inflation relative to the decadal average. The ten year average inflation in fuel was around 8.9 percent majorly contributed by the high inflation of year 2000-01. The years 2003-04, 2004-05, 2006-07, and 2008-09 witnessed high inflation in manufactured products mainly on account of high prices of raw materials such as basic metal alloys and metal products, non-metallic mineral products, and machinery and machine tools. The year 2008-09 was different as inflation in this year remained high on account of high international fuel and commodity prices. The year 2009-10 was an abnormal year due to global economic downtrend and unfavorable monsoon[6].

Recent Inflation trends in India (2010-11 to 2011-12)

The year 2010-11 was marked by strong inflation persisting with head line inflation averaging 9.6 percent (Table 1). Since December 2010, there was hike in vegetable prices caused by unseasonal rainfall during the post-monsoon and rising global commodity prices that resulted in significant cost-push and demand-pull inflation. Food products were the main drivers of price rise in WPI during April-July 2010. Subsequently, during August-November their share declined when non-food primary products turned out to be the main drivers. However, these price pressures spilled over to manufactured non-food products during December 2010-March 2011, which accounted for 61 percent of the price rise in this period[7].

During 2011-12, the WPI exhibited a sustained increase in the first half and slowed down during the latter half of the year. The financial year started with a headline inflation of 9.7 percent which touched double digit in September 2011 before coming down to 6.6 percent in January 2012[8]. The increase in WPI during the initial months of the year was driven by the factors that cause an increase in food prices, revision in the prices of fuel and an increase in manufactured product prices due to the pressure from

---

[6] GoI. (2011-12), *Ibid.*
[7] RBI. (2010-11). Annual Report 2010-11. *Governement of India* , pp. 2.
[8] GoI. (2011-12), *Op.cit.*

high input costs as well as strong demand. The decline in growth rate during 2011-12 was expected to ease the pressure on core inflation. However, the extent of moderation was constrained by further pressure from rupee depreciation and high global commodity prices.

The softening of inflation was due to the decline in the contribution of food, which started increasing from February 2012 as prices increased sharply after the seasonal decline. The contribution of non-food manufactured products remained strong despite the deceleration in growth. The contribution of fuel group to overall inflation remained significantly high throughout the year despite suppressed inflation from the administered prices of some petro-products, coal and electricity.

Primary food articles inflation showed a sharp decline during November 2011– January 2012, from above 10 percent to negative territory, largely due to seasonal decline in the prices of vegetables and a favorable base effect. However, food prices rebounded significantly, resulting in food inflation reverting to double-digit levels by April 2012. The prices of protein-based food articles have remained persistently high since October 2011[9]. As per mid-year analysis 2012-13, inflation as measured by WPI averaged 8.9 percent for 2011-12.

---

[9].RBI. (2010-11), *Op.cit.*

2.4 FOOD INFLATION IN INDIA

Meaning:

In general, food inflation is defined as persistent rise in the prices of food articles. Food inflation has been a serious cause of concern over the past few years. Price stability of the food articles is crucial for sustainable growth of the economy, as persistent inflation implies higher demand for agriculture commodity relative to supply. There is an urgent need to address the situation of changing consumption pattern and to respond with appropriate agricultural policies to keep food prices stable.

2.5 NATURE AND STRUCTURE OF FOOD INFLATION

India did not face double-digit inflation in food during the past several years despite severe droughts and decline in food output in some years[10]. Since year 2000 till year 2007, both food and non-food inflation was moderate, in the average range of 6-8%. Food prices in India started spiraling-up since mid-2008 onwards. The year 2010 witnessed overall inflation rate crossing the psychological threshold of 10% for

---

[10] Ramesh Chand, P. S. (2011, February). Managing food inflation in India: Reforms and policy options, Policy brief 35. *National Centre for Agricultural Economics and Policy Research, New Delhi* .

consecutive five months. Inflation based on year-on year wholesale price index (WPI) of primary food articles rules high at double digits in January 2011. The wholesale food prices in India touched a ten year high with food inflation rate at 18.21% for the week ended March 25, 2012. From Figure 4, it has shown that, the food inflation rate crossed 20% in December 2009 and again in February 2010.

Figure 4: WPI inflation in food and non-food commodities

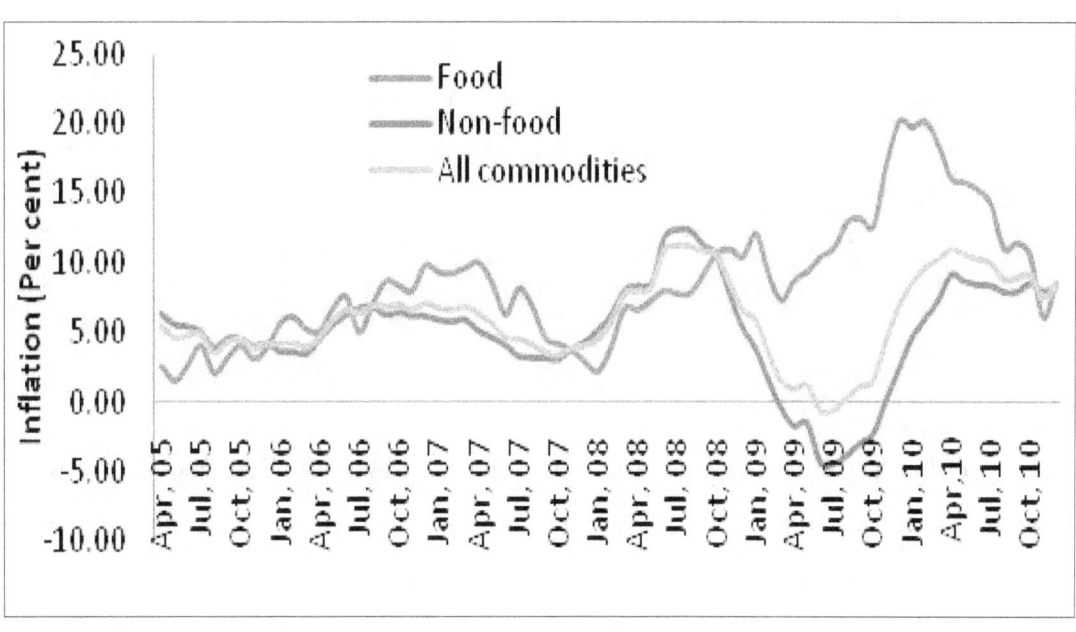

Source: GoI. (2011).

To understand the nature of food inflation, total food is disaggregated into primary food articles and manufactured food products with a weight of 59% and 41%, respectively. Primary food articles include cereals, pulses, fruits, vegetables, milk, egg, meat and fish, condiments and spices, etc., whereas the major components of manufactured food products are sugar, dairy products, vegetable oils, prepared food stuff and other processed items. From Figure 5, till January 2010 the rates of price rise in food articles and food products were more or less aligned with one another, but later, they followed disparate trends. Though the prices of food products declined sharply afterwards, food article inflation remained in double digit in the late-2010.

Figure 5: WPI Inflation in Food disaggregated

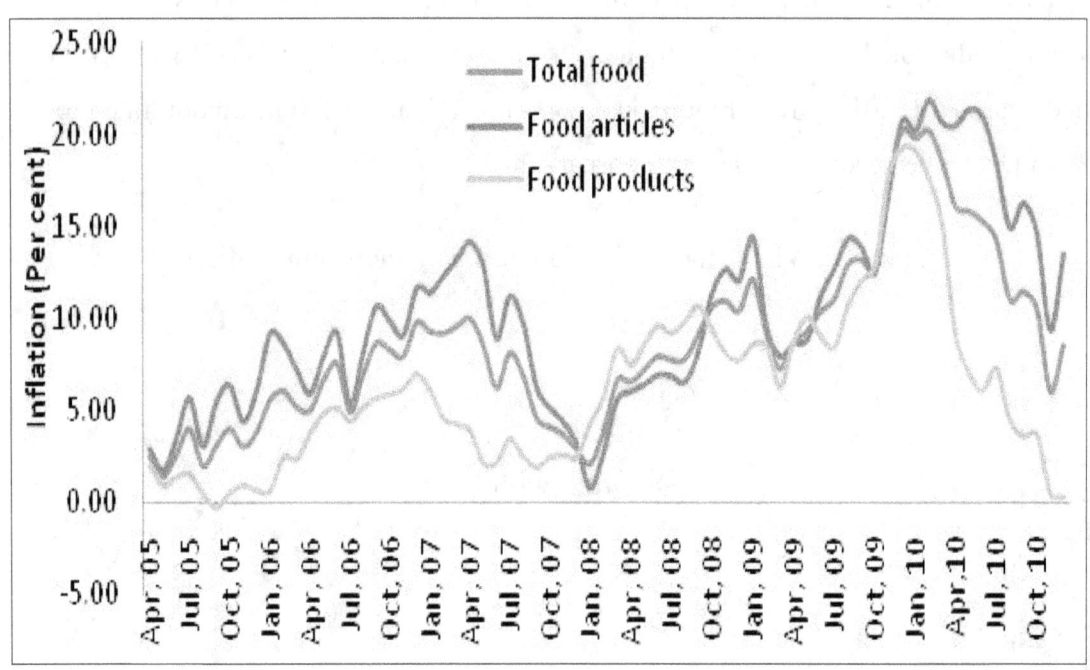

Source: GoI. (2011).

In 2008, high prices of food grains and manufactured food products contributed more towards inflation than any other commodity group. In between the first quarter of 2009 and last quarter of 2010, share of food grains in overall food inflation declined from 25% to 0.3%, while that of food products eased out from 32.3% to 6.8% (Figure 6). Commodities like fruits and vegetables, milk and meat group dominated overall food inflation in the fourth quarter of 2010. The overriding role of vegetables group in this quarter can be specifically attributed to the sudden spurt in prices of onion due to production deficit. Also, the structural demand-supply mismatch of agricultural commodity cannot be ruled out.

Figure 6: Contribution of various commodities to Food Inflation

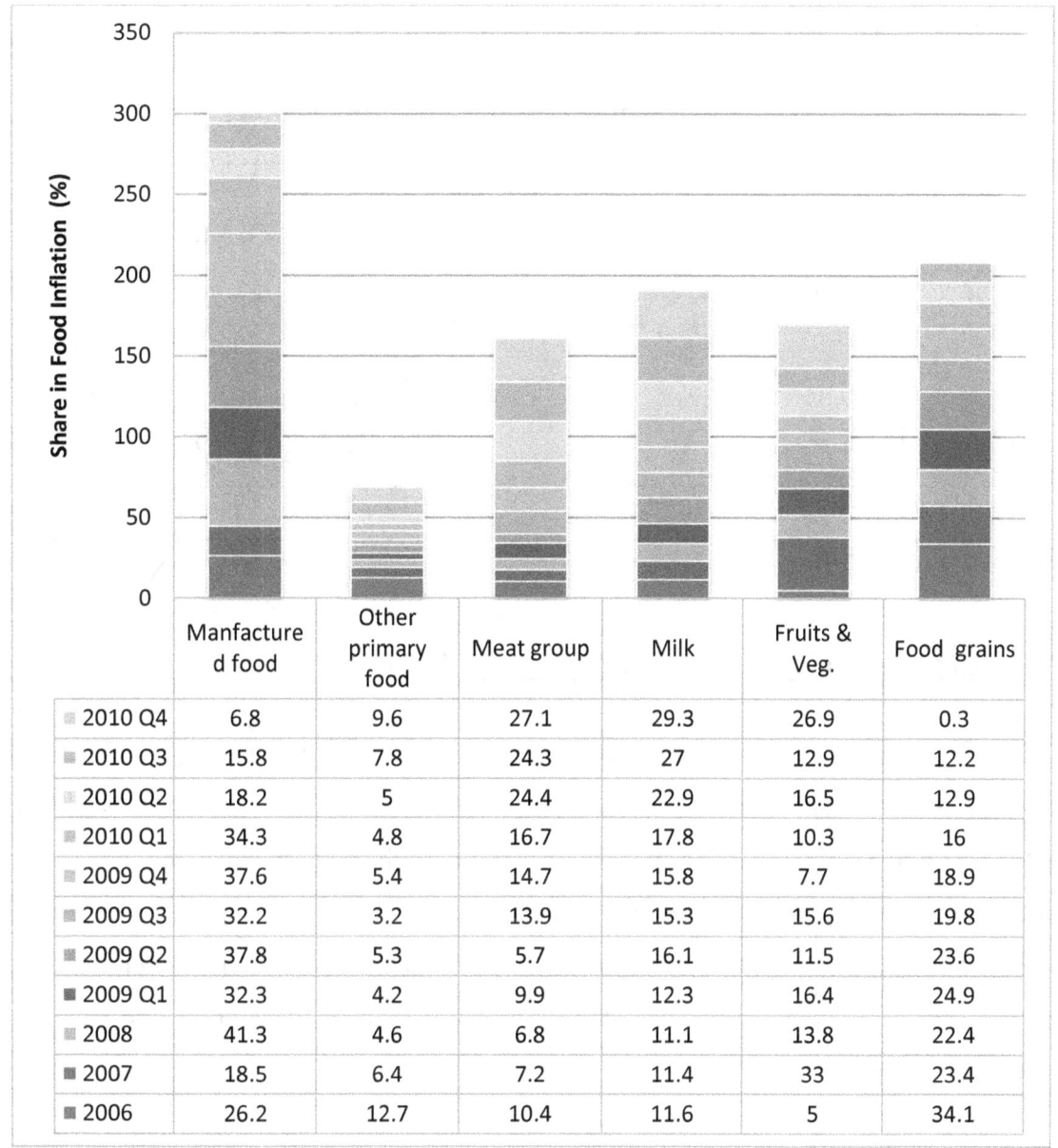

	Manfactured food	Other primary food	Meat group	Milk	Fruits & Veg.	Food grains
2010 Q4	6.8	9.6	27.1	29.3	26.9	0.3
2010 Q3	15.8	7.8	24.3	27	12.9	12.2
2010 Q2	18.2	5	24.4	22.9	16.5	12.9
2010 Q1	34.3	4.8	16.7	17.8	10.3	16
2009 Q4	37.6	5.4	14.7	15.8	7.7	18.9
2009 Q3	32.2	3.2	13.9	15.3	15.6	19.8
2009 Q2	37.8	5.3	5.7	16.1	11.5	23.6
2009 Q1	32.3	4.2	9.9	12.3	16.4	24.9
2008	41.3	4.6	6.8	11.1	13.8	22.4
2007	18.5	6.4	7.2	11.4	33	23.4
2006	26.2	12.7	10.4	11.6	5	34.1

Source: GoI. (2011).

The receding effect of food grains and manufactured food products and sustained influence of fruits, vegetables, milk and meat group can be seen from their rates of inflation during 2010 (Table 2). The food grains inflation weakened substantially from 19.5% in January 2010 to (-) 2.59% in December 2010. Similar was the case with manufactured food products, while the inflation rates of fruits and vegetables, milk and meat remained in double digits. In the case of onion, inflation was moderate in January

2010, remained negative from April to June 2010 before the sudden and sharp jump to 45.8% in December 2010.

Table 2: Trend in Inflation in major Food commodities: 2010

Month	Food Grains	Fruits & Veg.	Onion	Milk	Meat Group	Manuf. Food
January	19.49	7.89	7.0	26.59	31.60	19.16
April	11.05	14.32	-10.0	27.91	38.61	9.09
July	9.63	13.22	-7.5	26.06	31.42	7.34
October	3.89	12.39	22.3	21.04	27.37	3.75
December	-2.59	22.77	45.8	18.21	19.23	0.35

Source: GoI. (2011).

2.6 HIGH INFLATION EPISODES IN INDIA SINCE 1972

There have been seven episodes of high inflation in India since 1972. During these periods the headline WPI inflation was above 8.5 percent for more than seven months (Table 3). Most of these episodes resulted in high inflation persisting in the range of two to three years. Sustained inflation in the economy is a common phenomenon when inflation rises due to the drivers like crude oil prices, drought, currency devaluation etc. Moreover, food, fuel and core have been significantly contributing to high and persistent inflation[11].

---

[11] RBI. (2011-12). Annual Report 2011-12. pp. 32-33.

Table 3: High Inflation Episodes in India

Period	Average Inflation		Number of months
	WPI	CPI-IW	
July 1972- April 1975	19.3	19.4	34
May 1979- Dec 1981	15.7	11.1	32
Aug 1987-July 1988	8.8	9.6	12
Feb 1990- Dec 1992	11.3	11.7	35
Sep 1993- Nov 1995	10.0	9.9	27
May 2008- Nov 2008	10.2	9.1	7
Jan 2010- Nov 2011	9.6	10.7	23

Source: RBI Annual Report, 2011-12.

2.7 FOOD PRICES: GLOBAL VERSUS DEVELOPED, DEVELOPING AND LOW INCOME COUNTRIES

The International food prices saw a sudden upsurge between July 2010 and July 2011 by over 33%. This section compares the variation in food prices from 2000 to 2011 between global average and three set of countries. There is a huge difference in the way prices have varied between the three set of countries. Figure 7 shows the comparison of global food prices and prices of developed countries. Despite the global average increasing at a very fast rate, the developed countries like USA, France and Germany have been able to control their food prices by giving subsidies, etc. and have kept it stable.

Figure 7: Comparison of Global Food Prices and Prices of Developed Countries

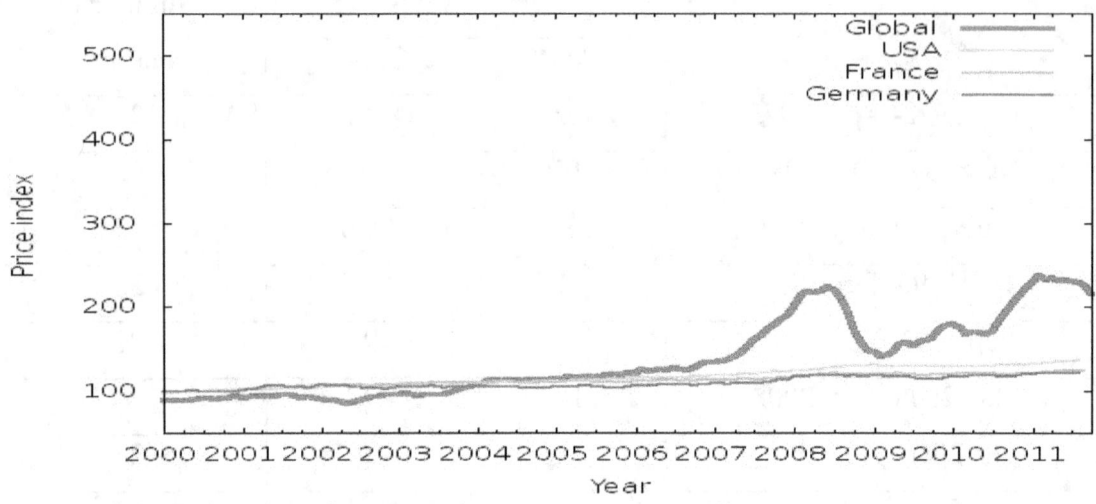

Source: Calculations based on FAO data.

Figure 8 shows the comparison of global food prices and prices of developing countries. The developing countries such as India and China have seen an increase in their food prices in line with that of global average. Unstable countries like Pakistan showed a consistent rise in food prices, even higher than world average since year 2008. This could probably because of insufficient fund to subsidize their food items at such high rates.

Figure 8: Comparison of Global Food Prices and Prices of Developing Countries

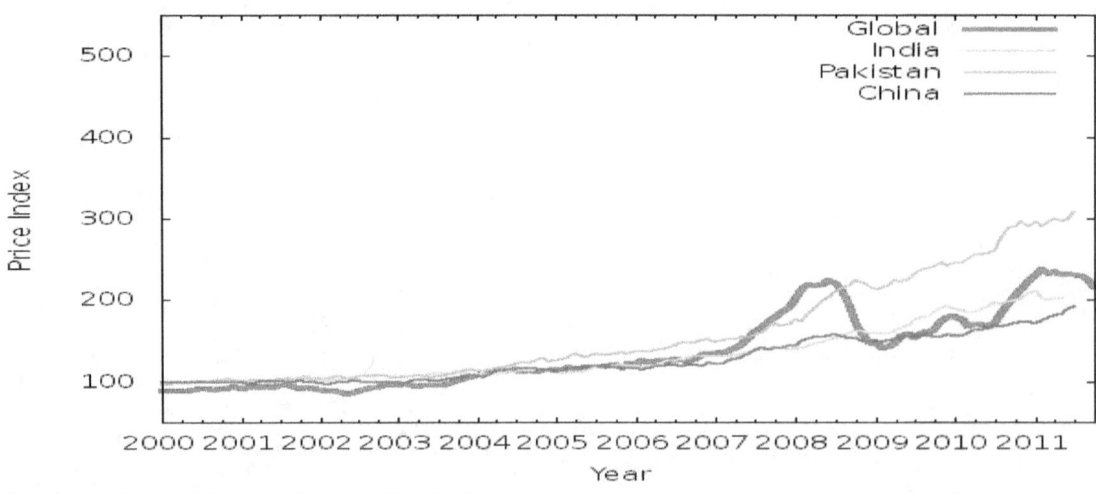

Source: Calculations based on FAO data.

Low income countries such as Ethiopia and Zambia have had prices significantly higher than the global average throughout the decade. However, South Africa has been slightly better off, but unable to keep the prices stable (Figure 9).

Figure 9: Comparison of Global Food Prices and Prices of Low Income Countries

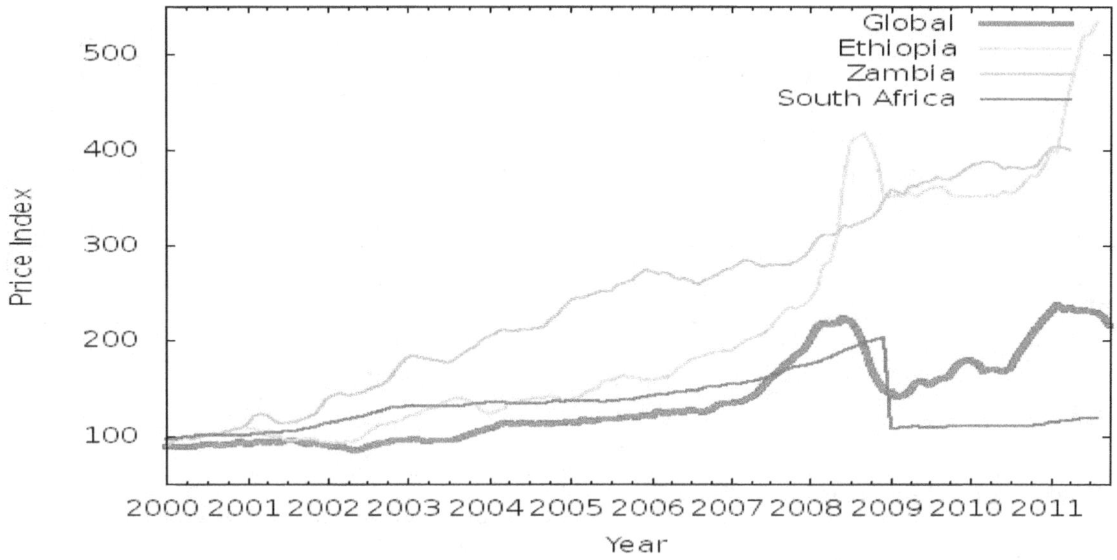

Source: Calculations based on FAO data.

2.8 INFLATION: INDIA VERSUS WORLD AND EMERGING & DEVELOP-ING ECONOMIES

In another comparison of average inflation rate between India and the world it has been observed that, in recent years India's inflation rate has been higher than the world's average. In the 2000s, there was a moderation in inflation all around the world. From period 2000-2007, the world inflation average 3.9 percent per annum. Even the emerging and developing economics (EDEs) had very high inflation showed an average annual rate of 6.7 percent. India's inflation rate was at comfortable level of 5.2 percent as measured by WPI and 4.6 percent as measured by CPI. In the post 2008 global crises period, inflation rose sharply both in advance countries and EDEs as the commodity and oil prices rebounded. Thereafter, the inflation rate moderated in advance countries and

EDEs. In India, inflation rate rose from 4.7 percent in 2007-08 to a high of 8.1 percent in 2008-09 and again fell to 3.8 percent in 2009-10 (Table 4). During 2010-11 and 2011-12 inflation in India has reached double digits before showing some moderation in 2012-13. The high inflation during year 2010 and 2011 was due to the combined effect of adverse global and domestic factors and demand and supply side constraints[12].

Table 4: India's Inflation above the World average

(Year –on-Year in percent)

	2000-07	2008	2009	2010	2011	2012	2008-12
	Average	Annual					Average
Global Inflation							
World	3.9	6.0	2.4	3.7	4.9	4.0	4.2
EDEs	6.7	9.3	5.1	6.1	7.2	6.1	6.8
Inflation in India							
WPI	5.2	8.1	3.8	9.6	8.9	7.6	7.6
WPI-food	3.8	8.9	14.6	11.1	7.2	9.1	10.2
WPI-NFMP	4.3	5.7	0.2	6.1	7.3	5.2	4.9
CPI-IW	4.6	9.1	12.2	10.5	8.4	9.9	10.0
Indian inflation data pertains to financial year, WPI- Wholesale Price Index CPI-IW- Consumer Price Index Industrial Workers			EDEs- Emerging and Developing Economies NFMP- Non-Food Manufactured Products				

Source: **(1)** FAO data.
(2) Office of Economic Advisors, GoI.

2.9 GROWTH OF AGRICULTURE SECTOR IN INDIA

The growth of agriculture sector has been fluctuating across the plans period (Figure 10). During Eight plan period (1992-97), the growth rate of agriculture sector was 4.8 percent. However, there was a downtrend in the beginning of the Ninth plan period (1997-02) and the Tenth plan period (2002-07) which accounted for growth rate of 2.5

---

[12] Mohanty, D. (2013, January 31). India Inflation Puzzle. *Speech delivered in the function of Late Dr. Ramchandra Parnerkar Outstanding Economics Award 2013 at Mumbai .*

percent and 2.4 percent respectively. The average annual growth rate of economy during the Tenth plan period was 7.6 percent against the crippling growth rate of 2.4 percent in agriculture, which was a cause of concern. In other words, the contribution of the agriculture sector in the country's GDP shows a gradual fall from the Eight plan period (1992-97) to Eleventh plan period (2007-2012). The trend of rate of growth during the period 1992-93 to 2010-11 was 2.8 while the average annual growth rate of agriculture & allied sectors in GDP during the same period was 3.2 percent. Eleventh plan period showed a recovery in the deceleration of agriculture growth occurred during Ninth and Tenth plan period. Food grains production in 2011-12 touched a new high of 250.42 million tonnes. Agricultural GDP growth has accelerated to an average of 3.9 percent during 2005-06 to 2010-11. As per the advance estimate of Central Statistics Office (CSO), agriculture and allied sectors are likely to grow at 2.5 percent during 2011-12 at constant (2004-05) prices. In the Twelfth plan drafted by Planning Commission, it is expected that the average growth rate of agriculture and allied sector may be 3.3 to 3.5 percent per year. Finally, it is clear from Table 5 that, there is a fall in the contribution of agriculture and allied sector in total GDP over the years. Table 6 shows India's position in world agriculture in 2008.

Figure 10: Growth Rates: GDP (overall) and GDP (Agriculture & Allied Sectors) – Five Year Plan Period wise

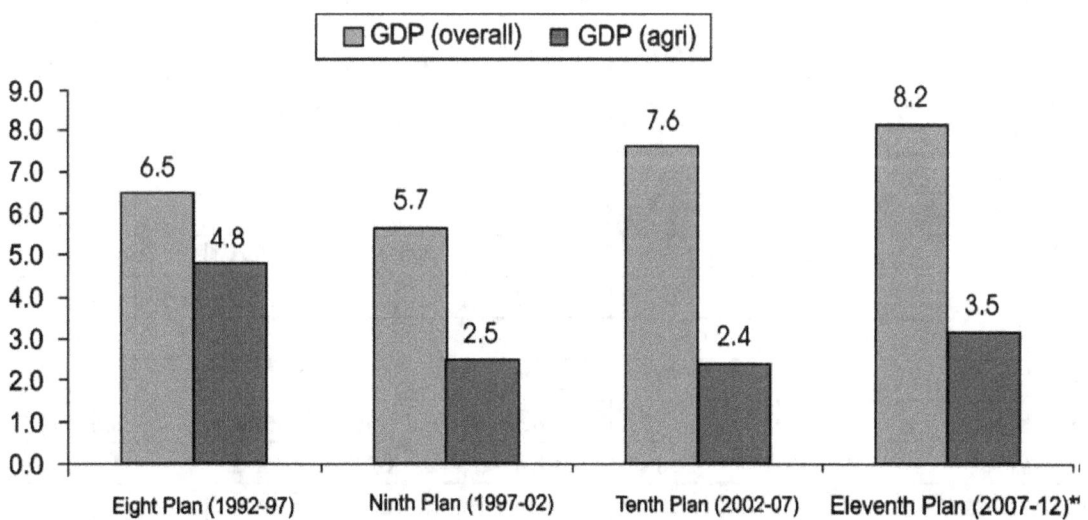

Source: CSO, MOSPI, GoI.
*Figures for the Eleventh Plan show growth for the first four years.

Table 5: Growth Rates: GDP (overall) and GDP (Agriculture & Allied Sectors) - Year wise

(Percent)

Period	GDP (overall)	GDP(Agriculture & Allied Sectors)	Contribution of Agriculture & Allied Sectors in GDP
2005-06	9.5	5.1	(-)
2006-07	9.6	4.2	17.4
2007-08	9.3	5.8	16.8
2008-09	6.8	- 0.1	15.7
2009-10	8.0	0.4	14.6
2010-11	8.6	5.4	14.2

Source: Central Statistics Office, MOSPI, GoI.

(-) indicates data not available.

Table 6: India's position in world agriculture in 2008

Item	India	World	% Share	India's Rank	Next to
1	2	3	4	5	6
1. Total Area (Million Hectares)	329	13442	2.4	Seventh	Russian Federation, Canada, U.S.A., China, Brazil, Australia
Land Area	297	13009	2.3	Seventh	Russian Federation, China, U.S.A., Canada, Brazil, Australia
Arable Land	159	1411	11.3	Second	U.S.A.
2. Total Population* (Million)	1181	6750	17.5	Second	China
Agriculture	583	2617	22.3	Second	China
3. Economically Active Population* (Million)					
Total	472	3178	14.9	Second	China
Agriculture	262	1295	20.2	Second	China
4. Crop Production (Million Tonnes)					
(A) : Total Cereals	267	2521	10.6	Third	China, USA
Wheat	79	683	11.5	Second	China
Rice (Paddy)	148	686	21.6	Second	China
Total Pulses	15	61	24.6	First	
(B) : Oilseeds					
Groundnut (in shell)	7	38	18.8	Second	China
Rapeseed	6	58	10.3	Third	Canada, China

5. Fruits & Vegetables (Million Tonnes)

(A) : Vegetables & Melons	90	932	9.7	Second	China
(B) : Fruits excluding Melons	67	580	11.6	Second	China
(C) : Potatoes	35	326	10.6	Second	China
(D) : Onion (Dry)	14	73	18.5	Second	China

6. Commercial Crops (Million Tonnes)

(A) : Sugarcane	348	1736	20.1	Second	Brazil
(B) : Tea	0.81	3.9	20.7	Third	China, Turkey
(C) : Coffee (green)	0.26	8.25	3.2	Seventh	Brazil, Vietnam, Colombia, Indonesia, Ethiopia, Mexico
(D) : Jute & Jute like Fibres	2.02	3.20	63.1	First	
(E) : Cotton(lint)	3.77	22.85	16.5	Second	China
(F) : Tobacco Leaves	0.52	6.88	7.6	Third	China, Brazil

7. Livestock (Million Heads)

(A) : Cattle	175	1372	12.7	Second	Brazil
(B) : Buffaloes	105	185	56.7	First	
(C) : Camels	0.63	24.73	2.5	Tenth	Somalia, Sudan, Ethiopia, Niger, Mauritania, Kenya, Mali, Pakistan, Chad
(D) : Sheep	65	1086	6.0	Third	China, Australia
(E) : Goats	126	864	14.5	Second	China
(F) : Chicken	584	18139.1	3.2	Fifth	China, USA, Indonesia, Brazil

8. Animal Products

(A) : Total Milk (000 MT)	109000	694235	15.7	First	
(B) : Eggs Total (000 MT)	3060	66103	4.6	Third	China, U.S.A.
(C) : Total Meat (000 MT)	4353.1	277848	1.6	Fifth	China, U.S.A., Brazil, Germany

9. Implements (Thousands numbers)**

Agricultural Tractors-in-use	3149	29320	10.7	Second	USA

* Estimated figure for 2008. ** Figure relates to 2007.

Source: FAO, Regional Office for Asia and the Pacific, Bangkok.

2.10 FACTORS CAUSING FOOD INFLATION

There are number of factors which cause food inflation. Some of the important factors are:

1) EXOGENOUS FACTORS

It includes the significant factors to the inflationary trend such as rise in global commodity prices and drought condition in the country. For example, in 2008, the international food prices rose to 23% after coming down to 7.2% and the deficient south-west monsoon during 2009 resulted in drought situation in several states in India.

2) STRUCTURAL FACTORS

In India, it is increasingly being viewed by several researchers and policy makers that there are structural elements included in the food inflation. They are:

Decelerating Production:

Annual growth of food grains in India has been decelerated from 2.8% in 1980 to 1.6% in 1990 and further 1.2% in 2000 onwards.

Growing Population & Per capita Income:

The population of India rose annually by 1.5% from 2004-05 to 2009-10 and the per capita income showed robust growth of 6.9% in the same period. In fact, the present level of average nutrition and food intake levels are way below the prescribed levels, which led to accelerated growth for food demand.

Changing Dietary Patterns:

The consumption basket is getting shifted from carbohydrate dominated diet to protein rich diet such as milk, pulses, eggs, fish, mutton etc. and vitamin diet such as vegetables & fruits with the increase in per capita income. The recent inflationary trend shows that, the key drivers of food inflation are protein items.

3) INSTITUTIONAL FACTORS

There are several features of the food sector in India that cause food inflation:

Inadequate Storage Facility:

In India, food storage capacity is inadequate and even not suitable for keeping food beyond a few months. This is basically true in case of perishable foods. In spite of bumper crop production in any year, the stock cannot be carried over to meet the shortfall in production in the next year[13].

Constraints in Importing:

In economy, to meet domestic shortages imports taken place to augment demand. For the commodity like edible oil the international market is quite big. Large public & private import houses regularly import edible oil resulting in keeping control over the domestic price of edible oil. However, it is not true for other commodities because of the constraints like import restrictions and insufficient availability in the international market.

Institutional Limitations:

Government regulations over imports, high import duties on food items like vegetables and fruits and shortage of private import houses in case of certain commodities.

Nature of the Market:

The size of international market in case of pulses is small relative to the demand for pulses in India. Presently, India imports approx. 30% of total pulses through international trade.

Hoardings & Speculations:

Due to hoarding, the prices of essential food items shoot up which is clear indication of the failure of the government regulations & policies in respect of food sector. Moreover, the speculation of food items in commodity market sometimes artificially raises the prices of the commodity in anticipation of inadequate supply in future.

Apart from the above factors, some of the factors suggested by Duvvuri Subbarao, Ex-Governor of Reserve Bank of India, are; i) shift in dietary habits towards protein

---

[13] Chand, R. (2010, February 27). Understanding the nature & causes of food inflation. *Economic & Political weekly,Vol. XLV No. 9* , pp. 10-13.

foods; ii) pressure stemming from inclusive growth policies; iii) large increases in MSPs of food grains; iv) shocks from global food inflation; and v) financialization of commodities.

2.11 INFLATION IN FOOD ARTICLES: A COMMODITY WISE ANALYSIS OF CAUSAL FACTORS

Role of Demand Side Pressure:

One popular reason for the spurt in the prices of the food items in recent years is the rising demand for high value food items like, pulses, milk, livestock, fishery, vegetables and fruits which is attributed by the rise in per capita income and structural shift in the dietary pattern. As the supply response to growing demand for these high value food items is weak, their prices continued to remain high. Table 7 & 8 shows the trend in MPCE at constant prices based on the NSSO surveys on quinquennial basis. Over the four year period i.e. from 2004-05 to 2009-10, the share of the high value commodities namely pulses, milk and milk products, egg, fish, meat, vegetables and fruits has increased (Table 7). It is difficult to conclude from the data that, the rising domestic pressures have contributed significantly to the food price spiral and the structural shift in food consumption towards high value food items. This calls for detailed examination of the food expenditure pattern as the demand side explanation for high food inflation reveals many infirmities.

First, except pulses, the increase in the expenditure share of other high value food items in 2009-10 was only marginal and not significantly different than in previous periods (Table 7). Second, the share of expenditure on fruits exhibited negative growth during 2009-10. Third, the expenditure on vegetables in 2009-10 is not new highs. Fourth, analysis of MPCE in real terms on various food commodities reveals that the expenditure on cereals, pulses, eggs, fish, meat, fruits and vegetables declined during 2004-2010 (Table 8). Also, the real MPCE on these food items in 2009-10 was the lowest since 1993-94. In case of milk the MPCE recorded an increase during 2004-10 both in terms of absolute amount and growth.

Table 7: Trends in percentage composition of MPCE (at current prices) on groups of Food Items in Urban India

(Share in total consumer expenditure on food)

Food Items	1999-2000	2004-05	2009-10
Cereals	25.70 (0.01)	23.65 (-2.04)	22.25 (-1.40)
Pulses & Pulse Products	5.90 (0.35)	5.03 (-0.87)	6.54 (1.51)
Milk & Milk Products	18.05 (0.11)	18.62 (0.57)	19.07 (0.45)
Egg, Fish & Meat	6.52 (0.33)	6.36 (-0.16)	6.60 (0.24)
Vegetables	10.69 (0.70)	10.47 (-0.22)	10.54 (0.07)
Fruits & nuts	5.03 (0.16)	5.29 (0.25)	4.06 (-1.23)

Source: (1) Household Consumer Expenditure in India 2007-08, NSSO 64th Round (Report No. 530), GoI.

(2) Key indicators of Household Consumer Expenditure in India 2009-10, NSSO 66th Round (Report No. KI (66/1.0)), GoI.

* Figures in the bracket are percentage point change over the years.

Table 8: Real MPCE on groups of Food Items in Urban India

(In Rs)

Food Items	1999-2000	2004-05	2009-10
Cereals	26.98 (24.64)	25.87 (24.43)	24.80 (23.44)
Pulses & Pulse Products	5.83 (5.33)	5.14 (4.85)	4.55 (4.30)
Milk & Milk Products	22.38 (20.44)	21.75 (20.54)	23.79 (22.48)
Egg, Fish & Meat	6.79 (6.20)	5.97 (5.64)	5.85 (5.53)
Vegetables & Fruits	18.06 (16.49)	17.57 (16.59)	16.09 (15.20)
Food Total	109.51	105.90	105.83

Source: (1) Ministry of Labour and Employment, Labour Bureau (Shimla), GoI.

(2) Central Statistics Office, MOSPI, GoI.

* Figures in the bracket shows percentage share in total food composition.

Role of Supply Side Factors:

It is known fact the oil prices are administered by the global crude oil prices and government's decision on price revision. Fuel prices are partially revised with a time lag in response to the international oil prices[14]. From September 2007 to 2008 and November 2009 to July 2010, in surging to the international oil prices, the WPI inflation rate of mineral oil remained high in India during March 2008 to Nov. 2008 and Jan. 2010 to July 2010. It appears that, the escalation in the domestic fuel price coincide with the rising prices of food items. Therefore, it can be revealed that the oil price increase has had an impact on food prices in India. During April 2009 to November 2009, the moderation in the mineral oil price has no effect on the food inflation. This is because of the agricultural supply shocks that occurred in 2008-09 and 2009-10.

Following food commodities witnessed high inflationary pressure due to supply side factors: rice, pulses, fruits, vegetables, milk, meat, fish, spices, tea, and coffee.

1) RICE

The production of rice was quite comfortable for the four consecutive kharif marketing seasons (KMS) (October-September) from 2005-06 to 2008-09. In fact, for the first time in the history the output of rice hovered above 90 million tonnes for four consecutive years since 2005-06 (Table 9). Despite this bumper crop production, the inflation rate of rice started picking up from November 2006 and touched a peak of 17.23 % in December 2008. The average rate of inflation in 2007-08, 2008-09 and 2009-2010 recorded at 11.30%, 14.83% and 12.31% respectively.

---

[14] Rakshit, M. (2009). India admist the global crisis. *Economic & Political Weekly, 44(13)* , pp. 94-106.

Table 9: Production and growth of Rice

Year	Production (In MT)	Year-on-Year (growth %)
2000-01	84.98	(-)
2001-02	93.34	9.84
2002-03	71.82	-23.06
2003-04	88.53	23.27
2004-05	83.13	-6.10
2005-06	91.79	10.42
2006-07	93.35	1.70
2007-08	96.69	3.58
2008-09	99.18	2.58
2009-10	89.09	-10.17

Source: Department of Agriculture and Cooperation, Ministry of Agriculture, GoI. (http://agricoop.nic.in/Agristatistics.htm)
(-) indicates data not available.

The upward movement in rice inflation from November 2006 onwards has coincided with the buffer stock position of the grain. The actual buffer stock of the government was close to the minimum norm between October 2006 and July 2008. The reason for this situation was the higher export of rice during 2005-06, 2006-07 and 2007-08 and the mismanagement of the food grain economy. Starting from 2000, India experienced high mountains of rice stocks due to significant increase in procurement of rice by the government (Table 10).

Table 10: Production and government procurement of Rice

Year	Production	Procurement	Procurement as % of production
2000-01	84.98	18.93	22.28
2001-02	93.34	21.12	22.63
2002-03	71.82	19.00	26.46
2003-04	88.53	20.78	23.47
2004-05	83.13	24.04	28.92
2005-06	91.79	26.69	29.08
2006-07	93.35	26.30	28.17
2007-08	96.69	26.29	27.19
2008-09	99.18	32.84	33.14
2009-10	89.09	32.59	36.58

Source: Handbook of Statistics on Indian Economy (2009-10), RBI.

Due to high minimum support prices (MSP), consumption of rice has fallen drastically[15]. In order to bail out of financial burden involved in managing the rice mountain, the government decided to open up the exports from 2001 at heavy discounts[16]. However, the export of rice was only a triggered factor but the inflationary pressure has sustained because of two reasons. First, the sharp increase in the MSP of rice for two consecutive KMS 2007-08 and 2008-09 jacked up the price of rice in open market (Table 11).

Table 11: Minimum Support Price of paddy inclusive of incentive bonus

(Rs per quintal)

Marketing Season	Common Trade	Grade 'A'
2000-01	510	540
2001-02	530	560
2002-03	530	560
2003-04	550	580
2004-05	560	590
2005-06	570	600
2006-07	620	650
2007-08	745/850*	745/880*
2008-09	900	930
2009-10	1000	980

Source: Department of Agriculture and Cooperation, Ministry of Agriculture, GoI. (http://agricoop.nic.in/Agristatistics.htm)
*From 12 June 2008

A high MSP was declared just to incentivize rice procurement in the light of the decline in wheat procurement during the Rabi marketing season (RMS) 2005-06 and 2007-08[17]. Second, Due to insufficient buffer stock, the Food Corporation of India (FCI) did not resort to sale of rice in 2007-08 and 2008-09 through open market sales scheme (OMSS). The buffer stock of rice increasing after August 2008 and went beyond manageable limits. The buffer stock of rice was made possible because of the high levels

[15] Chand, R. (2005). Whither India's Food Policy. *Economic & Political Weekly 40(11): 1055-62* .

[16] Anwarul Hoda, A. G. (2007). *WTO Negotiations on Agriculture and Developing Countries.* New Delhi: Oxford University Press.

[17] Sthanu R Nair, L. M. (2011, September 3). Wheat price inflation in recent times: Causes, lessons and new perspectives. *Economic & Political Weekly, XLVI No. 36* , pp. 58-65.

of production and procurement in the KMS 2008-09. The inflation rate continued to remain high in 2009-10. The factors responsible for high inflation in rice despite this favourable were (1) a hike in MSP in 2009-10 to Rs. 1000 and (2) deficiency in south-west monsoon in 2009 and unusual heavy rainfall in some parts of the country in late September and early October 2009. This has resulted in significant fall in rice production during 2009-10 KMS (Table 10).

2) WHEAT

Despite positive output of wheat between three consecutive RMS from 2007-08 (April-March) to 2009-10 and negligible export during 2007-08 to 2009-10, the WPI inflation in wheat was ruling high for most of the time during April 2008 to August 2010 (Table 12 and Table 13). The overall average inflation rate in wheat recorded at 8.41% during April 2008 to August 2010. Consequently, the buffer stock of government remained high during this period of high inflation due to the phenomenal increase in procurement in RMS 2008-09 and 2009-10 (Table 14).

Table 12: Production and growth rate in production of Wheat

Year	Production (in million tonnes)	Year-on-Year Growth (%)
2000-01	69.68	-
2001-02	72.77	4.43
2002-03	65.76	-9.63
2003-04	72.15	9.72
2004-05	68.64	-4.86
2005-06	69.35	1.03
2006-07	75.81	9.32
2007-08	78.57	3.64
2008-09	80.68	2.69
2009-10	80.80	0.15

Source: Department of Agriculture and Cooperation, Ministry of Agriculture, GoI (http://agricoop.nic.in/Agristatistics.htm).
(-) indicates data not available.

Table 13: Export and Import of Wheat

(In '000 tonnes)

Year	Export	Import
2000-01	813.49	4.22
2001-02	2649.38	1.35
2002-03	3671.25	-
2003-04	4093.08	0.46
2004-05	2009.35	1.39
2005-06	746.18	0.49
2006-07	46.64	6079.56
2007-08	0.24	1793.21
2008-09	1.12	0.01
2009-10 (P)	0.0293	160.08

Source: Department of Agriculture and Cooperation, Ministry of Agriculture, GoI. (http://agricoop.nic.in/Agristatistics.htm)
(-) indicates data not available.

Table 14: Production and government procurement of Wheat

(In million tonnes)

Year	Production	Procurement	Production as % of production
2000-01	69.68	16.36	23.48
2001-02	72.77	20.63	28.35
2002-03	65.76	19.03	28.94
2003-04	72.15	15.80	21.90
2004-05	68.64	16.80	24.48
2005-06	69.35	14.79	21.33
2006-07	75.81	9.23	12.18
2007-08	78.57	11.13	14.17
2008-09	80.68	22.69	28.12
2009-10	80.80	25.38	31.41

Source: Handbook of Statistics on Indian Economy 2009-10, RBI.

In order to arrive at the realistic understanding of the causes for high wheat prices during 2008-09 and 2009-10, it is required to examine the circumstances which were responsible for the building up of huge stock and the manner it was accumulated in 2008-09 and 20009-10. The reason for the government to increase wheat procurement and buffer stock in 2008-09 and 2009-10 is the fact that most part of the period between January 2005 and March 2008, wheat stock with the government were below the prescribed buffer norms. However, in order to avoid shortages the stock of wheat procured at higher MSP during 2008-09 and 2009-10 for three consecutive years from RMS 2007-08 (Table 15). Rising price of MSP of this kind was the cause for rising open market price of wheat[18]. Also, the historic high levels of procurement in RMS 2008-09 and 2009-10 might have deprived the private trade of adequate wheat, thereby causing an increase in the open market price.

Table 15: Minimum Support Price (MSP) of Wheat inclusive of incentive

(Per Quintal)

Marketing Seasons	MSP
2000-01	580
2001-02	610
2002-03	620
2003-04	620
2004-05	630
2005-06	640
2006-07	650
2007-08	850
2008-09	1000
2009-10	1080

Source: Department of Agriculture and Cooperation, Ministry of Agriculture, GoI. (http://agricoop.nic.in/Agristatistics.htm)

3) PULSES

Poor production of pulses in 2008-09 and 2009-10 witnessed a rise in inflation between August 2008 and July 2010 (Table 17). In response, to this situation India imported higher quantity of pulses during 2009-10 (Table 16). It has been observed from the historical data that, pulses imports do not fulfill the requirements of the supply to the extent of reducing the domestic prices due to predominance of the demand factor. Over the years, the production of pulses in India is highly inadequate as compared to the level of domestic consumption. Also, some of the popular pulses varieties are not produced in other parts of the world thereby limiting the imports.

---

[18] Basu, K. (2011, January 20). India's Food grain Policy: An Economic Theory Perspective. *Economic & Political Weekly, vol. XLVI No 5* , pp. 37-46.

Table 16: Export and Import of agricultural products

(In '000 tonnes)

Commodity		2005-06	2006-07	2007-08	2008-09	2009-10(p)
Pulses	Export	447.44	250.7	164.2	136.27	100
	Import	1695.95	22740.97	2835.05	2474.11	3448.35
Spices	Export	400.24	482.8	614.86	673.87	680.6
	Import	108.93	118.51	144.63	122.85	150.03
Tea	Export	162.86	185.63	197.39	207.46	208.55
	Import	18.75	23.29	19.73	25.16	33.64
Coffee	Export	177.68	213.65	178.3	174.08	177.23
	Import	24.94	5.71	9.35	14.19	16.55
Milk & Cream	Export	67.10	41.00	58.07	50.10	26.74
	Import	1.63	3.09	1.98	3.23	8.24

Source: (1) Department of Agriculture and Cooperation, Ministry of Agriculture, GoI. (http://agricoop.nic.in/Agristatistics.htm)

(2) Export Import data bank, Ministry of Commerce and Industry, Department of Commerce, GoI. (http://commerce.nic.in/eidb/Default.asp).

4) FRUITS, VEGETABLES AND MILK

The fall in production was primarily responsible for the rise in inflation rate of fruits and vegetables during 2008-09 and 2009-10. Though, vegetable production picked up in 2009-10 despite bad monsoon followed by floods in some parts of the country, the growth rate was not in line in relation to the trends in the recent past. Due to lower production of oil seeds in 2008-09 and 2009-10, the inflation in oil cake prices was high. The prices of milk and dairy products were soaring high as a result of the combined effect of rise in oil cake prices which is used as animal/cattle feed and the consistent fall in the production of milk since 2006-07 (Table 17). India is the second largest producer of milk in the world and the net exporter of milk and milk products (Table 16). However, in 2008-09 and 2009-10, the export of milk has taken a hit which was severe in 2009-10. Though the international prices of the dairy products were low during October 2008 and October 2009, India imported higher quantity of milk in the same period did not translate into lower domestic inflation of milk and dairy products. This may be because of the cost push effect of high inflation in oil cake and higher domestic demand for milk (Table 8).

Table 17: Year-on-Year growth of production of various Food commodities

(Percent)

Items	2005-06	2006-07	2007-08	2008-09	2009-10
Pulses	1.98	6.05	3.94	-1.29	0.14
Fruits	-7.54	7.60	10.11	4.39	2.47
Vegetables	10.03	3.23	11.70	0.49	4.77
Tea	4.64	2.54	1.43	-1.44	1.89
Coffee	-0.54	5.11	-9.03	0.11	10.41
Milk	4.97	3.91	3.87	3.53	3.23
Egg	2.21	9.74	5.52	3.39	8.03
Meat (Mutton)	3.81	16.93	-15.71	7.59	2.72
Fish (Marine)	1.33	7.39	-3.44	1.99	-9.70
Fish (Inland)	6.55	2.37	9.41	10.27	4.81
Spices	-53.98	6.69	10.22	-4.87	-3.11

Source: (1) Department of Agriculture and Cooperation, Ministry of Agriculture, GoI. (http://agricoop.nic.in/Agristatistics.htm)

(2) Indian Horticulture Database (Various issues), National Horticulture Board, Ministry of Agriculture, GoI.

(3) Basic Animal Husbandry Statistics (various issues), Department of Animal Husbandry, Dairying and Fisheries, Ministry of Agriculture, GoI.

(4) Handbook of Statistics on Indian Economy, 2009-10, RBI.

(5) Coffee Board of India.

(6) Spices Board of India, Cochin, Ministry of Commerce & Industry, GoI. (http://www.indiastat.com)

5) EGG, MEAT AND FISH

The reasons for the high inflation in egg prices were the fall in production in 2008-09 (Table 17) and higher prices livestock feed. The key product responsible for the high prices of meat during March 2008 to July 2010 was mutton. The production growth rate of mutton was also disappointing since 2007-08 (Table 17). This cause high inflation in mutton prices started from October 207 and continued thereafter. The prices of the inland fish pushed up between June 2009 and July 2010 due to the drastic fall in the production during 2009-10 compared to the previous year (Table 17). Similarly, lower production in two consecutive years from 2008-09 resulted in high inflation of marine fish from July 2008 to July 2010.

6) SPICES, TEA AND COFFEE

India is the leading producer and consumer of spices. Also, it was the world's largest exporter (in 2003) and fourth largest importer (in 2005) of spices. Despite higher production of spices each year, imports are necessitated to fulfill the domestic demand for it. The drop in the growth of spices production during 2008-09 and 2009-10 resulted in high inflation in spices (Table 17). However, the spices export was continued despite domestic demand which aggravated the supply-demand gap, thereby causing further rise in prices of spices.

India is world's second largest producer of tea and fourth largest exporter of tea. The rate of growth of tea in India was much lower from 2007-08 onwards compared to the previous three years (Table 16). However, export of tea remained high despite domestic demand. This suggests that export of tea was allowed to take advantage of the high price situation in the international market between February 2008 and April 2010. Thus, the high inflation in tea prices was the result of lower tea production, higher exports and high cost imports.

Inflation rate in coffee was high between March 2008 and April 2010 due to low growth of production in 2008-09 and higher consumption in 2008-09. There was significant jump in domestic consumption of coffee from 94,400 million tonnes to 1,02,000 million tonnes in 2009, an increase of 8.05%. This was the second highest jump in domestic consumption in coffee since 2000. However, the export of coffee did not witness any significant downward pressure in 2008-09 and 2009-10 (Table 16). On the contrary, coffee imports increased during the same. Though, the inflation in coffee at the global level was ruling negative between October 2008 and October 2009, imports could have provided some relief to consumers which are inadequate as compared to domestic demand.

2.12 PRODUCTION, NET EXPORTS & IMPORTS AND NET AVAILABILITY OF FOOD GRAINS IN INDIA

Food Grains Production:

In our economy, the demand for food grows naturally over time due to the population growth. In order to keep pace with population growth, food production has to grow consistently. But, in India, the availability and production have grown considerably very low. In year 2008-09, annual per capita availability of cereal was only 165 kg, which was of the level in year 2000. Agriculture and Food Processing Industries Minister Sharad Pawar released the third advance estimates of crop production for year 2010-11. As per the estimates, India has produced the highest ever food grains of 235.88 million tonnes in year 2010-11, breaking the earlier record of 234.47 million tonnes in 2008-09. In the previous year, the country produced 218.11 million tonnes. In year 2010-11, production of wheat and pulses were at all time high of 86.87 million tonnes and 18.24 million tonnes, respectively. Despite drought in some of the major rice producing areas in the country, food grains production reached the record level of 244.49 due to the significant production of wheat, pulses and coarse cereals (Table 18). During 2011-12, total food grains production reached an all time high of 259.32 million tonnes.

Table 18: Food production in India

(In million tonnes)

Year	Cereals			Pulses	Total Food Grains
	Rice	Wheat	Cereals Total		
2005-06	91.79	69.35	195.20	13.39	208.59
2006-07	93.35	75.81	203.08	14.20	217.28
2007-08	96.69	78.57	216.02	14.76	230.78
2008-09	99.18	80.68	219.90	14.57	234.47
2009-10	89.09	80.80	203.45	14.66	218.11
2010-11	95.98	86.87	226.25	18.24	244.49
2011-12	105.30	94.88	242.20	17.09	259.29

Source: Ministry of Agriculture, GoI.

Net Exports & Imports and Net Availability of Food Grains:

On the contrary, the handling of exports and imports of food stocks by the central government has contributed to domestic price rise in food grains. Table 19 shows that the net exports of food grains were large even in the period of rapid food grain price rise.

Table 19: Production, Net Exports & Imports and Net Availability of Food Grains

(In million tonnes)

Year	Cereals				Pulses		
	Production	Net Exports	Change in Govt. stock	Net Availability	Production	Net Imports	Net Availability
2005-06	162.1	7.2	(-)2.4	157.3	11.5	1.2	12.7
2006-07	170.8	3.8	(-)1.8	168.8	11.3	2.0	13.3
2007-08	177.7	7.0	(+)1.7	169	12.0	2.7	14.7
2008-09	197.2	14.4	(+)17.0	165.9	15.3	2.3	17.6
2009-10	192.4	7.2	(+)11.5	173.7	12.4	3.4	15.8
2010-11	178	4.7	(-)0.5	173.8	12.8	2.5	15.3
2011-12	198.2	4.2	(+)8.3	185.8	14.2	3.1	17.3

Source: Directorate of Economics and Statistics, Department of Agriculture and Cooperation.

Further, the increase in the central stockholding of food grains in the period of rising prices and inadequate infrastructure allow the food grains to rot and become unfit for human consumption. In India, the production of pulses is relatively low to fulfill the requirement, making India the largest importer of pulses, whose import drives the global prices up and leave the net domestic availability low relative to real need of the population.

2.13 DECLINING SHARE OF FOOD IN CONSUMPTION BASKET

From Table 20 and Figure 11, over the last two decades, since 1993-94, the share of food in the total consumption basket has gone down from a level of 54.7 percent to 38.5 percent in 2011-12.Subsequently, the share of non-food in the consumption basket has risen from 45.3 percent in 1993-94 to 61.5 percent in 2011-12. Also, from year 1993-

94 to 2011-12, the share decreases drastically in cereals and vegetables from 14 percent to 7.3 percent and 5.5 percent to 3.4 percent. In protein based items such as pulses, milk, eggs, meat & fish and condiments and spices the trend is flat especially from 2004-05 onwards. In an interview, Rajesh Shukla, Founder Director for Macro Consumer Research at National Council of Advance Economic Research (NCAER-CMCR) told PTI that, as the level of income increases, the share of food in total household expenditure decreases doesn't hold true, if we do not understand the distribution of food in consumption basket.

Table 20: Percentage share of Food & Non-Food in consumption basket (1993-94 to 2011-12)

Item group	Percentage share of Food & Non-Food Items in total consumption expenditure in Urban area				
	1993-94	1999-2000	2004-05	2009-10	20011-12
Cereals	14	12.4	10.1	9.1	7.3
Pulses	3	2.8	2.1	2.7	2.1
Milk & Milk products	9.8	8.7	7.9	7.8	7.8
Eggs, fish & meat	3.4	3.1	2.7	2.7	2.8
Vegetables	5.5	5.1	4.5	4.3	3.4
Fruits	2.7	2.4	2.2	2.1	2.3
Condiments & spices	2	2.2	1.7	1.5	1.7
Food total	**54.7**	**48.1**	**42.5**	**40.7**	**38.5**
Non-food total	**45.3**	**51.9**	**57.5**	**59.3**	**61.5**

Source: MOSPI, GoI (Press release, Key indicators of household consumption expenditure in India, 2011-12, 20th June 2013.pp-6).

Figure 11: Percentage share of Food & Non-Food in consumption basket (1993-94 to 2011-12)

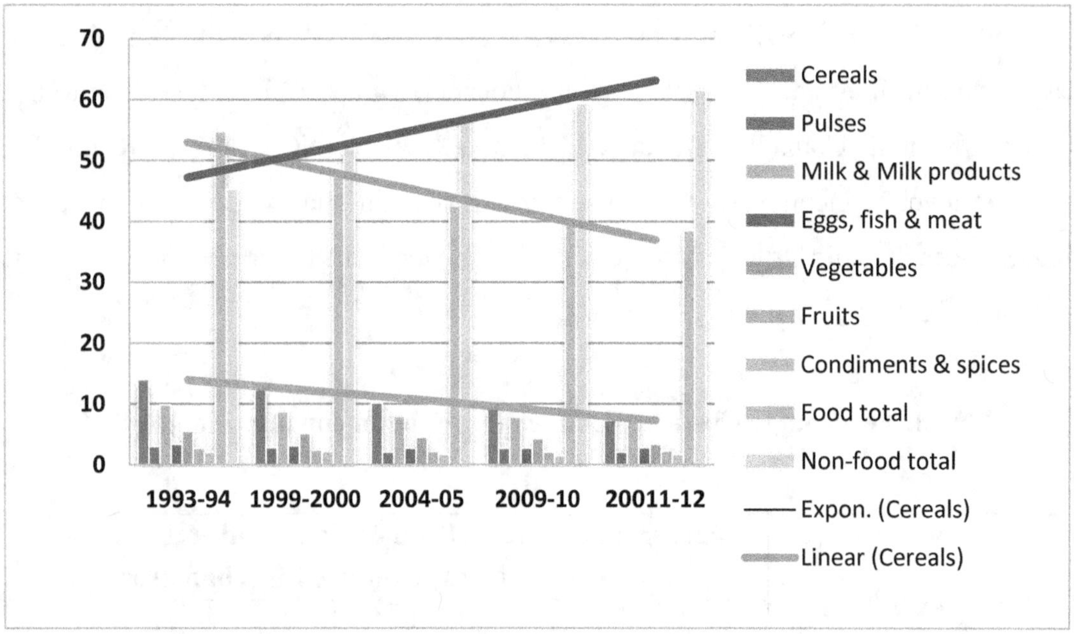

Source: MOSPI, GoI (Press release, Key indicators of household consumption expenditure in India, 2011-12, 20th June 2013.p-6).

2.14 FOOD GRAINS CONSUMPTION IN URBAN INDIA: BELOW THE AVAILABILITY

The Union Agriculture minister Sharad Pawar informed the Parliament that as per the household consumption expenditure survey carried out by National Sample Survey Office (NSSO) between 2004-05 and 2009-10, the per capita consumption of cereals and pulses declined in urban households (Figure 12). Pawar added, in order to augment availability of food grains for individuals, various incentives are being provided under different schemes like National Food Security Mission (NFSM), Rashtriya Krishi Vikas Yojana (RKVY) and National Horticulture Mission (NHM) to boost farm productivity[19].

---

[19] *Indian Express.* (2012, March 25). Retrieved from http://www.indian express.com/news/daily-foodgrains-availability-rises-by-over-25-g-in-2011/928186/.

Figure 12: Per capita consumption of Food Grains (per annum) in Urban area (India)

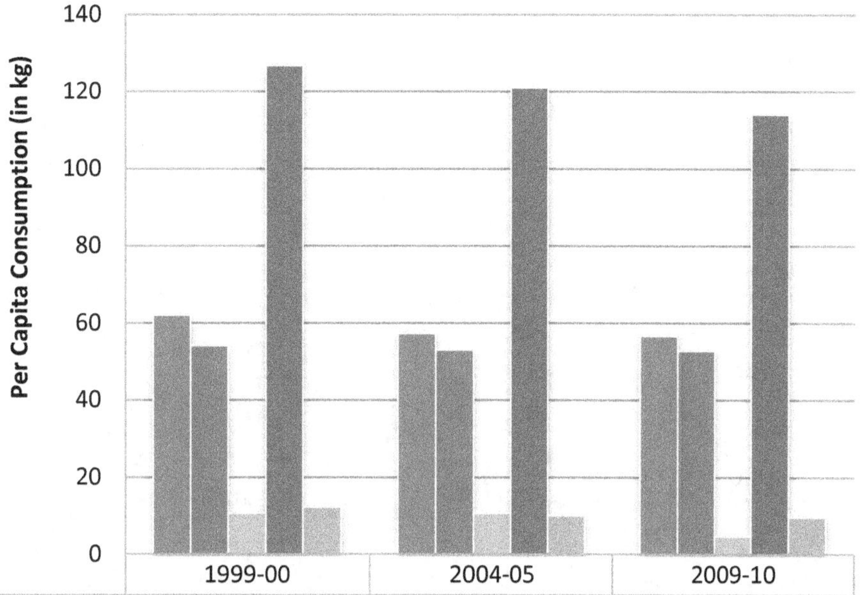

	1999-00	2004-05	2009-10
▪ Rice	62.05	57.31	56.64
▪ Wheat	54.14	53.05	52.82
▪ Coarse Cereal	10.59	10.59	4.6
▪ All cereal	126.78	120.94	114.05
▪ Pulses	12.17	9.98	9.6

Source: National Sample Survey Organization (55, 61 & 66th Round).

2.15 FOOD GRAINS AVAILABILITY IN URBAN INDIA: AT SATISFACTORY LEVEL

The per capita net availability of food grains has declined over the years from 2006-10 and then sharply increased in 2011. On the other hand, a study reveals that, the per capita requirement of food grains in India is 140 kg to 160 kg per annum which is in the range of per capita availability of food grains (Figure 13).

Figure 13: Per capita Net availability of Food Grains (per annum) in Urban area (India)

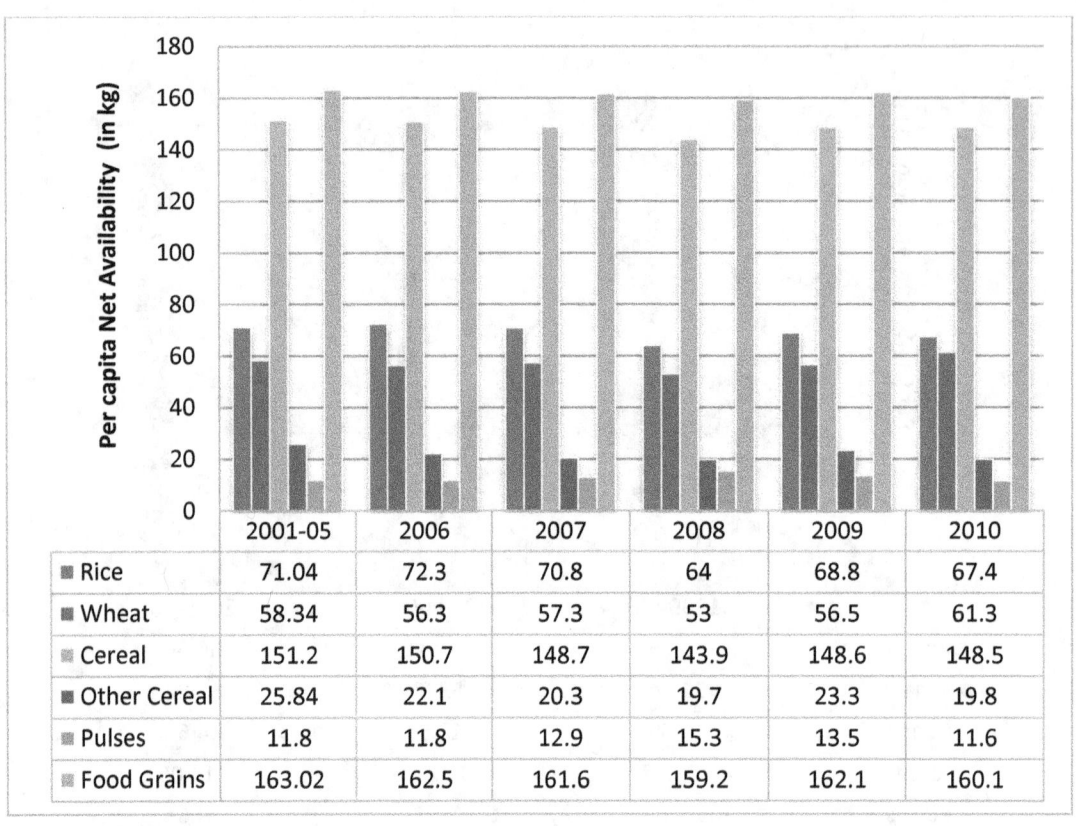

	2001-05	2006	2007	2008	2009	2010
Rice	71.04	72.3	70.8	64	68.8	67.4
Wheat	58.34	56.3	57.3	53	56.5	61.3
Cereal	151.2	150.7	148.7	143.9	148.6	148.5
Other Cereal	25.84	22.1	20.3	19.7	23.3	19.8
Pulses	11.8	11.8	12.9	15.3	13.5	11.6
Food Grains	163.02	162.5	161.6	159.2	162.1	160.1

Source: Directorate of Economics and Statistics, Department of Agriculture and Cooperation.

2.16 SHIFT IN DIETARY HABITS TOWARDS PROTEIN FOODS

A distinct feature of recent food price inflation has been the sustained price pressure in protein rich items (milk, pulses, fish, meat and eggs). Inflation in protein rich items has generally exceeded both headline (WPI) inflation and inflation in primary food articles (Figure 14).

Figure 14: Inflation in Primary Food Articles and overall Inflation

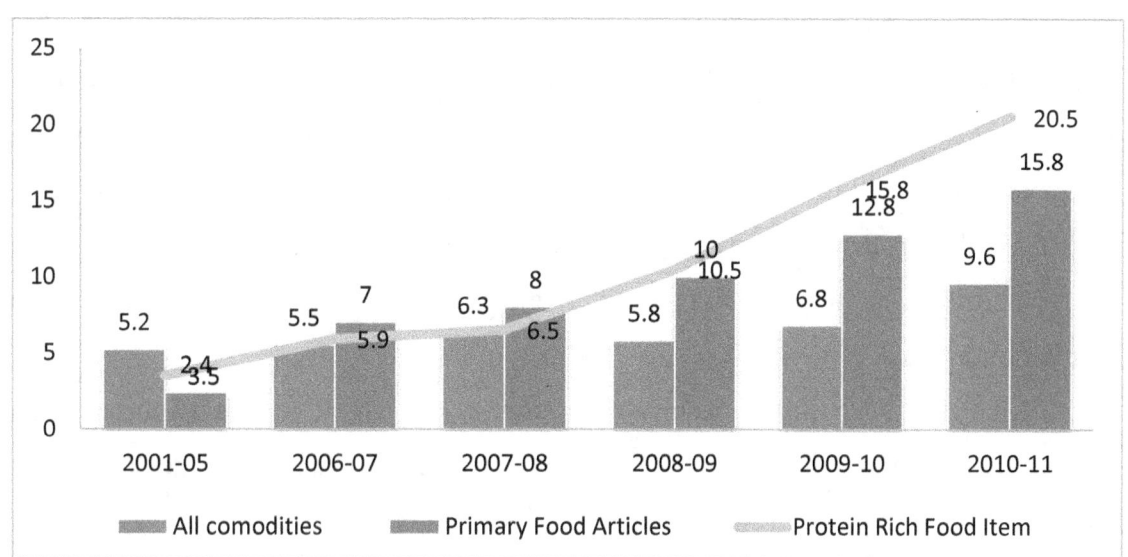

Source: NSSO Surveys.

2.17 OUTSIDE FOOD EATING IN MUMBAI: HIGHEST AMONG OTHER METRO CITIES IN INDIA

There are significant variations across cities in India, while the single largest expense across all location is food and population of Mumbai spends highest on outside food eating (Figure 15). This may be the reason for the fall in the share of household consumption expenditure on food in urban area.

Figure 15: Outside Food eating in Metro cities in India

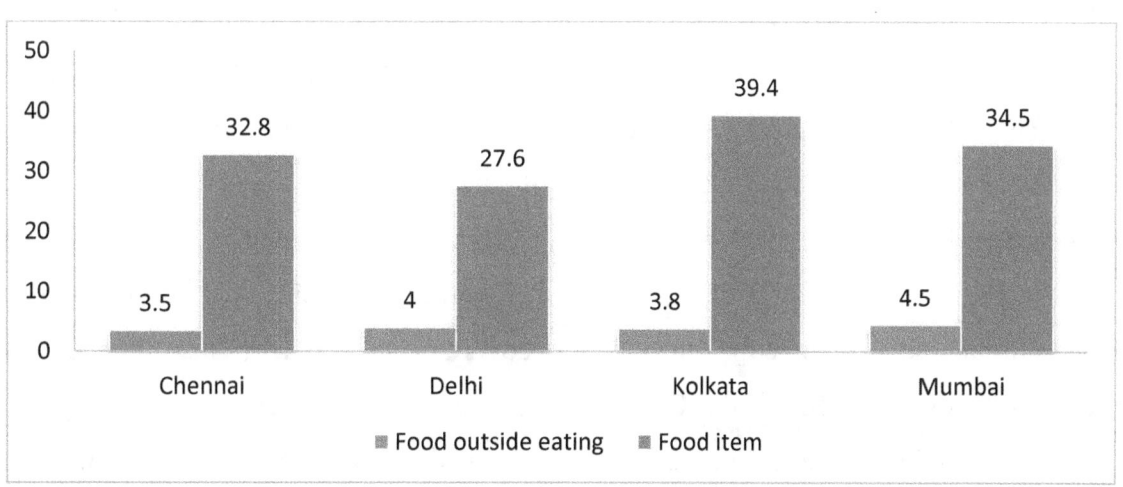

Source: www.atulvaid.com

73

2.18 MEASURES OF INFLATION

There are different ways of measuring inflation. One of the methods is Implicit Price Index (IPI) often called as Gross National Product (GNP) deflator which is defined as the ratio of GNP at current prices to the GNP at constant prices. Therefore, in computation of IPI all the goods and services produced in the economy are considered.

Another method of measuring inflation is Wholesale Price Index (WPI) which in many countries is termed as the Producer Price Index (PPP). WPI is the official measure of inflation in India.

Like, the WPI, the Consumer Price Index (CPI) is also used to measure the changes over time in the level of price of goods and services that a reference population acquires, use, or pay for consumption. The population that falls within the scope of an index is termed as the reference population. In practice, a CPI measures the cost of purchasing a fixed basket of goods and services. However with the launch of new CPI index, RBI started monitoring CPI inflation in its monetary policy. Of the three measures of inflation WPI and CPI are commonly used in India.

WHOLESALE PRICE INDEX (WPI)

Wholesale Price Index measures the change over time in the level of prices of commodities in the wholesale market i.e. price paid by wholesalers and producers, and does not take into account retail margins. The WPI measures the price change at the early stage of distribution system and has broader coverage in terms of commodities. Moreover, the price changes in the service sector are not duly accounted for in WPI, even though they are largely influenced by the inputs from the industrial sector. However, headline WPI inflation includes all commodities while core WPI inflation excludes volatile items such as food and fuel. As WPI measures price fluctuations in a more comprehensive way, it is widely used by government, banks, industries and business circles. The movement of WPI serves as an important determinant in formulation of trade, fiscal and economic policies by the government of India. The office of the Economic Advisors, Ministry of Commerce and Industry is responsible for compiling WPI and its release. The office published WPI for the first time, an index number of wholesale prices, with base week ended 19th August, 1939=100, from the week commencing 10thJanuary, 1942. Ever since the introduction of the WPI, six revisions have taken place introducing the new base years, viz. 1948-49, 1952-53, 1961-62, 1970-71, 1981-82 and 1993-94. Table 21 shows the evolution of WPI in India.

Table 21: Evolution of WPI in India

Base	Year of Introduction	No. of Items	No. of Price Quotations
Week ended 19th August, 1939	10th January, 1942	23	23
End August, 1939	1947	78	215
1952-53(1948-49 as weight base)	1952	112	555
1961-62	July, 1969	139	774
1970-71	January, 1977	360	1295
1981-82	July, 1989	447	2371
1993-94	April, 2000	435	1918
2004-05	September, 2010	676	5482

Source: MOSPI, GoI.

Method of calculation of WPI:

It is calculated on the principle of weighted arithmetic mean, according to Laspeyer's formula which has a fixed base year weighting diagram operative through the entire life span of the WPI series.

The formula is given as:

$$I= \sum (I_i * W_i)/ W_i$$

Where,

I= Index number of wholesale prices of sub-group/group/major group/all commodities

W_i= The weights assigned to the ith item/sub-group/group/major group

I_i= Index of the ith item/sub-group/group/major group

The weights have been assigned on the basis of entire wholesale transactions in the economy (Table 22).

**Table 22: Comparative statement of weights assigned to product groups
(WPI 1993-94 and 2004-05 series)**

Major Group/ Group	WPI series	
	1993-94	2004-05
All Commodities	100.000	100.000
Primary Articles	22.025	20.118
Food Articles	15.402	14.337
Non-food Articles	6.138	4.258
Minerals	0.485	1.521
Fuel & Power	14.226	14.910
Coal	1.753	2.094
Mineral Oils	6.987	9.364
Electricity	5.484	3.452
Manufactured Products	63.749	64.972
Food Products	11.538	9.974
Beverages, Tobacco & Tobacco Products	1.339	1.762
Textiles	9.800	7.326
Wood & Wood Products	0.173	0.587
Paper & Paper Products	2.044	2.034
Leather & Leather Products	1.019	0.835
Rubber & Plastics Products	2.388	2.987
Chemicals & Chemical Products	11.931	12.081
Non-Metallic Mineral Products	2.516	2.556
Basic Metals, Alloys & Metal Products	8.342	10.748
Machinery & Machine Tools	8.363	8.931
Transportation Equipments & parts	4.259	5.213
Other Industries	0.000	0.000

Source: MOSPI, GoI.

Table 23: Comparative statement of commodities and price quotations (WPI series 1993-94 and 2004-05)

Major Group/ Group	Number of commodities		Number of price quotations	
	1993-94	2004-05	1993-94	2004-05
All Commodities	435	676	1918	5482
Primary Articles	98	102	455	479
Food Articles	54	55	340	431
Non-food Articles	25	29	96	108
Minerals	19	18	19	40
Fuel & Power	19	19	72	72
Manufactured Products	318	555	1391	4831
Food Products	41	57	168	406
Beverages, Tobacco & Tobacco Products	11	15	49	102
Textiles	29	55	100	457
Wood & Wood Products	2	10	9	64
Paper & Paper Products	11	18	67	138
Leather & Leather Products	1	13	9	91
Rubber & Plastics Products	15	45	55	351
Chemicals & Chemical Products	69	107	276	1111
Non-Metallic Mineral Products	9	26	42	225
Basic Metals, Alloys & Metal Products	53	69	203	696
Machinery & Machine Tools	56	107	312	903
Transportation Equipments & parts	21	33	101	287

Source: MOSPI, GoI.

Figure 16 shows below broad breakup of components comprising WPI index.

Figure 16: Components of WPI Inflation

```
                              ┌───────┐
                              │  WPI  │
                              └───┬───┘
        ┌─────────────────────────┼─────────────────────────┐
┌───────────────────┐   ┌──────────────┐    ┌─────────────────────┐
│ Primary Articles  │   │ Fuel & Power │    │ Manufactured Products│
└───────────────────┘   └──────────────┘    └─────────────────────┘
```

Primary Articles
- Food
- Non Foods (Oil, Seeds & Fibers)
- Minerals

Fuel & Power
- Coal, LPG, Petrol, Electricity etc.

Manufactured Products

12 Industries
Food
Textile
Wood
Paper
Leather
Chemicals
Metals
Rubber & Plastics
Transport
Machinery
Non Metallic Minerals
Beverages & Tobacco

Source: Self complied.

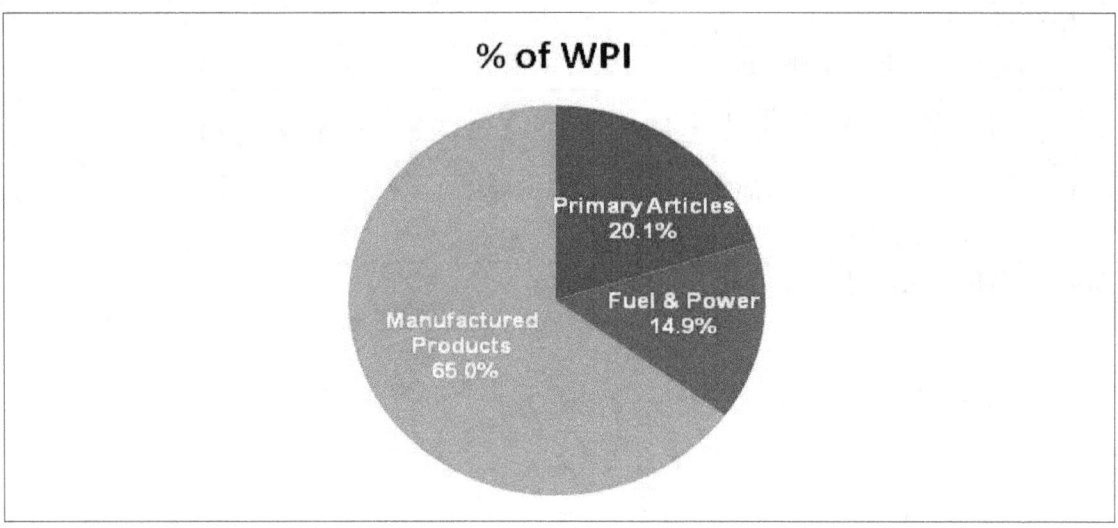

% of WPI

Primary Articles 20.1%

Fuel & Power 14.9%

Manufactured Products 65.0%

Source: Self complied.

Figure 17 shows that the major driver of inflation is generally primary articles particularly food articles and fuel & power.

Figure 17: WPI Inflation trend Post 2008 crisis

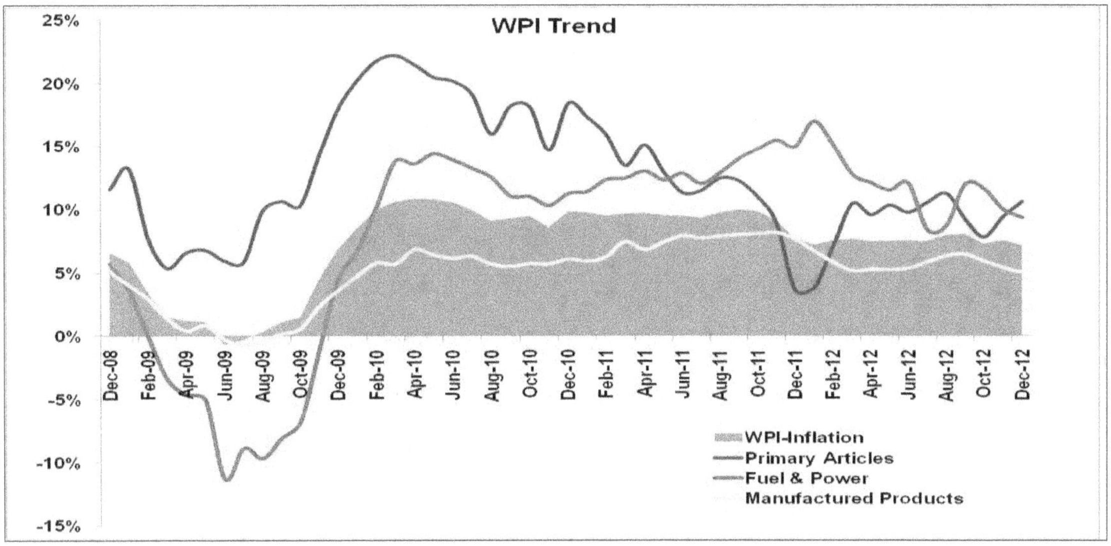

Source: Office of Economic Advisor, GoI.

Table 24: Wholesale Price Inflation (Average) from Year 2000-01 to Year 2011-12 (up to March 2012)

(Percent)

Year	All commodity	Primary articles	Primary articles of which		Fuel, Power, Light and Lubricants	Manufac-tured Products
			Food articles	Non-Food articles		
(Base: 1993-94=100)						
2000-01	7.2	2.8	3.0	2.4	28.5	3.3
2001-02	3.6	3.6	3.3	4.4	8.9	1.8
2002-03	3.4	3.3	1.8	8.2	5.5	2.6
2003-04	5.5	4.3	1.3	12.6	6.4	5.7
2004-05	6.5	3.6	2.6	0.7	10.1	6.3
(Base: 2004-05=100)						
2005-06	4.4	4.3	5.4	-3.3	13.5	2.4
2006-07	6.6	9.6	9.6	5.8	6.5	5.7
2007-08	4.7	8.3	7.0	11.9	0.0	4.8
2008-09	8.1	11.0	9.1	12.9	11.6	6.2
2009-10	3.8	12.7	15.3	5.5	-2.1	2.2
2010-11	9.6	17.7	15.6	22.3	12.3	5.7
2011-12	8.9	9.8	7.3	9.6	14.0	7.3

Source: (1) RBI, Handbook of Statistics on Indian Economy 2011-12.
(http://rbidocs.rbi.org.in/rdocs/publication/PDFS/232)
(2) RBI, Handbook of Monetary Statistics of India 2006-07.
(http://rbidocs.rbi.org.in/rdocs/publication/PDFS/690)

CONSUMER PRICE INDEX (CPI)

Consumer price index measures the changes over time in the general level of prices of goods and services that household acquire for the purpose of consumption. CPI numbers are used as a macroeconomic indicator of inflation, as a tool by government and RBI for inflation targeting and monitoring price stability and as a deflator in the national accounts. It is also used for indexing dearness allowances to employees against the increase in prices. CPI numbers are presently compiled and released at the national level reflect the fluctuations in retail prices pertaining to specific class of population in the country namely CPI-Industrial Workers (CPI-IW), CPI-Rural Labourers (CPI-RL), CPI-Agricultural Labourers (CPI-AL) and CPI-Urban Non-Manual Employees (CPI-UNME).

Figure 18: Components of CPI Inflation (Rural + Urban)

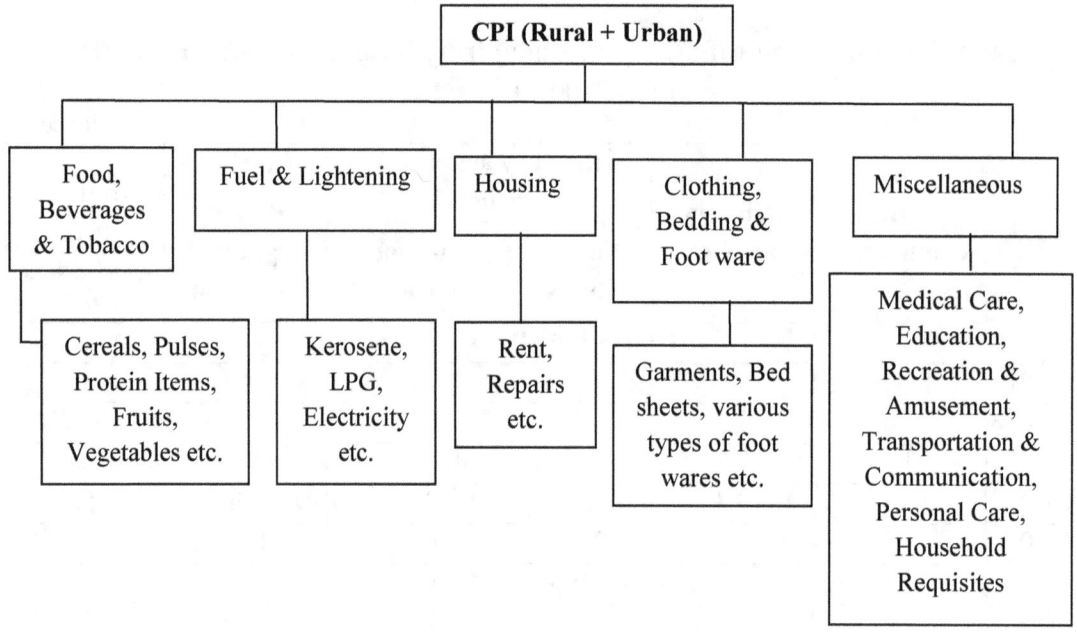

Source: Self complied.

CPI-Urban Non-Manual Employees (CPI-UNME) has been discontinued and a new index was launched in January 2011 with base year 2010 which measures changes in the prices of goods and services consumed by rural and urban population. Figure 18 shows a broad break up of CPI index.

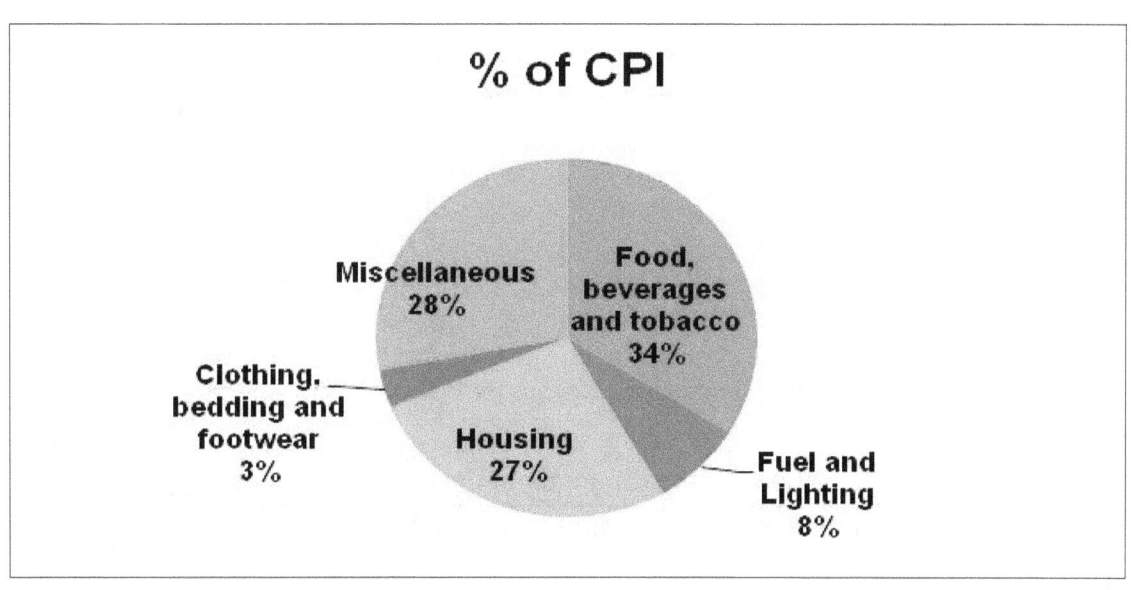

% of CPI

Source: Self complied.

Table 25: Consumer Price Inflation (Average) from Year 2000-01 to Year 2011-12 up to March 2012)

(Percent)

Year	Industrial Workers	Urban Non-Manual Employees	Agricultural Labourers
(Base: 1986-87=100 for AL)			
2000-01	3.8	5.6	-0.3
2001-02	4.3	5.1	1.1
2002-03	4.0	3.8	3.2
2003-04	3.9	3.7	3.9
2004-05	3.8	3.6	2.6
2005-06	4.4	4.7	3.9
2006-07	6.7	6.6	7.8
(Base: 2001=100 for IW)			
2007-08	6.2	5.9	7.5
2008-09	9.1	8.9	10.2
2009-10	12.4	13.0	13.9
2010-11	10.4	-	10.0
2011-12	8.4	-	8.2

Source: Handbook of Statistics on Indian Economy, 2011-12.

Method of Calculation of CPI

Following are the formulae used for the calculation of CPI:

1) Laspeyer's Formula
2) Paasche's Formula
3) Fisher's formula

The formula which is commonly used for Consumer Price Index would be

$$\frac{\text{Total cost of a fixed basket of goods in the current period}}{\text{Total cost of a fixed basket of goods inthe base period}} * 100$$

As already given, the fixed basket of goods and services would be determined on the basis of a family budget enquiry among the population group concerned. This enquiry would yield information on the consumption pattern of the families belonging to the group for which the survey data relate.

If the survey data related to the base period of the index series, as is generally the case, the above formula is the well known Laspeyer's formula. Thus, if the quantities of different goods and services consumed by an average family in base period are denoted by q_o's and the corresponding prices in the base period and current prices are denoted by p_o's and p_n's resp., the index for the current period I_n would be

$$I_n = \frac{\sum q_o p_n}{\sum q_o p_o} * 100 \qquad \ldots\ldots\ldots\ldots\ldots (1)$$

Thus, I_n is the cost of buying the goods and services (as purchased in the base period) at current prices. With every successive current period only p_n's in the formula will vary while the other terms are held constant over the whole life of the index series.

If the quantities of goods and services vary in each current period according to the current consumption patterns (family budget enquiry has to be conducted during every successive period), the formula above would be changed, replacing q_o's by q_n's. Thus, the formula would be

$$I_n = \frac{\sum q_n p_n}{\sum q_n p_o} *100 \dots\dots\dots\dots\dots \quad (2)$$

is known as Paasche's formula. It is seldom used in practice due to the operational difficulty of conduction of family budget enquiry during every successive period for which the index is compiled.

In normal economic situations, with the passage of time, the Laspeyer's index shows an upward bias. In contrast, the Paasche's index shows downward bias. A renowned econometrician, Irvin Fisher, constructed an ideal index as the geometric mean of the Laspeyer's index and Paasche's index . Since, the geometric mean lies in between the two; it gives the value nearest to the true cost of living index. The Fisher's ideal index is given as:

$$I_n = \left[\sqrt{ \frac{(\sum q_o p_n}{(\sum q_o p_o} * \frac{\sum q_n p_n)}{\sum q_n p_o)} } \right] *100$$

Majority of the Consumer Price Indices in different countries across the world are based on Laspeyer's formula due to its practical simplicity of compilation as the weights are determined in the base period which remain constant during the entire life of the index.

GAP BETWEEN WPI AND CPI

There are several distinguishing points between WPI and CPI:

1) There is a variation between WPI and CPI with CPI being higher by 2-3 percent.
2) Base year for WPI is 2004-05, while that of CPI is 2010.
3) Over the past several years, food has been the major contributor to inflation has higher weight in CPI than WPI.

4) Despite, service sector contributing to more than 60% of GDP, is not included in WPI, while CPI covers price changes in service sector.

2.19 GOVERNMENT MEASURES TO CURB INFLATION

Inflation in India has been a major cause of worry for both the government as well as central bank who take numerous measures to contain it such as:

1) **Fiscal and Administrative Measures**

- Reduced import duty to zero on wheat, onion, pulses, crude palmolein and 7.5 percent on refined & hydrogenated oils & vegetable oils.

- Duty free import of white and raw sugar was extended up to 30.6.2012; however import duty of 10 percent was instituted in June 2012.

- Banned export of edible oils (except coconut oil and forest based oil) and edible oils in blended consumer packs up to 5 kg with a capacity of 20,000 tons per annum and pulses (except Kabuli chana and organic pulses and lentils up to a maximum of 10,000 tonnes per annum).

- Imposed stock limits on selected essential commodities such as pulses, edible oil, and edible oilseeds and in the case of paddy and rice for specific seven states up to 30.11.2012.

- Banned export of onion for short period of time whenever required. Exports of onion were calibrated through the mechanism of Minimum Export Prices (MEP).

- Maintained the Central Issue Price (CIP) for rice (at Rs 5.65 per kg for BPL and Rs 3 per kg for AAY) and wheat (at Rs 4.15 per kg for BPL and Rs 2 per kg for AAY) since 2002.

- Suspended Futures trading in rice, urad, tur, guar gum and guar seed.

- To ensure adequate availability of sugar for the households covered under TPDS (Targeted Public Distribution System), the levy obligation on sugar factories was restored to 10 percent for sugar season 2011-12.

- Government allocated rice and wheat under Open Market Sales Scheme. Resumed the scheme for subsidized imported pulses through PDS in a varied form with the nomenclature, "Scheme for Supply of Imported Pulses at

Subsidized rates to States/UTs for Distribution under PDS to BPL card holders",
with a subsidy element of Rs. 20/- per kg to be paid to the designated importing
agencies up to a maximum number of BPL card holders for the residual part of
the current year and extended the scheme for subsidized imported edible oils
w.e.f. 1.10.2012 to 30.9.2013 with subsidy of Rs. 15/- per kg for import of up to
10 Lakh tonnes of edible oils for this period[20].

2) Budgetary and Other Measures

A number of measures were announced in Union Budget 2012-13 to
augment supply and improve storage and warehousing facilities. Government
launched a National Mission for Protein supplements in 2011-12 with allocation
of Rs. 300 crore. To broaden the scope of production of fish to coastal
aquaculture, apart from fresh water aquaculture, the outlay in 2012-13 was
stepped up to Rs. 500 crore. Recently, Government permitted Foreign Direct
Investment (FDI) in multi-brand retail trading. This will help consumers and
farmers as it will improve the selling and purchasing facilities.

3) Monetary Measures

The Reserve bank of India took number of conventional and
unconventional measures to augment currency liquidity and sharply reduced the
policy rates. In a period of seven months i.e. between October 2008 and April
2009, the repo rate was reduced by 425 basis points to 4.75 percent; the reverse
repo rate was reduced by 275 basis points to 3.25 percent; cash reserve ratio
(CRR) was reduced by cumulative 400 basis points of their net demand and time
liabilities (NDTL) to 5.0 percent and primary liquidity made available to the
financial system was over rupees 5.6 trillion or over 10 percent of GDP.

In October 2009 RBI showed a need to exit from monetary policy
stimulus. It was not so easy because of the two reasons; first, the year on year

---

[20] MoF. (2012-13). Mid-Year Economic Review 2012-13. *Ministry of Finance,
Government of India* .

headline inflation WPI had just turned positive and was mainly due to food inflation Industrial production had started to pick up but exports were still declining; secondly, most central banks across the world were in favour of continuing stimulus. On the other hand, consumer price inflation was high, household inflation expectations rising and surplus liquidity was substantial. These developments had inflationary consequences.

The RBI restored the statutory liquidity ratio (SLR) of bank to its pre-crisis levels. At the same time, monetary policy recognized that the economic growth was recovering from the crises slowed down and any tightening in the monetary policy would affect recovery. Subsequently, in January, 2010, the CRR of banks was raised by 75 basis points and the policy rate was increased for the first time in March, 2010 by 25 basis points. Between March, 2010 and October, 2011 the policy rate was raised by 375 basis points to contain inflation. The policy rates was raised from a historical low of 4.75 percent and inflation had risen sharply there was a scope for further tightening of monetary policy (Figure 19).

Figure 19: Real Policy Rate versus WPI Inflation

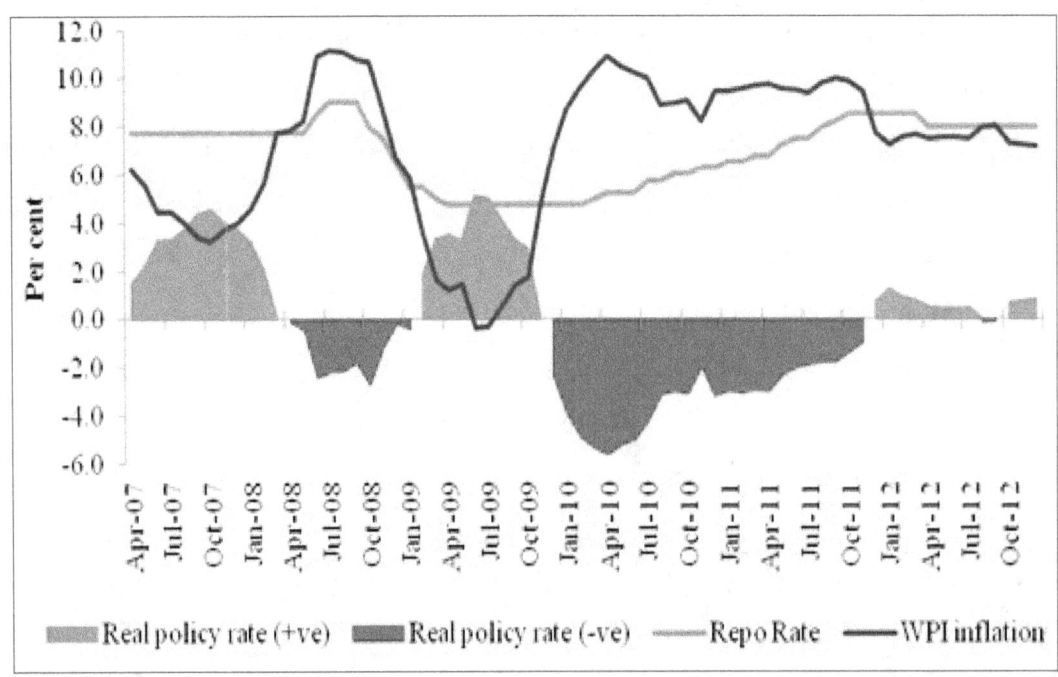

Source: http://www.rbi.org.in

2.20 OTHER EFFECTS OF FOOD INFLATION

1) Leads to Decline in GDP

The food inflation affects the middle class very badly. Indian consumer generally spends near about 50% his household income on food and any surplus remains goes to discretionary spending. Unfortunately, today, this is the segment which is experiencing the effect of high inflation. High food inflation pressurizes the consumers to cut back on their spending (on non-necessary items). This in turn will impact the consumption part of the GDP growth.

2) Investors Invest in Bank's Fixed Deposits

Most of the Indian investors do not invest in equity. They invest in bank's fixed deposits for a return of 8 to 10 %, which is much lesser than the rate of Inflation. Thus, a large section of the population is losing out on their purchasing power without realizing about it. For those who realize this, there is only one option to speculate in the stock markets and try to get returns which beat the annual inflation rate.

3) Second round of Food Inflation and cascading effect on Food Prices

If the government decides to raise the procurement price of agricultural commodities in a big way, it can lead to second round of food inflation. The government's decision to raise petrol and diesel prices will have a cascading effect on food prices as well.

4) Exacerbation of Inflation in Food importing countries

India, Argentina and other food-exporting nations, in response to global inflation and in order to protect their own consumers, imposed restrictions on exports. This is an understandable move, but it exacerbates inflation in food-importing countries.

2.21 REMEDIES TO TACKLE FOOD INFLATION IN INDIA

The remedies to tame the current food inflation in the economy can be classified in to short-term and long-term options. Some of the important measures discussed below are:

1) Increasing Supply of Food

The supply side constraints and structural deficiencies accelerating the food inflation in India can be corrected by taking concerted efforts over an extended period of time. As a short-term measure, supply shortages can be overcome by releasing government stocks of food and allowing imports by reducing import duties or reducing them to zero, whenever required. However, decision on export and import should be preceded by some planning based on market intelligence and supply-demand situation.

2) Deflating the Stimulus Package

There is a need to curb excess liquidity that was created in the system as a result of fiscal stimulus given over the past two years to ensure growth recovery. Also, there is a need for a calibrated winding down of this stimulus package by tightening the monetary and fiscal policies. In the effort, in the Third Quarter Review of Monetary Policy for 2010-11, RBI has increased the repo rate to 6.5 % and the reverse repo rate to 5.5%.

3) Setting up Commercial Intelligence Agency

Often the inability to pre-assess the market conditions due to inadequate information and timely dissemation at various levels aggravated inflationary pressures. The differences in the various national level databases pose a problem in assessing the real situation of the agricultural production as observed in the case of onions, cotton, sugar, etc. Efforts should be taken to ensure convergence of these databases that can help take stock of the supply situation and then address the issue of availability and its impact on prices realistically. There is a need to establish commercial intelligence agency that can maintain the records of production, stocks, and trade and also tracks prices and can generate advance signals to help tame abnormal soaring up of prices. It is important to identify triggers to set off automatically when the market prices of the commodities cross the targeted price bands. The future market which was introduced to control the prices of the commodities sometimes cause inflation due to the projections of the future prices of the commodities in the present. It is a need of time that there should be greater synergy between various agencies and departments dealing with production, stocking and trade.

4) Reform of the Mandi System

The recent food price inflation is seen to be driven by high value food items, with vegetables playing a major role. The prices are extremely volatile, it may be noted that the spread between wholesale and retail prices is quite large in case of vegetables. The main reason being fragmented supply chains and the predominance of commission agents. As a step towards reforming the mandi system, it is suggested that fruits and vegetables should be exempted or de-listed from the APMC act. The states should be incentivized to encourage direct marketing between farmers and buyers without having to pay any mandi fee or commission to the agents. This can be linked to the incentives under various programs such as National Horticulture Mission. Also, taxation on primary agricultural goods needs to be replaced by value added tax. Existing impediments in moving agriculture commodities need to be removed to allow free flow of goods across the country[21]. Private mandis and terminal markets could be the alternatives to traditional market structures. The private sector can be incentivized to upgrade marketing infrastructure through public private partnership and create competition to cut down the transaction costs.

5) Encourage Farm-Firm Linkages

Direct farm-firm linkages is an alternative to the Mandi system and there are success stories in the agriculture sector (for example, Safal (Mother Dairy), Mahagrapes (marketing wing of grape growers cooperative in Maharashtra, and the like) that can be further experimented and scaled up. There can be scope for various models, be it cooperatives, producer companies, etc., whereby farmers cluster together to do business with the public or private players. Investments in backward linkages in terms of supply of agri-inputs, extension and agri-advisory and risk mitigation can help strengthen the firm-farm linkages. Institutions dealing in land leasing and credit activities need to be reformed to induce greater linkages that at present are not very congenial to modern agribusiness practices. It is right time to remove all obstacles to private investments in

---

[21] Ashok Gulati, K. G. (2011, January 13). Agri-reform to tame food inflation. *The Economic Times, New Delhi* .

agri-marketing so as to improve competition, developing value chains that include storage and warehousing facilities and backend services for the farmers.

6) Enhancing Investments in Agriculture

Investments in agriculture have increased sharply in recent years for about 20% of agricultural GDP. It is surprising that, why these have not translated into higher agricultural growth. It is necessary to look at the nature of these investments and account for the period of gestation lag in order to assess the impact on growth. It has also been observed that, investments in the form of infrastructure may not be sufficient and it is time to measure progress of infrastructural development from the point of view of service delivery. There is a scope for greater investments from the private sector, particularly in the high value supply chains and the public sector can catalyze these investments by providing the right policy environment in infrastructure such as roads, markets, etc.

2.22 MIDDLE CLASS IN INDIAN CONTEXT

There is no official definition of the middle class, estimates ranging from 30 million to approximately 300 million people. The most generous estimates of the group's size, the middle class comprises less than 30 percent of the population[22]. NCAER's definition identifies the middle class as comprising of two sub-groups: seekers and strivers. Rajesh Shukla, Director, NCAER's Centre for Macro Consumer Research (CMCR) told to PTI that, as per the study, which uses 'household income' as the criterion, a family with an annual income between Rs. 3.4 Lakh to Rs. 17 Lakh (at 2009-10 price levels) falls in the middle class category[23]. As per 2000-01 prices, middle class classification was based on annual income of Rs. 2-10 Lakh. Currently India has 31.4 million middle class households (160 million individuals) which represent 13.1 percent of India's population. The percentage of middle class in the country's total population will

[22] DBResearch. (2010, February). The middle class in India: Issues and opportunities. *Deutsche Bank Research* , pp. 1-8.
[23]Shukla, R. (2011). *National Council of Advance Economic Research (NCAER).* PTI Interviewer.

increase to 20.3 percent by 2015 (i.e. 53.3 million households or 267 million individuals) and 37.2 percent by 2025 (i.e. 113.8 million households or 547 million individuals). McKinsey Global Institute (MGI) shows that within a generation, India will become a nation of upwardly mobile middle-class households. Figure 20 shows pyramid of classification of the population in to five classes, being the seekers are called as "lower middle class" and strivers are called as "upper middle class" people.

Figure 20: Pyramid of population Class-wise

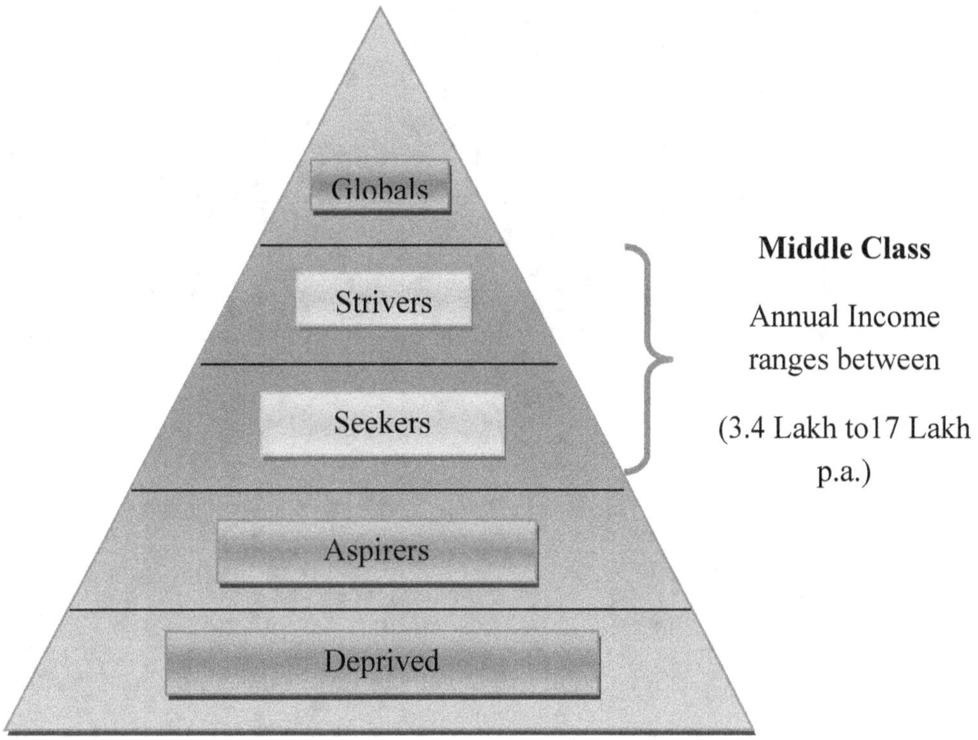

Source: MGI.

However, in a study, published in www.atulvaid.com, the author divide the whole population in to eight classes in the ascending order, starting from deprived, aspirers, seekers, strivers, near rich, clear rich, sheer rich and super rich. NSSO quinquennial surveys on consumption expenditure divide the whole population in to ten decile classes. The first decile class comprises of the bottom 10 percent of the population in terms of MPCE and the top (10th) decile class comprises of the top 10 percent of population.

2.23 PROFILE OF THANE CITY

Introduction:

Thane city is one of Maharashtra's major industrial towns and the district headquarters. It covers an area of 147 km^2 and has a population of 18,18,872 according to 2011 census. The city is located at the mean sea level on the northern part of the Konkan region. The city is also known as 'Lake city' because of the 35 lakes covering an area of about 40Ha.

Demographics & Culture:

It has predominantly Maharashtrian culture like its neighbouring city Mumbai and cosmopolitan culture as well. Majority of the people (over 76%) in Thane are Marathi speaking Maharashtrians. Besides Marathi, sizeable populations of North Indians, South Indians, Sindhis, Gujaratis and Marwari and other people from different religions live in Thane. Because of the huge industrial and residential boom, the city has witnessed a large number of immigrants from the nearby city of Mumbai as well as from other parts of the state and country. The current trend shows that the city is growing as a suburban dormitory town.

The intra city population analysis shows that, the central areas of the city are densely populated followed by areas of Mumbra and Kalwa. Wagle Estate and Vartak nagar have the largest population, whereas the least population is seen in the areas at Shilphata and Diva. The average female to male ratio in the city stands at 870 females per 1000 males, of which maximum in Naupada 948 and least in Balkum 802. The average number of members per households is 4.45; of which maximum 5.14 in Mumbra and minimum 4.14 in Kolshet. Average literacy rate of Thane city is 91.36 percent of which male and female literacy was 94.19 and 88.14 percent.

Thane city Ward-wise:

Thane city is divided into Nine Wards/ Prabhag Samities:

1) Uthalsar
2) Naupada
3) Kopari
4) Kalwa
5) Mumbra, Diva and Shilphata
6) Wagle Estate
7) Railadevi
8) Vartak Nagar
9) Owle, Manpada and Kolshet

CHAPTER 3: REVIEW OF LITERATURE

Chapter Highlights:

3.1 Introduction

3.2 Indian Studies related to Inflation and Food Inflation

3.3 Foreign Studies related to Inflation and Food Inflation

3.1 INTRODUCTION

To the best of my knowledge and belief, in the past and in the present work, no study has been done on impact of food inflation on household consumption expenditure in Thane city. This would be the first work by an individual on a subject of food inflation and how middle class consumers manage their household consumption expenditure on food articles.

In recent years, food inflation attracts lot of attention of the researchers & the policy makers and encourages them to conduct study on the causes, measure, effects, remedies to control food inflation etc. Very few studies have been done on effects of food inflation especially on management of household consumption expenditure by the middle class consumers in a city of high cost of living.

However, numbers of studies have been conducted in the form of NSSO surveys and research work done on food inflation, an attempt has been made by the researcher to understand and acknowledge the work of various researchers in the field of inflation and food inflation.

3.2 INDIAN STUDIES RELATED TO INFLATION AND FOOD INFLATION

(Gosh, 2011), in her article, "Food inflation in India", emphasizes on the rising prices of food items and nutritional deficiency. According to the author, in the recent period of rapid growth, lack of food security was a major failure of the development process and decline in the per capita calorie consumption is an indicator of pervasive hunger in India. She says, in the past two years, wholesale prices of food have risen by nearly 40 percent and retail prices have gone up even faster; the massive increase in the price of essential commodities is considered as a sign of material prosperity in India and increased demand for food is the success of the government schemes for the poor; the demand for food has been growing much slower than could be anticipated by both income and population growth; exposure of Indian food markets to the global price volatility by means of speculative financial activity in commodity futures. To remedy this situation, she suggests several measures to contain food inflation, such as; the medium term strategy should be to address the problem of agriculture and making food cultivation financially viable for farmers; a need for active role of public distribution system in moderating food price spikes and dampening inflationary expectations and tendencies of hoarders.

(Subbarao, 2011), in his presidential speech at the 25th Annual Conference of the Indian Society of Agricultural Marketing at Hyderabad on, "The Challenge of Food Inflation", emphasizes on the factors that are driving food inflation; i) shift in dietary habits towards protein foods; ii) pressure stemming from inclusive growth policies; iii) large increases in the minimum support prices (MSP) of food grains; iv) shocks from global food inflation; and v) financialization of commodities. According to him, inflation is a regressive tax and hurts the poor the most. The impact can be particularly severe in a country like India with a population of 1.2 billion, a per capita income of less than $1500 and a large share of food in the total consumption basket. The direct role of monetary policy in combating food price pressures is limited, but in the face of sustained high food inflation, monetary action may still be warranted to anchor inflation expectations. A lasting solution to food price pressures lies in a supply response that raises agricultural production and productivity, improves supply chain management and sets the right incentive framework for both producers and consumers. The outlook on food inflation in the short to medium term will be determined by the speed and quality of such a supply response by the Government.

(P&BD, 2010), observed that, the increase in public and private investment in the supply and distribution infrastructure is viewed by many as a key solution to control rising food inflation especially in case of preventing supply shock induced episodes. It is a need of time to invest in research and development of new technologies and their implementation. Also, the critical issue of irrigation infrastructure has been long neglected and what is required above all is systematic change in the government policy in the context of food sector.

(Chand, 2010), in his article, "Understanding the nature and causes of food inflation", emphasizes on the investments in expanding the storage capacity for various types of foods in both the public and private sectors. As India is a net exporter of food, a part of that export needs to be restored for the domestic consumption in order to bring stability. He suggest that, there is a need to change the food market regulation thereby encouraging the participation of private and public sector in the food market, trade and stock management for price stabilization. Also, there is need to set up a strong institutional mechanism, disseminate advance farming technologies and a food market regulator to look after the activity of hoarders and speculators.

(Mohanty, 2013), in his speech on the topic, "Indian Inflation puzzle", provides explanation that why inflation remained entrenched despite output gap being negative. The sustained level of high inflation is bad for economy as it imposes real cost which is borne disproportionately by different segments of the economy. In order to bring down inflation and anchor inflation expectation there is a need for policy action on several fronts. First, it is important to provide nutritional security not only to harness the demographic dividend arise from our sizeable young population but also to contain inflation. This requires addressing the supply-demand imbalance in the agriculture produce and modernizing the supply chain. Second, efforts are required to secure energy security for the country as the requirement of fossil fuel is met by imports. In order to reduce the burden of subsidy on petroleum products electricity generation should be improved to minimize the fall back option of diesel generation of power. Third, reliability of power supply and availability of necessary industrial raw materials are important for industrial capacity utilization and improvement in productivity. This will reduce reliance on imports of products for which domestic capacity exists. Fourth, it is important to maintain exchange rate of currency to smoothen the price pressure in commodities especially crude oil. This requires management of current account in balance of payment at the sustainable levels. Fifth, fiscal consolidation is important to encourage investments as well as maintaining price stability. Finally, while addressing credit constraints, monetary policy needs to be adjusted in such a way that we should move towards our potential growth in a non-inflationary manner.

(Anand Patil, 2012), in their paper, "Food inflation: An exploratory study", stated that it is a known fact that, to control inflation money supply in the economy is to be reduced thereby reducing liquidity. They have explained the situation by specifying the facts that, during 2009-10 the money supply growth has been only 8.6 percent till November 2009 compared to 9.4 percent in the corresponding period of 2008. The growth of the bank lending to the commercial sector has fallen from 11 percent in the previous year to 3.8 percent in the current year. They said that, reducing money supply is not the only solution to control inflation but it lies in releasing buffer stock with the government. They added, the government is sitting on a buffer stock of 65 million tonnes and it is a matter of great concern that why this stock has not been released at least in part in to the open market to curb inflation. The whole problem lies in the supply and distribution management and tight liquidity will cause trouble to various sectors, including farm sector.

(Sthanu Nair, 2012), in their paper, "Food price inflation in India (2008-2010) - A commodity-wise analysis of causal factors", examined the factors responsible for high inflation in various food commodities in India. The finding shows that, majority of food articles faced upside price pressure because of supply-side constraints. These commodities include fruits, vegetables, meat (mutton), fish (inland & marine), spices, tea, coffee and sugar. On the contrary, the prices of milk and eggs remained high even there is no shortage in the market. This was due to the cost push factor, particularly high inflation in the animal feed, resulting from a shortfall in production of oil seeds. In spite of high production, rice, the most important food grain exhibit high inflationary pressure due to the following two systematic problems plaguing India's food management: high MSP and stocking of grain stock in government depots at this higher MSP. Also, the draught situation in 2009-10 played a role in soaring rice prices. Except milk, the recent high food inflation cannot be attributed substantially to structural demand side factors relating to non-cereal food items. The global economy influenced the domestic food price scenario mainly through passing on high prices of crude oil. Only in case of tea and sugar, the world market had an influence on domestic prices due to costly imports. During the period 2008-2010, the world inflation was in the negative territory, but India was facing high inflation which was primarily due to domestic supply side constraints.

(Pons, 2011), paper on, "Food prices in India: Impact of rising food prices on welfare", examined the impact of food inflation on household welfare. The findings show that, consumption pattern has changed since 1993. Non-food expenditure has increased whereas household have diversified food consumption. Coarse cereals consumption has declined. The changes in the consumption pattern are highly responsible for the demand of higher value food items. Expenditure elasticities allow classifying commodities in to inferior (cereals), normal and luxury goods (fruit, non-food, beverage and meat). In urban areas, the demand is less elastics except for inferior goods. If the demand is less elastic, the inflation will impact severely the households as their consumption pattern would not change. The increase in fruit prices does not matter too much for the households but the increase in the prices of cereals and non-foods have a great effect on them. Different structures of inflation affect negatively different households. The most vulnerable are rural households whose consumption get affected with the increase in the prices of the food especially cereals. On the other hand, the rich households in the urban area are affected with the rise in non-food items. This resulted in the widening of gap between poor and the rich.

(Mittal, 2008), in her working paper, "Demand-Supply trends and projections of food in India", analyzed that the present demand for food is mainly due to growth in population and per capita income. As supply of food is constrained by low yield growth, a gap between supply and demand is narrowing down over the years for all the food items. For cereals, this gap is expected to be 21.19 million tonnes whereas it is projected at 16.96 million tonnes in 2026. The supply–demand gap for pulses, edible oil and sugar is expected to be negative in future. We need to have necessary policy initiatives to increase the supply or otherwise rely on the imports to meet the domestic demand. There is a huge gap between the average yield between India and most of the countries worldwide. This is an indicator of the yield potential that can be achieved through technological advancements. If we strive to achieve this yield levels, then the increasing demand of the country can be met in future.

(S.K.Goyal, 2001), presented that, in India, during the last four decades, the share of superior cereals (rice and wheat) has shown an increasing trend whereas the share of coarse cereals and pulses has shown a declining trend in total food grains production. The per capita consumption of cereal showed a declining trend in both rural and urban region.

The total per capita monthly consumption expenditure has increased by about six and seven times whereas the expenditure on food items exhibited a declining trend during this period. The food basket is found to be diversified showing high per capita consumption expenditure on protein diet such as meat, milk and milk products, vegetables and fruits. A deficit in cereals production in 2009- 10 is expected to be overcome by 2029-30. Pulses deficit in 2009-10 is further expected to increase gradually by 2029-30. With the estimated food grains production there is no danger to food security but this production can be achieved through increase in productivity by giving priority in agricultural research.

(Mittal, 2010), emphasizes on the use of demand models that makes the demand projections based on realistic assumptions which can help to frame medium and long-term agricultural policies. She added, the economy is moving to the demand-driven economy from being a supply-driven economy because of the high economic growth and increasing per capita income. It becomes essential to understand the changing consumption pattern and their responsiveness to the incomes and prices.

(Agrawal, 2011), analyzes that, food inflation is a major structural and policy issue. The decline in agricultural production has been over decades and the impact of rising prices has been felt now because of rising incomes. He suggests the solution to the problem of rising food prices lies in increasing investment in agriculture and productivity. The government raises MSP for various crops and initiates social programs to lower poverty and support agriculture. These policies lead to rise in fiscal deficits and inflation as the rural income increases. Food inflation is just a structural problem but a structural economic problem.

(Mittal, 2006), threw light on two issues such as food demand and food security. According to the author, demand for the food security depends on several factors such as growth of population, per capita income, urbanization, changes in tastes and future growth of the bottom most section of the population. She defines food security is a situation in which both food supply and demand are sufficient to meet nutritional requirements. Food security has number of dimensions that go beyond the production, availability and demand for food. At the household level, it refers to the ability of a household to secure adequate food to meet the dietary requirements of the members of the household.

(Praduman Kumar, 2009), in his paper, "Demand projections for food grains in India", estimated the future demand for food grains in India. He said that, looking at the current trends in food grains production, meeting future demand through domestic production appears to be difficult. There is a need for productivity improvements. Increasing demand for high value food commodities like fruits and vegetables is likely to cause a shift in area from staple food crops. Also, agriculture land is being used for non-agricultural activities. To meet the future demand of food grains the yield of crop has to be increased which requires a serious effort to sustain and improve the total factor productivity through research and development efforts.

(Ashima Goyal, 2010), in her paper, "Extracting information on inflation from consumer and wholesale prices and the NKE aggregate supply curve", emphasizes on the relationship between CPI and WPI. According to the author, consumer prices are a weighted average of the prices of domestic and of imported consumption goods, and producer prices feed in to final consumer prices, wholesale price inflation should cause consumer price inflation. Moreover, there exist a long term relationship between consumer and wholesale price inflation and the exchange rate. This suggests that CPI inflation should Granger cause WPI inflation, through the effect of food prices on wages and producer prices.

(Khalid, 2011), in her paper focuses on the causes behind the rising prices of food items and suggest solutions. According to Khalid, there are several reasons for food price spiral; first, the lack of infrastructure, despite bumper crop production there was no room to store Kharif harvest in September; second, hoarders are creating artificial shortages and fleecing people from time to time; third, the growing penetration of big corporate in the food economy, international trade in food, items and speculative futures trading in agriculture commodities has weakened the government's capacity to control the food prices; fourth, we are not producing enough to meet the demand of growing population;

fifth, the cuts in subsidies and price hikes of inputs like diesel and fertilizers also contributes to food inflation. Solutions to the above problem are; creating transport and storage infrastructure to the required extent; farm productivity should be raised by investing in water management and rural infrastructure; priority should be given in reducing risk due to poor monsoon.

(Lahiri, 2012), in his paper aims to model the behaviour of big retailers and middlemen who hoard perishable commodities, and adds to food inflation by creating artificial shortages. The paper shows the adverse effect of speculative buffering on average price and how import of food item and open market sale of government stock will help to reduce inflation.

(Kumari, 2013), in her paper represents the inflationary scenario for overall food products during the year 2011-12 with the major causes, impact and measures taken by Indian government to contain food inflation. According to Raj Kumari, the main drivers of food inflation are capital stock deficiency, demand side drivers, food price pressures, import price pressures, inflation expectations, etc. High inflation has adverse impact on growth through variety of channels; first, high inflation impacts investments and growth; high inflation results in moving of investments in financial assets to physical assets. The government should take measures to contain prices of essential commodities including ban on export and future trading in food grains, zero import duty on select food items, permitting import of pulses and sugar by PSU's, etc. In addition, state government are empowered to act against hoarders of food items by holding in abeyance the removal of restrictions on licensing, stock limits and movement of food articles under the Essential commodities Act, 1955. There is a need to examine the linkages and trade-offs between policy rate changes and growth of the economy. Government can play a role in expediting irrigation schemes and managing water resources.

(Ramya, 2011), in her article, "India- Food inflation demand driven", stated that, food inflation is driven by demand side forces or at least enduring lags in supply. This means it is also non-transient and calls for a monetary policy response.

(Pradeep Agrawal, 2012), attempts to understand the reasons for the rapid food price inflation witnessed in India over the last few years and to examine how it can be controlled through appropriate agricultural sector policies. According to the author, for every one percent increase in per capita income, the demand for per capita cereals and pulses is likely to decline by 0.05 percent and 0.02 percent respectively, while the demand for fruits, vegetables, milk and edible oil is likely to increase by about 0.55-0.6 percent and that of animal product such as egg, meat & fish is likely to increase by 0.38 percent. The projections shows that for annual per capita income growth of 4.8-7.8 percent, the annual per capita growth rate would decline by about 0.24-0.39 percent for cereal consumption, by 0.96-1.56 percent for pulses but increases by about 4-5 percent for all other food categories, such as fruits, vegetables, starchy roots, milk and edible oil, and 2-3 percent for fish and meat. Also, the per capita consumption of cereal, fruits and vegetables in India will approach that of developed regions such as United Kingdom by 2022. However, our consumption of Milk products and meat & fish will remain significantly below that of developed country levels even by 2022. India's total consumption of vegetables, fruits, oils and dairy products is projected to increase by about 60-70 percent over the next ten years while that of meat products will likely to increase by about 45 percent. The consumption of pulses will remain constant and that of cereals will increase by about 7-9 percent. He suggested several measures to control food price inflation such as reforms in the agriculture sector to increase food production by increasing the yield of crop; provide irrigation facilities to cover more land (55 percent of our cultivated land is still unirrigated); research in agriculture sector to find ways to increase land productivity by an additional one percent above the existing level to keep up with increasing demand; develop farmer's cooperatives like Amul; creating cold storage and transportation facilities; provide reasonable support prices for fruits and vegetables and encourage food processing and packaging sectors to reduce wastage and increase employment in rural areas.

(Angus Deaton, 2009), in the article, "Food nutrition in India: facts and interpretations", attempts to make sense of various puzzles, particularly the decline of average calorie intake during last 25 years. The findings of the study are: First, according to NSS data, the average calorie consumption in rural area was about 10 percent lower in 2004-05 than in 1983. The proportionate decline was larger in better- off sections of the population, and close to zero for the bottom quartile of the per capita consumption expenditure scale. In urban area, there was little change in average calorie consumption over this period. Second, the decline in per capita consumption is not limited to calorie but also applies to proteins and many other nutrients, the major exception being fat consumption, which was increased steadily in both rural and urban areas. Third, it would be difficult to attribute decline in calorie consumption to declining per capita incomes or the changes in relative prices. The per capita calorie consumption is lower today at a given level of per capita household expenditure and this applies across the expenditure scale, at low level of per capita expenditure as well as high. Fourth, the calorie requirements have declined due to better health as well as low activity levels. Fifth, close attention needs to be given to other aspects of food deprivation such as the intake of vitamins and minerals, fat consumption, the diversity of the diet and breast feeding practices, but it is yet to be taken on board in economic analysis of nutrition issues in India. Sixth, it is difficult to assess the welfare implication because of the considerable uncertainty about the causes of calorie decline. Some of the calorie decline may come from a better health environment or a reduction in the burden of hard labour.

(Vishwakarma, 2012), in his article, "Future scenario of food grains: A case study for gap between demand and supply", reveals that, as a part of medium and long term agricultural policy, there is a need for bridging the gap between supply and demand for food grains in order to enable the country to achieve higher rate of economic development on a sustained basis. According to the projections in the paper, it will be required to import rice and pulses around 12 to 15 million tonnes and 13 to 20 million tonnes respectively in 2012-13, 2017-18, 2022-23 and 2025-26 while wheat export of 14 to 15 million tones is required in all horizon years. In case of rice, there is a yield gap of more than 20 percent in most of the states and some shows the gap around 50 to 77 percent. It is estimated that these gaps can accomplish future demand of rice and pulses by adopting improved practices in agriculture in the respective states. Excess production of food grains can be utilized in food processing industries, fulfilling domestic demands, producing value added products and export after fulfilling the country's requirement. Public investment in different agricultural activities could make agricultural profitability and encourage private investment.

(Naveed Ahamad Lone, 2013), in his paper aims to explore the purpose of the inclusive growth agenda that is to make the inclusion of the most vulnerable and excludable sections of the society, and implementation of various programmes and policies under inclusive agenda has given rise to various macroeconomic issues. Food inflation neutralizes the positive effects of inclusive growth and the major challenge is how to insulate the beneficiaries of these programmes from the effects of food inflation. India needs to understand the intensity of food inflation and take measures for the spread of improved technology, develop farm structure, create an institutional environment.

(Ila Patnaik, 2011), in her article argued that CPI-IW should be used among the existing measures of inflation in India as the headline inflation rate. The CPI represents the bundle of households and therefore more relevant than any other measure of inflation. The CPI-IW measures the prices of food as accurately as the other measures. The CPI-IW included the price of services which is not included in any other measures of inflation. However, the WPI or PPI reflects the global prices of tradables expressed in rupees. The monetary policy of the central bank has a minimal role in influencing these other than through the exchange rate while the CPI has large share of non-tradables. Monetary policy has a much bigger role to play in influencing domestic non-tradable prices. Macroeconomic analysis and policy thinking in India needs to move away from a focus on WPI to CPI. The new index will help further to increase confidence in the use of CPI for policy making.

(Bathla, 2012), in her paper, "Volatility in Agriculture Commodity Prices in India: Impact and Macroeconomic and Sector-Specific Policy Responses", evaluates the magnitude of sensitivity of Indian agriculture to volatility in global commodity prices, exchange rate and surge in imports, and explores policy options that may neutralize their adverse effects, maintain price incentives and stability. Findings of the study reveal that, wheat prices to be increasingly driven by an incentive structure arising out of liberal exchange rate, trade and other policies and a greater access of domestic markets to international markets. Wheat is backed by administered price and procurement which provide cushion against shocks caused by an unexpected plunge in its global market price. Empirical results indicates that sudden disturbances caused by a fall in the world price, tariffs and currency appreciation are relatively more pervasive than support price and rainfall in changing the incentive structure, exports and imports. Overall results indicate that wheat could be sensitive to exogenous impulses caused by external conditions. Moreover, hike in the support prices may increase domestic price but prevent higher exports. Appropriate and timely adjustments in tariffs together with changes in support price and operation of open market sales of public stocks may help to counter the adverse effects of likely divergences, maintain incentive structure and price stability in a market driven economy.

(Prachi Mishra, 2011), in her paper uses a disaggregated commodity level and high frequency dataset to provide forensic account of inflation in India over the last two decades with a focus on food prices. The findings show that, the commonly overlooked fact that low inflation has been a rare occurrence in the Indian economy. In the last two decades. The long term inflation exhibits a U-shaped pattern with a structural break in 2000 and inflection point in 2002 (2003 for CPI). There is an evidence for a moderate correlation between international and domestic food price inflation with significant variation across commodities. Moreover, the correlation is low when the world prices are high than when they are low. Food inflation measured by WPI is typically higher than non-food inflation. There is some variation over time in the contribution of specific commodities to food price inflation. The top contributors are milk and fish, sugar, rice and wheat, onions, potatoes, and to lesser extent edible oils. The findings of this paper may have several policy implications. First, both the central bank and other branches of the government can play a meaningful role in tackling the inflation problem. Given the high weight of food in overall inflation and the importance of supply factors or more structural and less interest sensitive demand factors in explaining food price inflation, the hope is that the RBI can control overall inflation by curbing the demand for non-food items that are more interest sensitive. Controlling non-food inflation may have little effect on overall inflation particularly if the central bank targets an inflation rate with CPI-based indices which have relatively smaller weight on non-food items (31-54 percent). Second, tighter monetary policy would reduce the aggregate demand and incomes of households and in turn reduce the demand for food. If food demand is relatively income inelastic, then monetary policy is likely to have limited effects in curbing food price inflation. Third, given than food has a high weight in the consumption basket and that food price inflation has been consistently above non-food by itself calls for focusing on headline rather than core measures of inflation.

(Chhibber, 2013), in his article in the newspaper, Business Standard, argued that, without better understanding of inflation , policy makers are shooting wildly in dark and could end up making costly policy mistakes with huge unwanted consequences. The RBI surprised the marketers by increasing the repo rate in the last monetary policy announcement. Many economists and business groups have criticized the RBI, as they assert that inflation is related to supply-side factors and therefore tighter monetary policy will have little effect on it and hurt growth without helping control inflation. These differences of opinion persist unless we get the better understanding of the causes of inflation. In the past, WPI and CPI inflation closely moved together but over the last five years they have consistently diverged largely due to food inflation which has a much bigger weight in the composition of the CPI Index. The procurement price of cereal has been rising very rapidly, well above the increase in the cost of production by almost 15-60 percent, causing food inflation. As a result, the food subsidy has increased from around 40,000 crore in 2008-09 to over 80,000 crore in 2012-13, and it is likely to increase further in 2013-14, as the new food bill is implemented. The rapid increase in purchase price has two effects: it increases the grain prices in the open market and increases the food subsidy bill, which adds to the fiscal deficit. Instead of releasing the excess of buffer stock, India has arranged for largest export of grain ever in its history in 2012-13, exporting 10.1 million tonnes of rice, 6.5 million tonnes of wheat and 4.8 million tonnes of corn, as domestic prices were below international prices. The rising wages of agricultural laboures also cause food inflation. The solution to manage inflation is not a food story alone, but food does play a central role. The food inflation must be managed by supply side factors but on the demand side the burden must not be on the monetary policy alone, fiscal policy must play a key role as well.

(Venkitaramanan, 2009), in his article in the newspaper, Business Line, believed that, it would be futile to tighten liquidity to combat inflation, when food prices are unresponsive to monetary policy. He added, it is surprising that the government has not released food from its ample buffer stocks or gone in for imports. The rise in the food prices has provoked various commentators to call for drastic action by the RBI. He suggested that, government should take effective action to increase supplies in the market by releasing food stocks at least in part and enabling import of those commodities which are in short supply.

(Sitikantha Pattanaik, 2011), in his working paper, "Why Persistent High Inflation Impedes Growth?: An Empirical Assessment of Threshold Level of Inflation for India", reveals that, the grease effect of inflation for growth as suggested by conventional Phillips curve does not hold true after a threshold level of inflation. Because of the excessive emphasis on growth maximizing level of inflation, the welfare cost of inflation and risk to growth are often ignored in the empirical estimation. The objective of the central bank tries to balance both by setting an inflation target which is not very far below the estimated inflation target to pose any risk to growth, but still lower than the threshold to minimize the welfare cost associated with any positive rate of inflation. This paper provides three layers of justifications to explain why high inflation impedes growth, from economic analysis, cross country evidence, and economic theory. Empirical estimates suggest a growth maximizing inflation rate of 6 percent in the economy. It is possible that the estimated threshold numbers may change over time, reflecting the changing structure of the economy and the causes of inflationary pressure. Past estimations of threshold inflation have been in the range of 5-7 percent and would have expected some moderation over the last decade, which reflects the benefits of reforms and globalization on inflation through higher productivity and competitive efficiency gains. Since, this paper suggests the threshold of about 6 percent one would presume that persistent shocks would have neutralized the expected softening impact of globalization and reforms on the threshold level of inflation. RBI's medium-term objective of 3.0 percent inflation consistent with India's broader integration into the global economy also reflects the normal expectations from reforms and globalization. If these expectations materialize, the threshold level would also decline over time. Recent findings, however, suggests that commodity price pressures have persisted, despite weak growth in advanced economies. On the domestic front, growing demand supply imbalances in certain food items also reflect an emerging structural source of price pressure. If food and fuel prices together become a perpetual source of sequential price pressure, it is unlikely that the threshold inflation would moderate to below 6 percent level in the near-term.

(Ashok Gulati S. J., 2013), in his discussion paper, "Farm trade: tapping the hidden potential", presents India's potential to farm trade. According to the author, India's agri-exports during the FY 2011-12 were more than US$ 37 billion against an import of around US$ 17 billion. India emerged as the world's largest exporter of rice, replacing Thailand and Vietnam and largest exporter of beef (buffalo) meat, exporting 1.7 million tonnes worth almost US$ 3 billion, beating Brazil, Australia and US. The analysis says that, India is consistently net exporter of agri-products during the last two decades. Indian agriculture has increasingly integrated with the world markets but relatively less than the entire Indian economy. The agri-trade (exports plus imports) as a percentage of agri-GDP, which was about 5 percent in 1990-91 and it is more than three times of that, touching 18 percent in 2011-12. It is still not very impressive as compared to the share of total trade in goods and services as a percent of India's GDP that has increased from 17.5 percent to 59.1 percent over the same period. India's agricultural exports constituting 11.9 percent of India's total exports and agricultural imports constituting only 3.4 percent of India's total imports in 2011-12, indicating India's comparative advantage in agriculture. India's share in total global exports of agri-products has increased from 0.8 percent in 1990 to 2.1 percent in 2011. This share is more than India's share in global merchandise exports i.e. 1.7 percent in 2011 (0.6 percent in 1990). Thus, from this point of view, Indian agriculture likely to have a greater comparative trade advantage than manufactured goods. However, it needs to be appreciated that India's agri-trade policy has been relatively restrictive and unstable. The success of the agri-sector against this backdrop, therefore, requires a more supportive and liberal trade policy that can help push growth and prosperity in rural areas. An analysis of the of agricultural trade over the last decade reveals that the traditional agri-exports of India, such as tea, coffee, cashews, spices, etc. have been over taken by new commodities like rice and maize, cotton, meat, guar gum, and the like, with the biggest change being noticed in cotton. India has also emerged as the largest importer of edible oils and pulses. A significant change has been the imports of raw cotton. A comparison of international prices and domestic prices for major crops shows that Indian agriculture is very much in tune with global markets for major agri-products. In several commodities, our domestic prices are below free on board prices indicating our trade competitive advantage. But the trade policy orientation has not promoted resource allocation in line with inherent competitive advantage, and thus has not allowed Indian agriculture to reap the efficiency gains from trade (Ashok Gulati T. K., 1999).

(Soumyatanu Mukherjee, 2012), in his paper, "Reasons and Impact of Soaring Food Prices in India", analyzes the possible reasons behind food price hike in India. He concluded that, two types of factors played a culminating role in increasing the food prices; the exogenous factors (such as public investment) were present in the preceding periods but the severity have increased and there are others new endogenous factors which were also present (such as NREGA). Endogenous factors could also be termed as demand driven factors, which had an important role to increase the demand for essential food articles. Apart from these factors another important factor has been the impact of crude oil prices. As crude oil prices increased internationally the transportation cost also increased. Lack of policy implementation by the government also aggravated the situation.

(Rajmal, 2009), in his paper, "Transmission from International Food Prices to Domestic Food Prices- The Indian Evidence", presents an analytical review of trends in international and domestic food prices and attempts to explore the nature of transmission from international food prices to domestic food prices in India. While domestic and international food prices have moved in the same direction in the current decade, the Indian food prices have remained lower than international prices, in absolute terms, growth rate and volatility. This indicates that, the rise in international prices have had limited effect on domestic food prices in India. The main reason is that, in India the prices are generally determined by domestic supply conditions in relation to demand with dependence on imports only at the margin for most of the food articles. However, in case of edible oils, imports are more relevant which helped to contain the price pressures domestically. The surge in world food prices has been accompanied by depreciation of US dollar or rupee that has neutralized certain portion of the increase in food prices in domestic market. Domestic commodities specific policy implications have also contributed towards stabilizing domestic prices relative to change in world prices. Nevertheless, domestic price is increasingly becoming susceptible to global developments with the gradual opening up of the economy. The global outlook for food grains and edible oils production remains mixed. While close monitoring of domestic and international prices followed by trade and fiscal measures along with import and food management can help in the short-run. There is a need for a comprehensive agricultural revamp programme in the long-run as demand-supply mismatches in the case of major agricultural commodities such as wheat, pulses and edible oils pose large imports of these commodities. Also, there is a need for augmenting the production and productivity of these commodities. Despite the relatively limited shares of imported commodities and the predominant role of domestic supply conditions in influencing food prices in India, policy should focus on enhancing investment in agriculture so as to facilitate stable supplies and prices that could offer long term incentives for production and protection to poor.

(Michael Debabrata Patra, 2013), in their paper, "Post-Global Crisis Inflation Dynamics in India: What has changed", explores the sources of inflation persistence in the recent period. The cross-sectional distribution of inflation shows that supply side shocks in the form of relative price increases, particularly of food, influenced the aggregate prices. Inflation persistence, based on univariate analysis, increased in the post global crisis period. Shocks to inflation will require forceful and more than proportionate policy responses. High degree of interest rate smoothing - 'baby steps' could be imparting persistence to the inflation process. The debate on the appropriate monetary policy framework for India is being overtaken by impending legislative changes. A flexible inflation targeting framework of constrained discretion appears to be the overwhelming choice.

(Raghav Gaiha, 2005), in his study analyze some aspects of state intervention in the food grain market in India and to assess how it has impacted on food grain productivity, accumulation of stocks, wholesale and consumer prices, and exports. The findings reveal that, state intervention in food grain marketing in India especially in rice and wheat aims at protecting producers against sharp reductions in prices and ensuring adequate availability and access of low income households to food grains. The subsidies involved, however, grown rapidly and contributed to large to fiscal deficit in recent years. Moreover, the benefits of the subsidies have accrued mostly to large farmers in a few of the major wheat and rice producing states. Although targeting has improved with the switch to the Targeted Public Distribution System (TPDS), a large proportion of the poorest remains excluded for various reasons (e.g. non-availability of the item in ration shops, unsatisfactory quality, etc.). A major concern is the role of the MSP as a deterrent to the shifting of wheat and rice production to northern and eastern states, which possess highly favourable agroecological conditions. For a regionally more differentiated agricultural strategy that would be sustainable over the longer term, it is vital that these states shift to a more diversified agricultural sector, growing less water-intensive and higher value crops (World Bank, 2005). Alongside, larger investments in rural infrastructure (e.g. roads, better maintenance of surface irrigation) and agricultural support services (e.g. research and extension) are a major priority. The specific concerns raised by our analysis are; growing subsidies have slowed down the yields of wheat and rice by constraining public investment in agriculture. A related and plausible concern is that, higher private investment mainly in ground water exploitation may have resulted in negative externalities for other farmers in the same village by lowering the water table. The MSPs have had significant positive effects on wheat and rice procurement. Wheat and rice off-takes fall with higher MSPs, as the gap between market and subsidized prices narrows down. Food grain stocks have grown as a consequence of higher MSPs but at a diminishing rate. The inflationary effects of hikes in the MSP are corroborated. The Wholesale Food Price Index (WFPI) is very sensitive to the MSP, and the former in turn raises the Consumer Price Index for Agricultural Labourers (CPI-AL). As rural poverty varies positively with increases in the CPI-AL, the effects on the poor are larger than just lower food entitlements. Exports were feasible only with subsidies. So, hikes in the MSP, leading to higher food stocks, and export subsidies to reduce these stocks was created. Various options have been proposed to replace the present form of the MSP such as; freezing of the MSP at current levels with a view to phasing it out, and deploying the resources in improving farmer access to technical advice, credit and rural infrastructure, to facilitate a shift to higher value crops and agribusiness activities; more specific proposals include investment grants to induce a shift from food grain production to higher value crops and agribusiness; contract farming and income support measures (e.g. a lump sum annual or seasonal payment to farmers based on crop area cultivated); and strengthening of other schemes (e.g. National Rural Employment Guarantee Scheme).

(Vaid, 2006), in his article, "India Profiles: Consumer Incomes & Spending Patterns", summarize that, there is tremendous boosts in prosperity, both nationally and at regional levels. The increase in income has been examined at a city level, rather than as a homogeneous trend. Distinct regional and city specific variations in spending habits, consumption baskets and eating preferences are observed across the country.

(Basu, 2011), in his article, "India's Food grain Policy: An Economic Theory Perspective", explains that, the simultaneous occurrence of high food inflation in the economy and large food grain stocks has been a matter of concern. The paper aims to understand the fundamentals of our food grain market and policy that lead to this situation and to suggest for policies, rectifying this. The central argument of the paper is that, it is imperative that, we look at the entire system of food production, food procurement and the release and distribution of food. The paper argues that, there are two different motives for food grain procurement by the state; to provide food security to the vulnerable and to even out food grain price fluctuations from one year to another. Moreover, how we procure the food has an impact on how we release the food, and vice versa. Inspired by the sight of food grain going waste, it is often made out that, our central problem persist in poor food grain storage. This paper disagrees with this popular view. While, no doubt we should improve our storage facilities, it is important to be clear that this in itself will not lower the price of food. To achieve that, we need to redesign the mechanics of how we acquire and release food in the market.

(Praduman Kumar S. M., 2006), in his article, "Agricultural Productivity Trends in India: Sustainability Issues", explains that, the sustainability issue of the crop productivity is fast emerging. The productivity attained during the 1980s has not been sustained during the 1990s and has posed a challenge before the researchers to shift the production function by improving the technology index. It has to be done by appropriate technology interventions, use of natural resources and harnessing bio-diversity. During the Green Revolution era, large investments were made on research and development for the irrigated agriculture. However, in recent years, agriculture has been experiencing diminishing returns to input-use and a significant proportion of the gross cropped area has been facing stagnation or negative growth in total factor productivity (TFP). The sharp fall in the total investment, more so in the public sector investment in agriculture has been the main cause for the deceleration of agricultural growth and development (Kumar, 2001). Moreover, the ratio of amount spent on extension to that on research has been falling. A vast untapped yield potential still exists in the country. This coupled with the second-generation technologies and heterogeneity in production environment warrants much more intensive extension efforts. Extension services need to be strengthened by scaling-up investment levels and improving the quality of extension. The first step in this direction should be to increase the availability of operating funds. This will result in accelerating the TFP growth, improving sustainability of the crop sector and minimizing the yield gap in the region. The problems of water logging and soil salinity may develop sooner or later in many irrigation project areas due to over-irrigation and deep percolation and seepage losses in the absence of a suitable drainage system. The problem is likely to aggravate further in future if proper soil management practices, including provision of suitable field irrigation channels and drainage system, are not undertaken. Due to the degradation problems, growth in TFP has not made headway across a substantial area of the country for major food crops. Over-irrigation and alarming rates of groundwater depletion in the IGP have caused land degradation and other environmental problems. The findings of the study have significant policy income groups, because the former spends a much larger proportion of its income on implications on the supply of agricultural commodities, and the national food and household nutritional security. An increase in agricultural investments especially in research and development, is urgently needed to stimulate growth in TFP. Recognizing that there are serious yield gaps and that there are already proven paths for increasing productivity, it is highly pertinent for India to maintain a steady growth rate in TFP. As TFP increases, the cost of production would decline and the market prices would stabilize at a lower level. Both the producers and consumers will benefit. The fall in food prices will benefit the urban and rural poor. More than half of the required growth in yield to meet the target of demand must be achieved from research efforts by developing location-specific and low input-use technologies with emphasis on the region/sub-regions/districts where the current yields are below the potential national average yields.

(Janak Raj, 2008), in his paper, "Imported Inflation: The Evidence from India", provides an analytical and empirical perspectives on imported inflation in the Indian context. Sources and commodity-wise trends in imported inflation are analyzed during the last four decades, suggests that, at the global level, export of inflation from oil exporting countries is significantly higher than that of industrial and non-oil developing countries including Asia. At the same time, despite low domestic inflation, export of inflation from industrial countries is significantly higher than that of non-oil developing countries. Inflation in India is positively influenced by import price, capital flows and exchange rate. Based on a non-parametric approach, import price inflation on an average accounts for about 1 to 2 percentage points increase in domestic inflation. Within the framework of the vector error correction and co-integration model, about 5 percentage point increase in import prices contribute to 1 to 1.5 percentage point increase in domestic prices. In terms of variance decomposition analysis, capital flows have a greater impact on domestic inflation, deriving from the former's association with exchange rate and import prices.

(Singh, 2011), in her working paper, "Inflation in India: An Empirical analysis", presents that, high inflation in India has become a major issue among both academics and policymakers. It is one of the biggest obstacles to growth and a major policy challenge for the governments. This paper analyzes the trends in inflation over the past five years, particularly food inflation, and examines the demand and supply side factors behind surging food prices. It argues that, demand for several food items in India exceeds their current supplies, and leads to high prices. It further contends that, this demand-supply imbalance is attributable to structural inefficiencies, including distribution of food products. Pointing out that monetary policy responses are unlikely to prove effective in reducing food prices, the paper emphasizes on the importance of increasing agricultural productivity and reforming retail trade policies for long-term results.

(Janak Raj S. M., 2011), in his paper, "Measures of Core Inflation in India: An Empirical Evaluation", attempts to analyze six exclusion-based measures of core inflation in India based on new series of WPI (2004-05=100). These are: WPI excluding food; WPI excluding fuel; WPI excluding food and fuel; non-food manufacturing; WPI excluding fuel and basic metals and metal products; and WPI excluding fuel, metal group and non-food primary articles. These measures were tested for volatility, un-biasedness and tracking the trend and predictive power. While WPI excluding food and WPI excluding food and fuel did not perform well in terms of volatility, the remaining four measures broadly satisfied the conditions relating to volatility, un-biasedness and tracking the trend and predictability of future inflation. A key property of core measure is that, it should not revert to headline inflation. It was found that, of the above four measures, all except non-food manufacturing revert back to headline inflation indicating that supply side shocks spill over to these core measures of inflation. This finding was further corroborated by granger causality and inflation persistence tests. Thus, non-food manufacturing, which the Reserve Bank uses as a measure of demand side pressures, is the only measure which satisfies all the properties of a core measure. A core measure of inflation is not an end in itself, but rather a means to achieve low and stable inflation by serving as a short-term operational guide for monetary policy.

(A. Ganesh-Kumar, 2007), in his paper, "Food grains Policy and Management in India", suggests that, the changing scenario demands a much different role for government in the future than it has exercised in the past. Food security is more important than food grains availability. Economic forces, led by market demand, domestically and globally, if allowed to operate, will drive the road to diversification. The private sector will provide the leadership. Increased incentives can contribute to "get prices right". Strengthened institutions can change the rules of the game in addition to the organizations in which they are embedded. Increased investment can provide the physical infrastructure and technologies to create and move inputs, services, and commodities. The role of government, therefore, should be to provide; 1) public goods, particularly infrastructure and research and 2) policies to facilitate, guide, and monitor an inclusive process so that the pace of transition accelerates and benefits are distributed widely. Unbundling the government objectives and instruments/institutions for public intervention is required to improve the efficiency of the current system of food grains management and to enhance the government's capacity for meeting its distributional goals for welfare improvement. The key to successful reforms of the food management system is to decouple the government's consumer welfare objectives from producer protection objectives. Producer interests should be protected not through public price stabilization programmes, but by allowing a free play of market forces. Accordingly, the Targeted Public Distribution System (TPDS) should be strengthened and it should cater only to the poor. Private marketing should be strengthened through reform of the Agricultural Produce Marketing Committees (APMC) Act, abolishing the Essential Commodities Act (ECA), permitting direct purchases from farmers, eliminating movement and storage controls, facilitating warehouse receipts, strengthening futures markets, and opening imports and exports to the private sector. Decouple MSP as protection against price risk (support prices) from using it to augment income. Market prices should be stabilized based on transparent rules in an open economy environment (i.e., free of movement, storage and trade restrictions) within a band bordered by CIF and FOB prices by using a variable tariff policy consistent with World Trade Organization (WTO) rules (within the bound rates). When domestic prices tend to reach the upper (CIF) level of the band, tariffs may be lowered enabling greater imports and also buffer stocks may be released, both of which will help lower the prices. When domestic prices tend to reach the lower (FOB) level of the band, tariffs may be increased to curtail imports and additionally the government may also procure grains at market prices to boost demand. Futures markets for grains are a useful institution that can give guidance about the future direction of change of the band itself.

(Vivek Moorthy, 2011), in his working paper, "Rising Food Prices and India's Monetary Policy", reveals that, the divergence between different CPI inflation measures is minimal, there is an unequivocal case for much tighter monetary policy. As the composition of the GDP changes, notable divergence between different CPI inflation measures may arise. However, a population weighted CPI, if calculated, would then provide an overall accurate indicator of inflation. Two immediate avenues for future research are suggested by this paper; First, examining the links between inflation and procurement price hikes, using a combination of statistical and event study methodology and second, the impact of supply shocks should be investigated by carefully examining the links between abnormal rainfall and weather and output and prices on a commodity by commodity basis, for which good data exists in India. More broadly, various matters pertaining to obtaining a unified consumer price index representative of the population need to be given their long overdue attention.

(Jha, 2006), in his paper, "Inflation Targeting in India: Issues and Prospects", evaluates the case for inflation targeting in India. The author argued that, inflation control cannot be an exclusive concern of monetary policy in a country such as India with a substantial poverty problem. The rationales for IT is then spelt out as are some nuances of the practical implementation of IT. The paper provides some evidence on the effects of IT in developed and transition economies and argues that although IT may have been responsible for maintaining a low inflation regime it has not brought down the inflation rate itself substantially. Further, the volatility of exchange rate and output movements in transition countries adopting IT has been higher than in developed market economies. The paper then discusses India's experience with using rules-based policy measures (nominal targets) and elaborates on the reasons why India is not ready for IT. It is further shown that, even if the Reserve Bank of India wanted to do it but could not pursue IT since the short-term interest rate does not have significant effects on the rate of inflation.

(Gokarn, 2011), in his speech on, "Striking the Balance between Growth and Inflation in India", highlighted that, the inflationary situation is India's most significant near-term macroeconomic challenge. There are some factors, global and domestic, that are clearly outside the purview of monetary influence, but that doesn't mean that monetary policy does not have a role in addressing factors that it does influence demand pressures and the risks of inflation becoming generalized through expectations and price-setting actions. To the extent that growth may be impacted, it must be understood as a short-term trade-off, with positive consequences for long-term performance. Finally, the contribution of supply forces, which the author has highlighted with the example of proteins, but which also exert pressure elsewhere, can only be addressed by increasing supply. Measures to do this are an integral part of a long-term inflation management strategy.

(Elumalai Kannan, 2011), in her working paper, "Analysis of Trends in India's Agricultural Growth", discussed the trends and patterns in the growth of the crop sector at the national and state levels. It has also estimated crop output growth model to analyze its determinants at the all India level. The cropping pattern in India has undergone significant changes with a significant shift from the cultivation of food grains to commercial crops. The area under coarse cereals, which is generally cultivated in dry regions, has declined by 13.3 percent between triennium ending (TE) 1970-71 and TE 2007-08. The performance of pulses in terms of area and output was not impressive during the study period. Nevertheless, increase in crop yield has been a major factor for accelerating crop production in the country since late 1960s. The use of modern varieties, irrigation and fertilizers were important aspects of higher growth in crop production in the country. The crop output growth model indicates that the enhanced capital formation, better irrigation facilities, normal rainfall and improved fertilizer consumption will help to improve crop output in the country. However, technological and institutional support for a few crops like rice and wheat have brought significant changes in crop area and output composition in some regions. Rice accounted for only 15.4 percent of gross crop area in TE 1962-65 and it increased to 23 percent in TE 2003-06 in North West India. Similarly, wheat area almost doubled in these periods. The expansion of area under these two crops resulted in a contraction of area under coarse cereals, pulses and oilseeds in that region. In the central region, the share of cotton increased in the 1980s and constituted about 10 percent of total value of crop output in recent years. Apart from this, the annual growth in yield during 1967-68 to 2007-08 for major crops was worked out to below. In comparison with the FAO data, yield per hectare of rice in China was 6.56 ton and in USA it was 7.67 ton against the all India average of 2.15 ton. Similarly, the yield of wheat in China was 4.76 ton and in USA it was 3.02 ton against the all India average of 2.71 ton. Hence, there is potential for enhancing yield of major crops through better soil and water management, profitable crop rotation, innovative marketing, genetic engineering and investment in farm education and rural infrastructure.

(Khundrakpam, 2012), in his paper, "Estimating Impacts of Monetary Policy on Aggregate Demand in India", estimated the impact of monetary policy on aggregate demand in India on the basis of quarterly data from 2000Q1 to 2011Q1. The overall impact on aggregate demand is then decomposed to observe the differential impact among the various components. It finds that an interest rate hike has a significant negative impact on the growth of aggregate demand. However, the maximum impact is borne by investment demand growth and import growth. Impact on private consumption growth and exports growth are relatively far more subdued, while there is hardly any cumulative impact on government consumption growth as it increases after some marginal fall initially. Variance decomposition analysis indicates that interest rate accounts for a significant percentage of the fluctuation in the growth of all the components of aggregate demand, except government consumption. Further, interest rate channel completely dominates exchange rate channel in monetary transmission, though the latter channel has non-negligible impact on investment and imports.

(Rahman, 2012), in his working paper, "Characterizing Food Prices in India", focuses on the empirical characteristics of WPI of food products in India. Using univariate time series techniques, the author examined the trend and cyclical properties of the selected price series. Rice and wheat, commodities with an effective MSP are characterized by smaller amplitude and phase suggesting that the government intervention in the cereals market lowers price variability. Relative price of rice and wheat shows a significant decline owing to positive productivity shift. Amongst other food products where MSP exists but procurement does not take place, the coarse cereals have shorter cycles since they are short duration crops. Pulses exhibit periods of boom more regularly than slumps. Also, they display a secular upward trend. Highly perishable products such as fruits and vegetables exhibit greater price variability, mainly attributed to greater amount of seasonality and lack of adequate storage facilities. Internationally traded food products such as spices and condiments are highly volatile owing to larger amplitude and cycle duration. A common feature which the author finds across all commodities is that, there is asymmetry in the duration spent in boom and slump. More importantly, it is found that, the price cycles do not have a consistent shape i.e. the extent of price change during boom and slump is independent of the duration spent in that state. Forecasting prices in that case become almost impossible, since the direction and magnitude of any future shock is unpredictable. Hence, it becomes difficult to prescribe appropriate countercyclical policy prescriptions and timing of government intervention.

(Shukla, 2011), in his article in the news paper, The Economic Times, emphasizes on the changing consumption pattern of rural and urban households. According to him, urbanization may alter food consumption and impact food demand. Consumption behavior is typically determined by two sets of factors; one, intrinsic factors comprising values, attitudes, cultures, education, etc, which determine consumer preferences; and two, a set of extrinsic factors such as disposables income, time availability and family composition, which determine the individual's capacity to fulfill his preferences. He added, as the level of income increases, the share of food items in total household expenditure declines for households in both urban and rural sectors. The expenditure on non-food items might surpass that on food items in the coming decade. Although, the absolute expenditure on food has gone up, what we are referring to is the distribution of expenditure among various categories expressed as a percentage of total expenditure. Looking at the distribution of expenditures on various categories within the broad food and non-food categorization, what is evident, and this hold true for both rural and urban areas, is that the proportion of expenditure on cereals has gone down sharply. It has gone down by 11% points in rural areas, from 26% in 1987-88 to about 16% in 2009-10, whereas in urban area it has fallen down by 6% points, from 15% in 1987-88 to 9% in 2009-10. The sharpest rise over the decades in non-food category is observed in education, medical expenditure, consumer durables goods, conveyance and toilet articles. These changes make it imperative to understand how consumer perception is evolving especially with regard to food habits and life style choice. Thus, to depict consumption patterns accurately, income specific estimates are likely to provide a better understanding of the distinctive sub-groups within the broad rural-urban split.

(Mohanty, 2012), in his speech on, "The importance of inflation expectations", at S. P. Jain Institute of Management & Research, Mumbai, tries to clarify that, people's belief about future inflation is an important factor in shaping inflation trends. It is not so clear that, how these inflation expectations are formed; are they formed purely on the basis of past experience or in a forward looking manner after processing all information or a combination of both. The Reserve Bank's household expectations surveys suggest that, expectations are formed adaptively with learning, but there is a dominance of food inflation in shaping overall household inflation expectations. Such behaviour of inflation expectations underscores the need for the Reserve Bank to continue to monitor in the Indian context, an array of measures of inflation, both overall and disaggregated components to assess the underlying inflationary pressures. Second, even professional forecasters, who are considered more rational, have moved up their inflation expectations. This suggests that, food inflation is acquiring a structural character feeding into inflation expectations rather than treating higher food prices as a temporary shock, households are assessing this as a permanent structural factor. This has inflationary implications in terms of higher wage-price spiral. If worker's and producer's inflation expectations go up than the latter's demand for wage increases is more likely to be acceded to by the former. If such wage increases are in excess of productivity increase they will be inflationary, making the inflation process persistent and raising the costs of disinflation. Third, in 2007–08, professional forecaster's medium to long term inflation expectations in the range of 4.0– 5.5 percent was well in line with the Reserve Bank's comfort level and what can be considered growth enhancing threshold level of inflation. Subsequently, as the actual inflation performance has deteriorated, medium to long term inflation expectations have also risen to a range of 6.0–7.3 percent. This underscores the need that, the current level of inflation ought to be brought down to better anchor inflation expectations which is vital for maintaining price stability in an enduring manner.

(Dev, 2010), in his paper, "Rising Food Prices and Financial Crises in India: Impact on Women and Children and Ways of Tackling the Problem", examine the analytical issues that relate to the pathways leading to the impact of the rising food prices and the global financial crisis on households, particularly women and children. The findings reveals that, the poor and vulnerable were significantly lagging behind in terms of human development, and social and financial security even before the onset of the food and global economic crises, which have further undermined their food security and livelihoods. The coping strategies adopted by the affected people could also have an adverse impact on the food security and human development of women and children. The volatility in food prices and the financial crisis can continue to pose a threat to the food and nutrition security of the country. The pathways that lead to poor outcomes in terms of the nutrition, health and education of children due to an increase in food prices can be grouped into the following four heads: 1) impact on poverty; 2) macro-economic impact and its effect on employment and the social sector; 3) impact on nutrition and social protection programmes; and 4) impact on women's well being and intra-household decisions. The cumulative impact of all these outcomes is reflected in two ways: (a) rise in household poverty, and (b) effect on child-specific factors. The financial crisis is also likely to have a negative effect on agriculture and the food security of the country. It may be noted that social inequality is high across all the states in India. The stimulus package offered by the Government needs to be aimed at the agricultural sector and primary food producers. Another view is propagated by the National Commission for Enterprises in the Unorganized Sector (NCEUS), which highlights the urgent need to protect the livelihood security, employment and income levels of the poor and vulnerable sections, which would also stimulate the overall economic growth.

3.3 FOREIGN STUDIES RELATED TO INFLATION AND FOOD NFLATION

(Walsh, 2011), in his working paper, "Reconsidering the Role of Food Prices in Inflation", clarifies that, the food prices are generally excluded from measures of inflation either due to their transitory nature or their higher volatility. However, in lower income countries, food price inflation is not only more volatile but also on average higher than non-food inflation. Food inflation in many cases is more persistent than non-food inflation, and shocks in many countries are propagated strongly into non-food inflation. Under these conditions, and particularly given high global commodity price inflation in recent years, a policy focus on measures of core inflation that exclude food prices can misspecify inflation, leading to higher inflationary expectations, a downward bias to forecasts of future inflation and lags in policy responses. In constructing measures of core inflation, policymakers should therefore not assume that excluding food price inflation will provide a clearer picture of underlying inflation trends than headline inflation.

(Idrees. M., 2012), in their paper, "Welfare impacts of food price inflation in Pakistan", examine the welfare effects of price changes on food items in Pakistan between two survey data of 2001-02 and 2005-06 which were taken from Household Integrated Economic Survey of Pakistan. The rationale of the study is related with the outsized budget shares of food items including in the consumer basket. Food expenditures are mainly inelastic in nature. However, the expenditures on non-food commodities can be overdue. The present study focuses on the magnitude of the cost involved in increasing the welfare among various income groups, using equivalent income and equivalent variation method. There are considerable differences in the composition of the consumption basket between rich and poor, therefore, the survey data of both years is disaggregated into four sub-samples according to the expenditure levels of rural-urban segments based on head count index. The results indicate the degree of vulnerability increases among the poorest households when staple food price increases. While in case of meat, this percentage change is low for poorest. It is evident that cereals, pulses and dairy products are the major source of welfare in urban, rural and overall Pakistan.

(Tom Capehart, 2008), in his report, "Food Price Inflation: Causes and Impacts", presented that, the U.S. food prices rose 4% in 2007 and are expected to gain 3.5% to 4.5% in 2008. Higher farm commodity prices and energy costs are the leading factors behind higher food prices. Farm commodity prices have surged because 1) demand for corn for ethanol is competing with food and feed for acreage; 2) global food grain and oilseed supplies are low due to poor harvests; 3) the weak dollar has increased U.S. exports; 4) rising incomes in large, rapidly emerging economies have changed eating habits; and (5) input costs have increased. Higher energy costs increase transportation, processing, and retail costs. Although the cost of commodities such as corn or wheat are a small part of the final retail price of most food products, they have risen enough to have an impact on retail prices. Generally, price changes at the farm level have a diminished impact on retail prices especially for highly processed products. The impact of higher food prices on U.S. households varies according to income. Lower-income households spend a greater portion of their income on food and feel price hikes more acutely than high-income families. Higher food costs impact domestic food assistance efforts in numerous ways depending on whether benefits are indexed, enrollments are limited, or additional funds are made available. Higher food and transportation costs also reduce the impact of U.S. contributions of food aid under current budget constraints.

(Worako, 2009), In his draft, "Analysis of Changes in Food Consumption pattern in Urban Ethiopia", explained that, the consumption expenditure on different food items are generally used as main yardstick for measuring standard of living in developing nations. Study of temporal changes in consumption patterns provides an insight into status of welfare changes and helpful in planning future investment decisions. In Ethiopia, since early 1990s several efforts have been taken by the government to alleviate poverty at national level. Thus understanding changes in urban consumption pattern provide valuable policy information on the effectiveness of policies designed to alleviate poverty. Accordingly, this paper investigates the phenomenon of changes in consumption expenditure in urban Ethiopia using two rounds (1994 and 2004) household survey data. The results from the decomposition of per capita consumption into different demographic and economic factors confirm that urban household consumption patterns started to shift from staple food grains to high value food products. The simulations and estimated income elasticity of demand for cereals, pulses and spices found to be much lower than those of non-staple high value products which are consistent with earlier findings. This ongoing transition in food consumption pattern will affect domestic food market that, supply side policy intervention highly recommended to meet increasing demand for high value food items.

(Bullard, 2011), in his article, "Measuring Inflation: The Core Is Rotten", argued that, U.S. monetary policy needs to de-emphasize on core inflation. Core inflation is not the ultimate goal of monetary policy. The author considered four classes of arguments for a focus on core inflation and found all of them wanting. Core versus headline inflation has been a long-standing issue for the Federal Open Market Committee (FOMC). The focus on core inflation in the United States seems to be more entrenched than in many other countries. The older ideas justifying this focus have rotted over time. The headline measures of inflation were designed to be the best measures of inflation available. The Fed should respect the construction of the price indexes as they are and accept the policy problem it poses. To do otherwise may create the appearance of avoiding responsibility for inflation. There is widespread agreement that headline inflation is the goal variable of monetary policy with respect to prices. Normally one would want to operate directly in terms of the goal variable, whenever possible. The concept of core inflation suggests that somehow an intermediate target strategy with respect to price inflation is optimal for U.S. monetary policy. In addition, the U.S. focus on core inflation tends to damage Fed credibility. Many other central banks have solidified their position on this question by adopting explicit, numerical inflation targets in terms of headline inflation, thus keeping faith with their citizens that they will work to keep headline inflation low and stable.

(Johnson, 2008), in his working paper, "Food Price Inflation", explained that, the nominal price of globally traded food has accelerated starting in 2003 and has been rising annually at double-digit rates. The price of globally traded food relative to that of manufactured exports of the advanced economies has accelerated due to the demand for globally traded food crops. There has been a shift in the contribution to global growth of the emerging and developing countries and is likely to continue for some time. Increased interest on the part of global investors in holdings of commodity futures contracts and mutual funds focused on commodities has contributed to the rise in the level of food prices recently. Although, it may change inventory behavior, because this trading does not reduce the quantity of food available for consumption, it does not seem likely to be an important factor in raising the sustained trend in food prices. Agricultural production has been maintained over the past five years, but it has not increased to meet the rise in demand. As a consequence, stocks of the major food crops are down. Corn production devoted to use, as ethanol accounts for much of the gains in supply of that crop. The most promising source of increased supply going forward to match the rising demand is increased yields in many of the world's agricultural producing countries. Although the conclusion that global food prices are likely to continue to rise in relative and real terms cannot be unambiguously established. Changes in monetary, agriculture, and trade policy would follow accordingly. Central banks, including the Fed, should manage future inflation risks by putting significant probability on the outcome that food prices continue to rise over the medium term. They should lessen the importance placed on the behavior of core measures of inflation and raise that placed on headline inflation. Those central banks that still manage the exchange value of their currency, particularly those from large emerging market economies, should move to an exchange rate regime with greater flexibility. In light of current and prospective upward pressure on the relative price of food, policy officials should move away from measures that control and hence distort prices experienced by consumers and producers. If subsidies are continued, they should not be in the form of price supports. In particular, officials should avoid imposing arbitrary and nonmarket relative prices within the agricultural sector that influence supply decisions by producers. Officials should move away from land-use policies that were designed to manage surpluses. Policies that contribute to raising agricultural yields where those are subpar should be adopted. Efforts to improve the infrastructure in the agricultural sector should be enhanced. Measures to restrict exports of agricultural products should be used only temporarily and as an emergency response to a critical problem. Over the medium term, such measures should be ended. Policies to liberalize market access for agricultural products should be adopted. Efforts to achieve success for the Doha Round should be strengthened.

(Elizabeth Frazao, 2007), in their report on, "Food Spending Patterns of Low-Income Households", examines the benefits of Food Stamp Program, which low income households can use to purchase food in grocery stores. Research shows that the program is successful in increasing the amount of food purchased and eaten by program participants, who numbered more than 26 million each month in fiscal 2006. However, the rise in obesity and diet-related chronic diseases has focused increased attention on how the program can promote not just an adequate quantity of food (that is, calories), but also healthier food choices, that bring consumption more in line with Federal dietary recommendations. Fruit and vegetable consumption is particularly low, and the perceived high cost of these foods has been suggested to be a barrier to food stamp participants purchasing and consuming them. This raises the question of food purchasing power as a barrier to making more healthful food choices.

(Reiko Miskelly, 2011), in their paper, "Food Price Increase in the Pacific Islands", summarize that, the vulnerability assessments carried out in 2009 and late 2010 indicate that, the more remote and import-dependent Pacific Island economies of Kiribati, FSM, RMI, Tuvalu, Tonga are particularly exposed to the economic costs of higher global fuel and food prices. Fiji, Solomon Islands, and Vanuatu are also vulnerable due to high inflation and structural issues such as the widely dispersed geographic structure of the population, gender inequality and rural/urban divide and the growing poverty in the urban centers. Across the six Pacific Island Countries, monitored by sentinel monitoring system, a majority of vulnerable families surveyed reported increased economic stress in meeting food expenditure due to rising food prices. Market surveys in sentinel sites confirm these findings with the cost of some staple food items up by as much as 50-100% since 2009. Increasing numbers of vulnerable families are resorting to subsistence agriculture, gardening and fishing when possible to supplement food and income. This offers a window of opportunity for government to promote local diverse food production and diversification of diet using local food. The food price increase will take a toll on the poorest households particularly those living in urban areas due to their higher expenditure on food compared to the rural people who have the option of resorting to subsistence farming. Nutrition concern is increasing as family shift their food to cheaper and low quality food such as tin fish, noodles, and turkey tails. Government current policy response is limited to price control and tariff exemption in most of countries and policy measure to protect the vulnerable is almost non-existent in high risk countries to buffer the impact of the increased food price particularly on the most vulnerable. More consumption targeted policy measures such as food and possibly cash assistance particularly targeting the urban poor as well as production oriented policy intervention targeting rural poor, warrant the immediate consideration. Promotion of breast milk for infant food security and community based awareness and interventions building on resilience should be accelerated. The most vulnerable Pacific Island Countries have been experiencing the social impacts of increased food and fuel prices since 2008 and the consecutive global economic crisis during 2009-10. Continuing natural disasters pose an additional strain on families and communities. Without proactive policy responses, countries long-term development and progress will be undermined.

(Gabriel A. Huppe, 2013), in their report on "Food Price Inflation and Food Security: A Morocco case study", reviewed food price inflation and its effects on food security. The authors found that, food prices are driven by multiple interrelated factors, such as the growing demand from developing countries, energy prices, bio-fuel policies, weather-related production shortfall, the growing scarcity of viable agricultural land and under-investment. Drought conditions in the U.S. and Eastern Europe and other weather-related production shortfalls drove food prices to drastic levels in the summer of 2012. Other factors that were identified in this recent crisis include bio-fuels policies, such as U.S. ethanol quotas, speculation in agricultural markets and food derivatives, rising food production costs due to high energy prices, and exchange rate swings such as a weakening U.S. dollar. A study by Oxfam has shown that, not only food prices projected to continue increasing, but they will also be more volatile in the future especially due to climate change. According to the UN, global food production will need to rise by 50 percent by 2030 to meet demand as continued population and economic growth will put upward pressure on demand. Prices are expected to be 10–30 percent higher in the next decade (OECD & FAO, 2012). In this review, the authors suggested a number of measures that have been taken by national governments in response to food price inflation; these include the reduction or elimination of food taxes, export restrictions, price controls, drawing on food grain stocks, safety net measures, input market intervention, investments to increase productivity and improve distribution networks, strengthening supportive institutions, land policies and water management systems, trade agreements and the removal of trade barriers. They also established a framework for assessing national food security and trade based on a review of the drivers of food price inflation, the projection of future food prices and the impact of these on food security.

(IFPRI, 2008), in the policy brief, "High Food Prices: The What, Who, and How of Proposed Policy Actions", highlighted that, the continued population growth, expanding demand due to income growth, and emerging climate change point to the future challenges for agriculture production. Without deep action, the current food price crisis merely foreshadows the events of coming decades. The high agricultural prices imply a fundamental revaluation of agricultural production and the natural resources it depends on especially land and water. The challenge is to soundly manage the transition to the new economics of agriculture and the food system and to facilitate stable supplies and prices that offer long-term incentives for agricultural production and help protect the poor. Science plays a key role in this transition in the long run. Although long-term price trends should be allowed to govern resource allocation, steps should also be taken to reduce short-term cyclical volatility. All of these goals make up a complex long-term agenda. When the current crisis ends, policy must not return to business as usual. If it does, the next crisis will hit even harder.

(Mahabub Hossain, 2005), in his paper, "Food Security and Nutrition in Bangladesh: Progress and Determinants", analyzed that, despite impressive achievements in increasing food grain and reducing instability in prices, long-term food and nutrition problems remain. Bangladesh has yet to achieve comprehensive food security that resolves the problems of inadequate food intake and chronic malnutrition among poor people. Solving these problems will require decisive action by the government, the private sector and individual households. A more efficient Public Food Distribution System (PFDS) can play a central role in government's food policy and make a significant contribution to the food security of households who receive transfers. Several steps could be taken to increase efficiency of food grain procurement and distribution. Increasing flexibility in setting procurement prices is one option. Using domestic tenders for food grain procurement could be even more efficient, particularly if tenders are designed with significant penalties for non-delivery and appropriate specifications of food grain grades and standards. A better understanding of poverty dynamics and linkages between adverse shocks (such as massive floods and droughts), rural income, credit markets and nutrition is important. Appropriately targeted income transfers, credit programs and insurance mechanisms in times of crisis may have very high payoffs in reducing poverty and improving food security in the medium terms through minimizing debt and the effects of large decline in income in both the short and the medium term. These interventions should be part of a broader social protection strategy of safely nets that is both cost-efficient and achieves maximum coverage. In view of the extreme pressure of population on limited natural resources, development and dissemination of improved production technology must continue to sustain the growth in food production. Within food grains, research emphasis could benefit by including improvements in grain quality as well as with yield, and developing shorter maturity rice varieties to facilitate expansion of area under pulses, oilseeds and vegetables that might address the issue of un-balanced nutrition in the diet. Among crops, the research strategy must accord higher priority to high-valued, non-food grain products. Continued facilitation of the import of new seeds and production technologies will be necessary for Bangladesh to capitalize on technological advancement made in international agricultural research centres. Public investment in agricultural research in Bangladesh has remained low compared to India, Pakistan, Sri Lanka and other East Asian countries.

(John M. Ulimwengu, 2009), in their working paper, "How Does Food Price Increase Affect Ugandan Households?", examines that, the poor households that already spend much of their income on food are responding to soaring food price by eating less, buying less nutritious food, and cutting other relevant expenses. Uganda has not yet experienced the negative impact of current soaring food prices with similar intensity as other African countries. However, since the beginning of 2008, signs of price hiking start occurring. Using the comprehensive UNHS 2005-06, the author estimated the net impact of increase in food price, accounting for both price and profit effects. The results suggest that, farmers are expected to increase crop supply in the face of price increase, more so in rural areas than in urban areas. The authors also found evidence of substitution effect between crops. Using the multimarket approach, decrease in consumption as a result of price increase is offset by a substantial increase in farmer's income. The profit effect shows potential for the crop producers to improve their welfare or at least limit its loss in the face of price increase. Accounting for substitution effects, our results suggest that the impact of rising food prices may be mitigated by some households that will attempt to substitute more expensive food items with cheaper ones. With respect to access to agricultural cropping and marketing services, the results suggest that, households with positive income impact have better access to agricultural services than the non-gainers. On average, their access to extension and National Agricultural Advisory Services (NAADS) is also higher than that of other households. As pointed out by many others, efficient responses should mitigate current as well as potential future impact of high food prices and help poor rural and urban households to benefit from the opportunities that the increased demand for food creates for farmers. From the findings, it is obvious that policy response based on demand elasticities alone will tend to favour consumers at the expense of producers. Programs such as food and cash-based social protection systems should target both individual and geographical attributes.

(Josef L. Loening, 2009), in their working paper, "Inflation Dynamics and Food Prices in an Agricultural Economy: The case of Ethiopia", analyzed the determinants of inflation in Ethiopia by estimating error correction models for cereal, food and non-food consumer prices and the CPI using monthly data from January 1999 to November 2008. The main finding is that, in the long run, domestic food and non-food prices are determined by the exchange rate and international food and goods prices. In the short to medium run, agricultural supply shocks and inflation inertia strongly affect domestic inflation, causing large deviations from long-run price trends. Money supply growth affects food price inflation in the short run, though excess money supply does not seem to drive inflation in the long run. The results suggest a challenging time ahead for Ethiopia, with the need for a multi-pronged approach to fight inflation. Forecast scenarios suggest monetary and exchange rate policies need to take into account the cereal sector, as food staple growth is among the key determinants of inflation, assuming a decline in global commodity prices. Implementation of successful policies will be contingent on the availability of foreign exchange and the performance of agriculture.

(ESCAP, 2011), in the policy briefs, "Rising food prices and inflation in the Asia-Pacific region: causes, impact and policy response", shows that, given the strong link between food price inflation and overall inflation in the chain of causation, the single most important policy initiative that developing countries in the region can adopt is to give priority to boost the agriculture sector in the years ahead. Such an approach will not only increase the output of food and non-food crops but reduce poverty as well. It needs to be borne in mind that, despite migration to the cities, 80 percent of the Asia-Pacific poor still reside in rural areas and lack access to adequate land, agricultural inputs, finance and markets to benefit from the higher food prices that have come about since 2008. This state of deprivation needs to be addressed in order to improve the food supply response and make growth more sustainable and inclusive. ESCAP has also observed in the past that a prosperous rural economy depends not only on agriculture but also on non-farm activities, including agro-industries, commerce and other services. Such activities provide additional sources of income for rural households above and beyond agriculture. They also contribute to a more balanced pattern of rural development. Indeed, a more prosperous rural economy reduces incentives for rural-to-urban migration, easing pressures on urban infrastructure and the provision of public services in cities. Increasing food production is a fundamental objective not only to contain inflation in the short and medium terms but also for long term sustainable development. Finally, when faced with a temporary supply shock, countries should avoid actions that meet national needs but make the problem worse for other countries. At the regional level, it is necessary to support mechanisms for improving emergency access to food through stock sharing and fewer restrictions on the release of stocks to other countries under emergency conditions. Over the long term, more serious efforts should be made to shift production of both food and non-food crops from agriculturally stressed areas in the region where arable land and water availability is declining to areas, even outside the Asia-Pacific region where such pressures have not yet emerged.

(Braun, 2008), in his report, "Food and Financial Crises: Implications for Agriculture and the Poor", suggests that, the successful resolution of the food crisis should be measured not primarily by declines in food prices, but by significant declines in the number of food-insecure people. A new boost in technological and policy innovation is essential for achieving this goal. The CGIAR and national agricultural research systems have key roles to play in building a sustainable and resilient agricultural system through solid research insights and innovative policy approaches. The world's poor and food-insecure people need a bailout through agricultural growth, stable food markets, and protection of their basic nutrition. Such a bailout not only is an ethical and humanitarian imperative, but also makes economic sense.

(Steindel, 2007), in his paper, "A Comparison of Measures of Core Inflation", evaluate several proposed measures of core inflation. Other studies have addressed this issue, but there has been little commonality in their underlying approaches. Thus, a key feature of this analysis is to provide a more consistent basis on which to judge the performance of the candidate core inflation series. One possible outcome from the study was that, a single core inflation measure would emerge as dominant in its performance. The author noted the unremarkable performance of the conventional ex-food and energy series. Consequently, the general practice of identifying core inflation with an ex-food and energy series instead of an alternative series does not seem to be justified based on analysis. Although the results of this study do not rule out the potential usefulness of core inflation measures, there appear to be difficulties associated with how best to employ the current set of candidates. One possibility is to weight various criteria and then select the core inflation measure that yields the best performance. However, this approach would be influenced by the highly subjective process of ranking the importance of the criteria. Another possibility is to acknowledge that, different core inflation measures seem better suited to performing different tasks, and then adopt the appropriate core inflation measure as the guide for a particular stated purpose. However, this approach would introduce the inconvenience of keeping track of a variety of core inflation measures. Moreover, in the policy area, it could require that a central bank provide the public with a clear understanding of each series. Finally, a central bank could consider the adoption of a model-based measure of core inflation. However, this approach would then face the previously cited difficulties of choosing the particular definition of core inflation and communicating it to the public. Taken together, these considerations and our results present challenging avenues for future research.

(Stephen G Cecchetti, 2008), in his paper, "Commodity prices and inflation dynamics", investigated aspects of the impact of the rise in food and energy prices on the level and dynamics of headline inflation. It has been found that, in recent years core inflation has generally not tended to revert to headline inflation in a majority of countries considered. This evidence suggests an absence of strong second round effects of higher commodity prices on inflation in a majority of countries over the period considered. The evidence also suggesting that, in recent years, food price inflation has tended to have greater additional explanatory power for future headline inflation than energy price inflation, and seems to have been somewhat more persistent. However, the sample period starting in 2003 when commodity prices started to rise is relatively short, so that the power of the tests might be relatively low for drawing firm conclusions.

(Francisco H. G. Ferreira, 2011), in their working paper, "Rising Food Prices and Household Welfare: Evidence from Brazil in 2008", estimate the welfare consequences of these food price increases, and their distribution across households. Since, Brazil is a large food producer with a predominantly wage-earning agricultural labor force, the estimates include general equilibrium effects on market and transfer incomes, as well as the standard estimates of changes in consumer surplus. While the expenditure (or consumer surplus) effects were large, negative and markedly regressive everywhere, the market income effect was positive and progressive, particularly in rural areas. Because of this effect on the rural poor and of the partial protection afforded by increases in two large social assistance benefits, the overall impact of higher food prices in Brazil was U-shaped, with middle-income groups suffering larger proportional losses than the very poor. Nevertheless, since Brazil is 80 percent urban, higher food prices still led to a greater incidence and depth of poverty at the national level.

(Torres, 2013), in his paper, "The Impact of Food Price Shocks on the Consumption and Nutritional Patterns of Mexican Households", presented that, around the world, food security of households and persons has been affected by recent shocks in food prices. Although, in México there is some evidence about the effects of food price inflation on household's consumption patterns, little is known about magnitudes and how food price inflation affects differentially people's food security depending on their food poverty condition. As expected, price elasticities and the resulting nutrient elasticities are inelastic. Distinguished by their food poverty condition, households present differentiated consumption patterns and use different diversification strategies to cope with food price increments. People in non-food poverty condition have diversified consumption patterns, opposing to people in food poverty condition that spend more than 25% of their food budget in cereals, which is the main source of nutrients. As a consequence of the expenditure and consumption patterns, the nutrient quantities acquisition of people in food poverty condition is quite sensitive to changes in cereals prices and vegetables prices. In contrast, for people in non-food poverty situation, nutrients quantity purchase is more sensitive to changes in meat and dairy prices. Rising food prices in cereals and vegetables could aggravate the disparities in the nutritional content of food acquisition and could contribute to deteriorate the nutrimental condition of the most vulnerable population. In this context, this research provides further information to enhance the efficiency of food policy interventions by improving the quality of the targeting. Effective targeting is the result of geographical indicators, observable individual or household characteristics and program restrictions. Paradoxically, the greatest food security gains typically does not come directly from food or feeding programs, but indirectly through policies that encourage poverty reduction. However, careful targeting is fundamental for long term programs that address the food insecurity of the most vulnerable population.

(Min Bahadur Shrestha, 2012), in his paper, "The Impact of Food Inflation on Poverty in Nepal", expressed that, as people differ in terms of their needs, consumption patterns and food position (as net buyer or net seller), the effects of food price changes will also be different from one household to another. Depending on household's position as net seller or net buyer of staple food, increase in prices of staple food would raise the income of households that are net sellers and add to the hardship of the households that are net buyers. Hardship of the poor people increases because they have to spend a larger share of their income on essential foods and less is left to spend on other items. Since the population below poverty line spends 72 percent of their total expenditure on food in Nepal, the impact of food price rise is severe on the poor section of the population. The findings of this study suggest that overall poverty is likely to increase between 4 and 12 percentage points, and the food poverty between 6 and 20 percentage points as a result of the food price rise ranging from 10 percent to 30 percent. It means that a food price hike of 10 percent will push 1 million new consumers into overall poverty, while 6.7 million existing poor populations would experience even harder lives. Therefore, policy makers need to focus on containing food price hikes and maintain a sizable food buffer. In this context, short and long term policy responses are required to prevent the reoccurrence of the food crisis and food price hikes in the future. These responses include lowering domestic food prices by reducing taxes on imports of key staples, boosting domestic food production, establishing regional food buffers, providing cash transfers and subsidies and promoting second generation concept among agricultural cooperatives.

(Christopher Adam, 2012), in their working paper, "Food Prices and Inflation in Tanzania", concluded that; First, money growth and hence the stance of monetary policy matters for inflation both in the long run and in the short run. `Monetary or demand-side effects also feed food and fuel price inflation, particularly in the short run. Second, however, the food price inflation is predominantly driven by supply-side factors including both domestic agricultural output shocks and by the pass-through from world prices for food and fuel. The inflation transmission from world food prices is, however, relatively weak and attenuated, and is much stronger when world prices rise than when they fall. Third, the effect of domestic supply conditions on food price inflation points to the asymmetric effects of trade policy in Tanzania, while food imports appear to respond reasonably rapidly to domestic production short-falls. The capacity to export surplus food production is much more muted so that market adjustment in this case occurs through falling prices, other things equal. This result has important implications for trade policy and production incentives in agriculture. Although, a much closer analysis of cross-border prices is required before firm policy conclusions can be drawn. Fourth, headline inflation exhibits strong seasonality, consistent with weak price-stabilizing effects of trade and incomplete storage. Non-food inflation is, by contrast, broadly non-seasonal. Finally, prices in Tanzania in general are flexible, more so for the food and energy sub-components but even in the traditionally sticky-price domain of core inflation there is little evidence of persistence. Some of the adjustments to equilibrium are somewhat prolonged, but conditional on these error-correction effects, inflationary shocks dissipate rapidly with half-live being little more than one month.

(Abebe Shimeles, 2013), in his working paper, "Rising Food Prices and Household Welfare in Ethiopia: Evidence from Micro Data", analyzes welfare implications of rising commodity prices in Ethiopia based on household budget surveys. The findings suggest that, a rise in relative prices of such necessities as cereals would lead to a large deterioration in the welfare of households in urban areas. In rural areas generally land-rich households tend to benefit significantly from the recent surge in food prices, while the land-poor and typical farm households tend to experience negative growth. Thus, price shifts in favour of agriculture could aggravate poverty conditions in rural areas. Simulated Gini computed from simple demand systems indicate worsening income distribution in urban areas due to price shifts that would exacerbate the already dire poverty conditions. The paper also reported own and cross-price elasticities mainly for cereals to gain insight into magnitude of demand shifts due to income and price changes.

(Niimi, 2005), in his working paper, "An Analysis of Household Responses to Price Shocks in Vietnam: Can Unit Values Substitute for Market Prices?", examines the robustness of Deaton's widely used method for estimating consumer responses. While unit values, ratios of expenditures to quantities purchased, are often employed in demand analysis as proxies for missing market prices, Deaton argues bias is likely to result as a consequence of both quality effects and measurement error. Hence he proposes a procedure that corrects the bias and enables price elasticities to be obtained in the absence of explicit price information. Given the availability of market price data and unit values in Vietnam, this paper estimates a food demand system and investigates the usefulness of Deaton's method. It also takes the analysis a step further to the existing literature by computing the welfare impact of price changes to see how Deaton's method performs in this context. The results demonstrate that Deaton's method generates materially different price elasticities from those estimated with market prices. However, it produces relatively similar results for the welfare analysis. Deaton's procedure therefore appears to be valid in welfare analysis at least in the case of Vietnam, but the findings also indicate that its use by policy makers should carry a strong health warning.

(Luis A.V. Catao, 2010), in his working paper, "World Food Prices and Monetary Policy", suggests policy implications; One is that the rationale for broad CPI targeting as currently adopted by many central banks is strengthened once we allow for the role of food in utility. This rationale reinforces considerations related to transparency and avoidance of ad hoc criteria to define the "core" component in CPI, as well as the credibility gains that might arise from targeting a broader price index. Second, the case provided for CPI targeting and implicit partial offset of imported food inflation therein also rectifies some of the regressive distributional bias associated with the usual prescription that monetary policy should focus on offsetting the sticky-price distortion. To the extent that food and other commodity prices are less sticky and determined under a more competitive market structure, this prescription implies that central banks should be more lenient towards inflation or deflation in those sectors. The weight of food in overall spending is higher among poorer households which are also precisely the ones with more limited access to credit markets to smooth real purchasing power fluctuations arising from shocks to relative food prices. Thus strict PPI targeting has a regressive distributional bias that CPI targeting mitigates. Third, the results suggest that, central banks should not be too lenient to shocks to food prices even if they are imported and that choosing a target that leads to more accommodative response to such a shock can be welfare inferior. If all central banks follow this prescription, this would help mitigate the externality problem associated with uncoordinated/inward oriented policy responses to world price shocks when central bank's target PPI or the exchange rate. Less accommodative policy based on broad CPI stabilization would thus be more conducive to keep global inflationary pressures in check as well as its converse whenever commodity prices tank. This might mitigate the need for greater international policy coordination that is not easily attainable in practice.

(Paul R. Masson, 1997), in their working paper, "The scope for Inflation Targeting in Developing Countries", examines the relevance of inflation targeting (IT) for developing countries. It delineates the prerequisites and building blocks of this monetary policy framework and discusses some features of its implementation in advance economies. The paper identifies two major prerequisites for adopting an IT framework; first, the ability to carry out a substantially independent monetary policy especially one not constrained by fiscal considerations; and second, freedom from commitment to another nominal anchor like the exchange rate or wages. A country satisfying these two requirements could choose to conduct its monetary policy in a manner consistent with IT, defined as a framework containing an explicit quantitative target for future inflation, a commitment for this target as an overriding objective, a model for predicting inflation, and an operating procedure for adjusting monetary instruments in case forecast inflation differs from its target. These fairly stringent and technical requirements of IT cannot be met by many developing countries because seigniorage remains an important source of financing and/or because there is no consensus that attainment of low inflation should be the overriding objective of monetary policy. It has been concluded that, the way to improve the monetary and inflation performance of developing countries may not be through the adoption of a framework akin to IT, at least not in the real term.

CHAPTER 4: RESEARCH METHODOLOGY

Chapter Highlights:

4. RESEARCH METHODOLOGY

Research Methodology is a way to systematically solve the research problem.

4.1 RESEARCH DESIGN

A research design is a logical and systematic plan prepared for directing a research study. A research design is a master plan specifying the methods and procedures for collecting and analyzing the needed information[24]. It is a framework or blue print that plans the action for the research project.

Research Purpose:

The purpose of the study is to better understand the phenomenon of food inflation, to know the relative importance of food articles in food basket and how lower middle class consumers manage their household consumption expenditure on food articles. This study is analytical and exploratory in nature.

Research Method:

The best research method to use for a study depends on that study's research purpose and the accompanying research questions. In this study, quantitative approach is used whose results are based on numbers and statistics that are presented in figures. Furthermore, this approach is considered useful when conducting surveys with set answering alternatives. The qualitative aspect of the study cannot be ignored.

Research Strategy:

The overall strategy should be determined from the research questions, the characteristics of the phenomenon studied, and the expected type of results in mind. In this study, survey method is adopted which allow for collection of a large amount of data from a sizeable population in a highly economical way. Moreover, survey method is

---

[24] Zikmund, W. G. (2010). Business Research Methods. *Cengage Learning, New Delhi* , pp. 65

based on interviews and conducted over a short period of time; cross-sectional study is best suited.

4.2 SAMPLE DESIGN

Sample design is a plan for drawing sample from a population.

Relevant Population:

The population relevant to a survey depends upon the research problem, the objectives of study, the geographical area selected for the survey and the operational definition of the unit of study. The study is conducted in Thane city (i.e. the area covered by Thane Municipal Corporation) among the population of lower middle class households.

Sampling Frame:

In this study, population of Thane city has been divided into nine wards/prabhag samities and each ward is considered as a stratum from which the samples were drawn.

Sample Size:

This refers to the number of items to be selected from the universe to constitute a sample. The size of the sample for this study is 500 lower middle class households selected on the basis of the criteria that, their household income should fall in the range of 3.4 Lac to 10 Lac per annum, only service should be the source of income and the number of members in the family should be at least four.

The formula used to calculate the sample size for infinite population is given as[25]:

$$S= (((Z)^2*P(1-P))/e^2)$$

Where,

S= the sample size

---

[25] J.K.Sachdeva. (2011). Business Research Methodology. *Himalya Publishing House* , pp. 156-175.

Z= the normal variate for confidence level (1.96 for 95% confidence level)

P= probability of the proportion of people falling into the group in which we are interested in the population (30 percent)

e= the proportion of error we are prepared to accept (+/- 4%)

So,

Sample Size, S= $((1.96)^2*0.3(1-0.3)/(0.04)^2=$ **504.21**≈ **504**

Sampling Technique:

The technique which is used to draw a sample from the population is stratified sampling, "Stratified sampling is a variant on simple random and systematic methods and is used when there are a number of distinct sub-groups, within each of which it is required that there is full representation. A sample is constructed by classifying the population in sub-populations (or strata), based on some well known characteristics of the population such as age, gender and socio economic status[26]".

4.3 DATA COLLECTION

For collection of data, secondary as well as primary data collection methods were used.

Secondary Data:

Secondary data comprises of various sources which already existed in the published form such as research papers in referred journals, articles, websites, books, magazines, manuals, reports, newspaper, etc. Selection of the papers was done on the basis of their relevance to the study and contribution to the body of knowledge.

Primary Data:

Primary data were collected by conducting structured interviews during the months from August, 2012 to January, 2013 (being period of rainfall and festivals) when the prices of food items are relatively high. The questionnaire were filled up among the respondents (LMCHs) selected from nine wards of Thane city. The questionnaire consists

---

[26] J.K.Sachdeva. (2011), Op.cit. pp. 154-155.

of closed ended questions with multiple response options based on five point Likert scale[27]. Part-I of the questionnaire covers the demographic characteristics of the respondents (2018 respondents were met to fill up Part-I of the questionnaire); Part-II and Part-III of the questionnaire covers the research questions. The respondents were identified as lower middle class households (LMCHs) for conducting interviews on the basis of criterion set in the Part-I of the questionnaire. After confirming to sufficient number of respondents fulfilled the criterion, 550 respondents were randomly selected and interviewed for part-II and Part-III of the questionnaire. Finally, after deliberations, exactly 500 completely filled questionnaires were selected for analysis.

Construction of questionnaire is a very difficult task as the whole conclusion of the research depends upon how questionnaire is drafted. The questionnaire refers to a series of questions asked to individuals in order to obtain statistically useful information in relation to the topic. Properly constructed and responsibly administered questionnaire becomes a vital instrument by which statements can be made about specific groups or people or entire population.

4.4 ANALYSIS OF DATA

Data analysis refers to the computation of certain measures along with searching for patterns of relationship that exists among data-groups[28].

In the process of analysis, relationships or differences supporting or conflicting with original or new hypotheses should be subjected to statistical test of significance with what validity data can be said to indicate any conclusion.

Irrespective of the statistical package that we are using, deciding upon the right statistical test to be used in analysis can be a daunting exercise. In order to select right statistical test, following points needs to be considered; 1) the question we want to

---

[27] Vagias, W. M. (2006). Likert-type scale response anchors. *Clemson International Institute for Tourism & Research Development, Department of Parks, Recreation and Tourism Management, Clemson University* .

[28] C.R.Kothari. (2009). Research Methodology (Methods & Techniques). *New Age International Publishers* , pp. 122-123.

address; 2) the level of measurement of our data and 3) the design/layout of our research. After considering the above three points, it should also be clear in our mind what we want to achieve.

The primary data collected from survey is processed on SPSS.20 and tested for significance at 5% level of significance by using statistical tools such as Karl Pearson's correlation - to measure the degree and direction of relationship between variables, Linear regression - to measure the nature and extent of relationship between variables, Factor analysis - to analyze the factors (food items) on which consumption expenditure get affected in terms of quantity, quality and frequency. Also, Reliability analysis has been conducted to measure the consistency of the collected data.

4.4.1 CORRELATION ANALYSIS USING SPSS

In general, correlation analysis looks at the relationship between two variables in a linear fashion.

Null Hypothesis, H_{01}:

There exists no significant relationship between impact of food inflation on household consumption expenditure on food composite and individual food items.

Alternate Hypothesis, H_{a1}:

There exists significant relationship between impact of food inflation on household consumption expenditure on food composite and individual food items.

SPSS procedure for Correlation:

1) Enter the values under the variable in the data view.

Figure 1: Correlation Analysis- Survey data (Entries under the variable in data view)

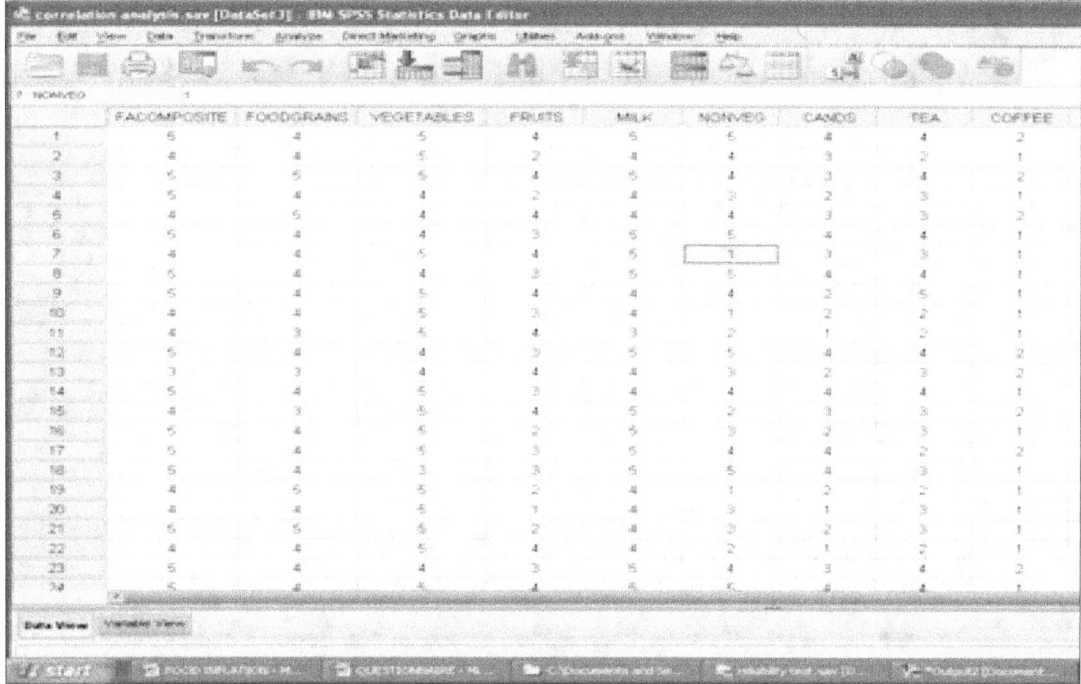

2) Select ➜ **Analyze** menu ➜ **Correlate** ➜ **Bivariate…..**

Figure 2: Correlation Analysis - Correlate option

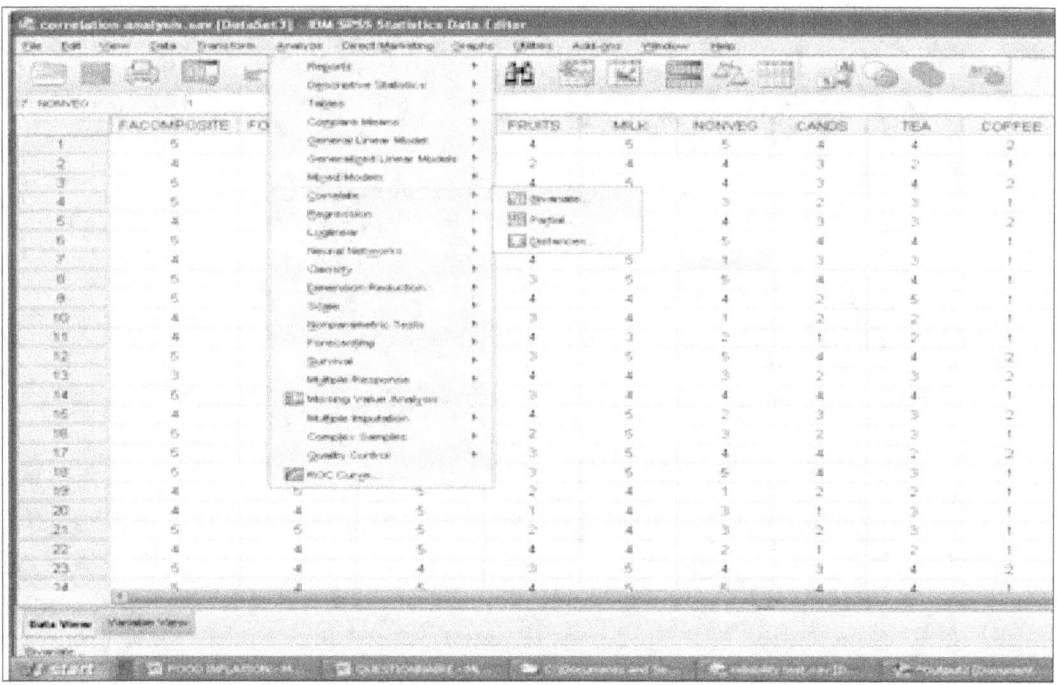

3) Open the **Bivariate dialogue box**. Following dialogue box will open.

Figure 3: Correlation Analysis - Bivariate dialogue box

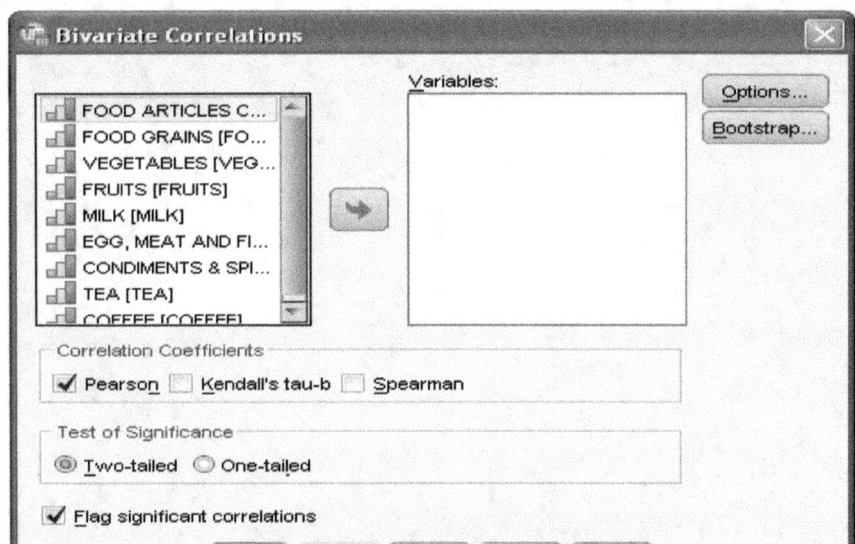

4) Select the variables and send it in **Variables** list box by clicking **right arrow** button. Similarly do this for other variables. Click **Pearson** check box and **Flag significant correlations** check box. See that test of significance is set according to the requirement.

Figure 4: Correlation Analysis – Variables list box

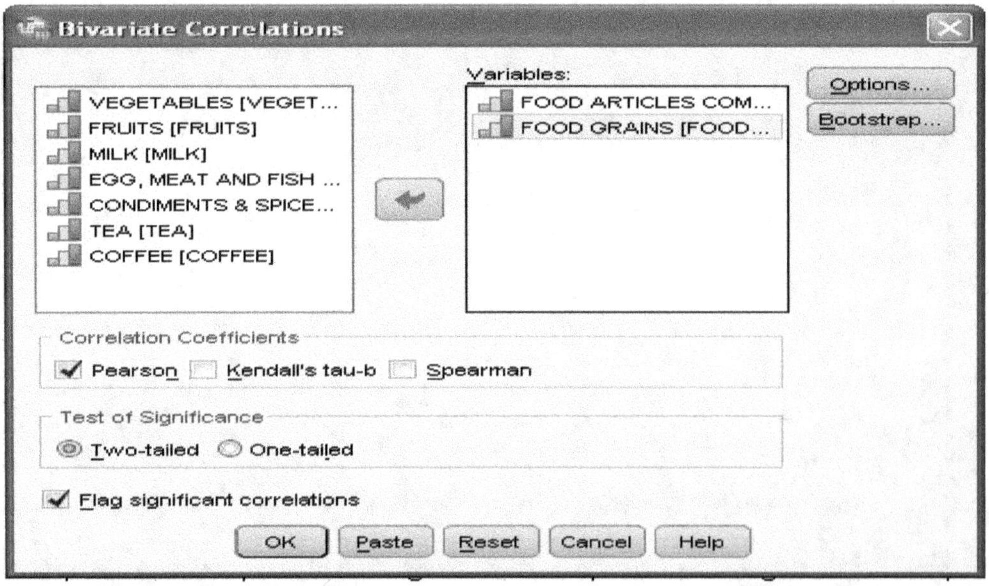

5) Click **Options…** button to open its sub dialogue box. Select the **Statistics** and **Missing values** options according to our requirement. Click **Continue** to close the sub dialogue box. The previous dialogue box will appear again.

Figure 5: Correlation Analysis – Options sub-dialogue box

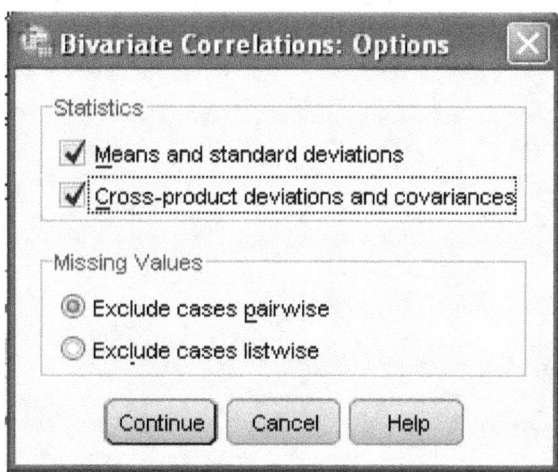

Click **OK** to open the output viewer (See Page No. 166).

4.4.2 REGRESSION ANALYSIS USING SPSS

To determine the extent of relationship between two variables, regression analysis is used. In this, the change in the value of one variable (independent) gives rise to corresponding change in the value of other variable (dependent).

Null Hypothesis, H_{02}:

There exists no significant change in household consumption expenditure on food composite with the corresponding change in individual food items along side high food inflation.

Alternate Hypothesis, H_{a2}:

There exists significant change in household consumption expenditure on food composite with the corresponding change in individual food items along side high food inflation.

SPSS procedure for Regression Analysis:

1) Fill the data view with following data.

Figure 1: Regression Analysis - Survey data (Entries under the variable in data view)

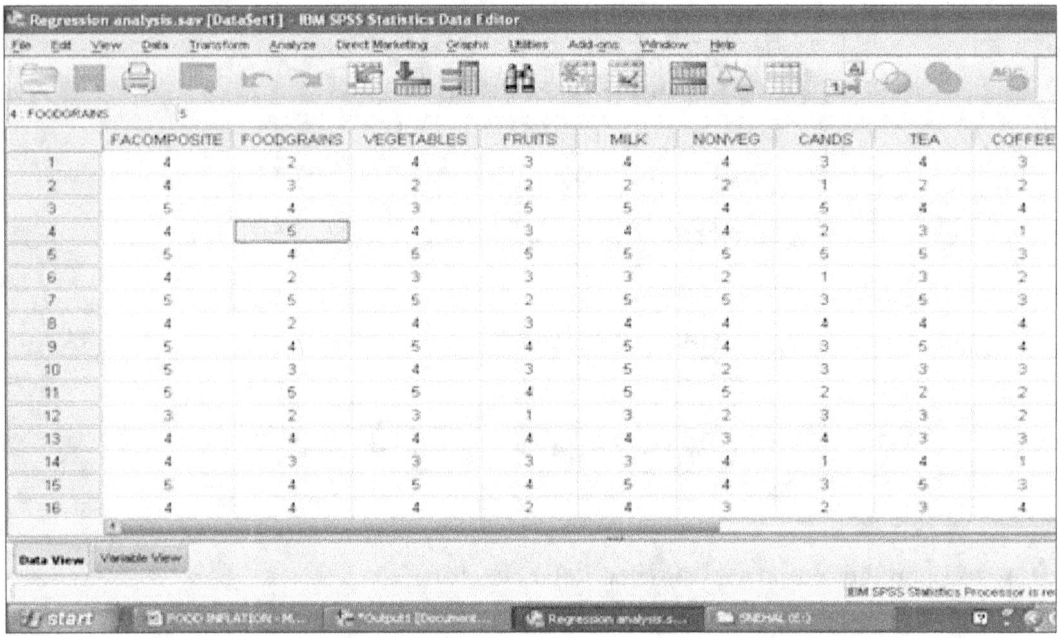

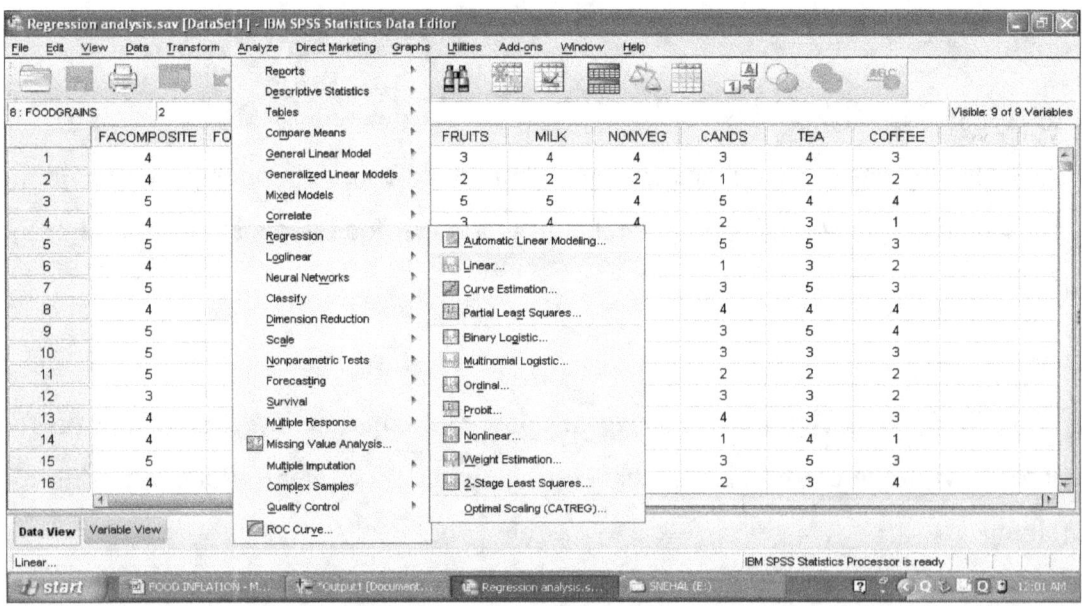

2) Select ➔ **Analyze** menu ➔ **Regression** ➔ **Linear Regression……**

Figure 2: Regression Analysis – Regression option

3) This will open Linear Regression Dialogue box. Select the dependent variable and send it in **Dependent** list box by clicking upper **right arrow** button. Similarly, select the independent variable and send it in **Independent(s)** list box by clicking second **right arrow** button, as shown in the figure below. Similarly enter other independent variables in **Independent(s)** list box.

Figure 3: Regression analysis – Linear Regression dialogue box

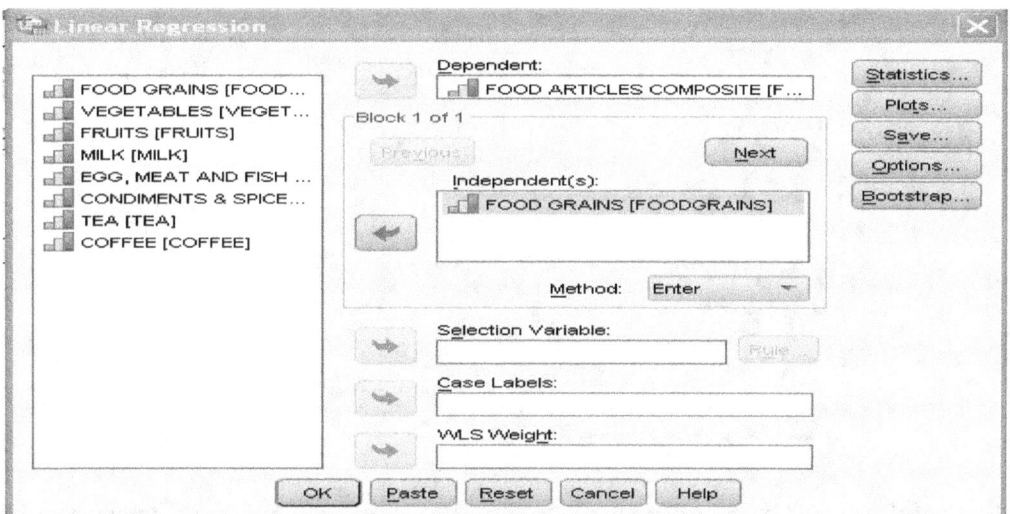

5) Click **Statistics…**button to open its sub dialogue box. Select the required statistics as shown in the figure below. Click **Continue** to close the sub dialogue box. Previous dialogue box will reappear.

Figure 4: Regression Analysis - Statistics sub-dialogue box

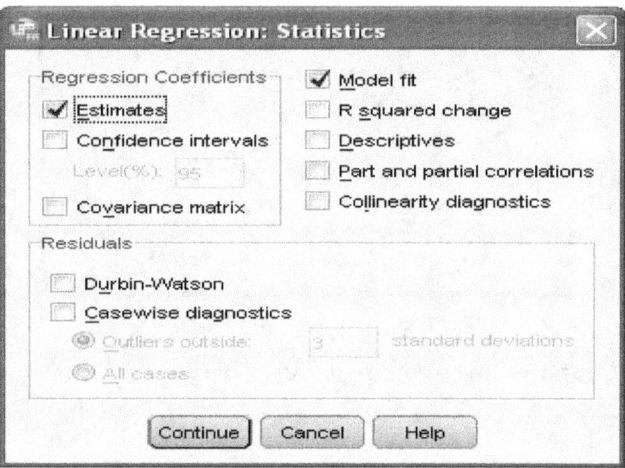

5) Click **Plots…**to open **Plots** sub dialogue box. Select the plots as required by us. Click **Continue** to close the sub dialogue box. Previous dialogue will reappear.

Figure 5: Regression Analysis – Regression - Plots sub-dialogue box

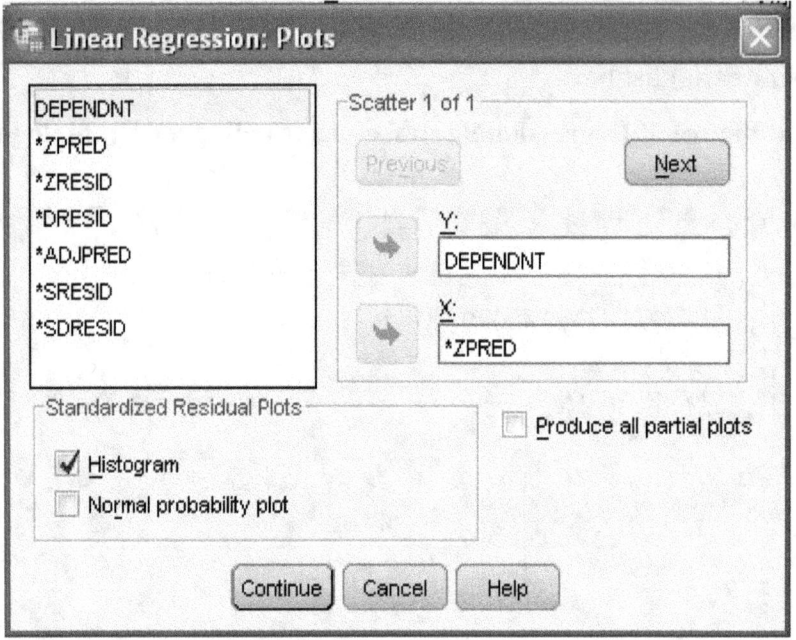

6) Click **Options….** To open **Options** sub dialogue box. Select the options as required by us. Click **Continue** to close the sub dialogue box. Previous dialogue box will reappear.

Figure 6: Regression Analysis - Options sub-dialogue box

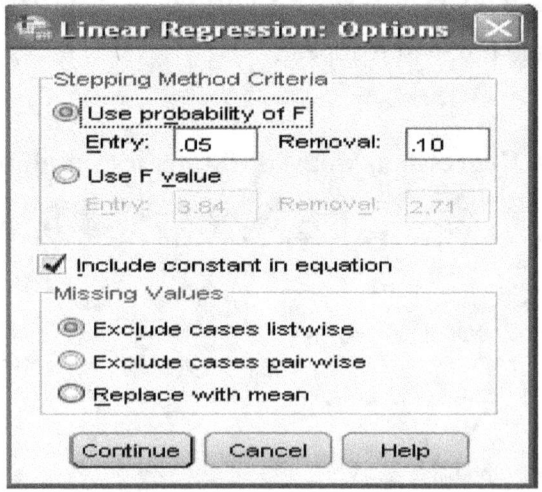

Click **OK** to see the output viewer (see page no. 170)

4.4.3 FACTOR ANALYSIS USING SPSS

Factor analysis is a statistical approach that can be used to analyze interrelationships among a large number of variables and to explain these variables in terms of their common underlying dimensions (factors). In summarizing the data, factor analysis derives underlying dimensions that, when interpreted and understood, describe the data in much smaller number of concepts than the original individual variables (S.L.Gupta, 2011).

SPSS procedure for Factor Analysis:

1) Make a data file based on the eight factors/variables as shown in the figure below.

Figure 1: Factor Analysis – Variable view

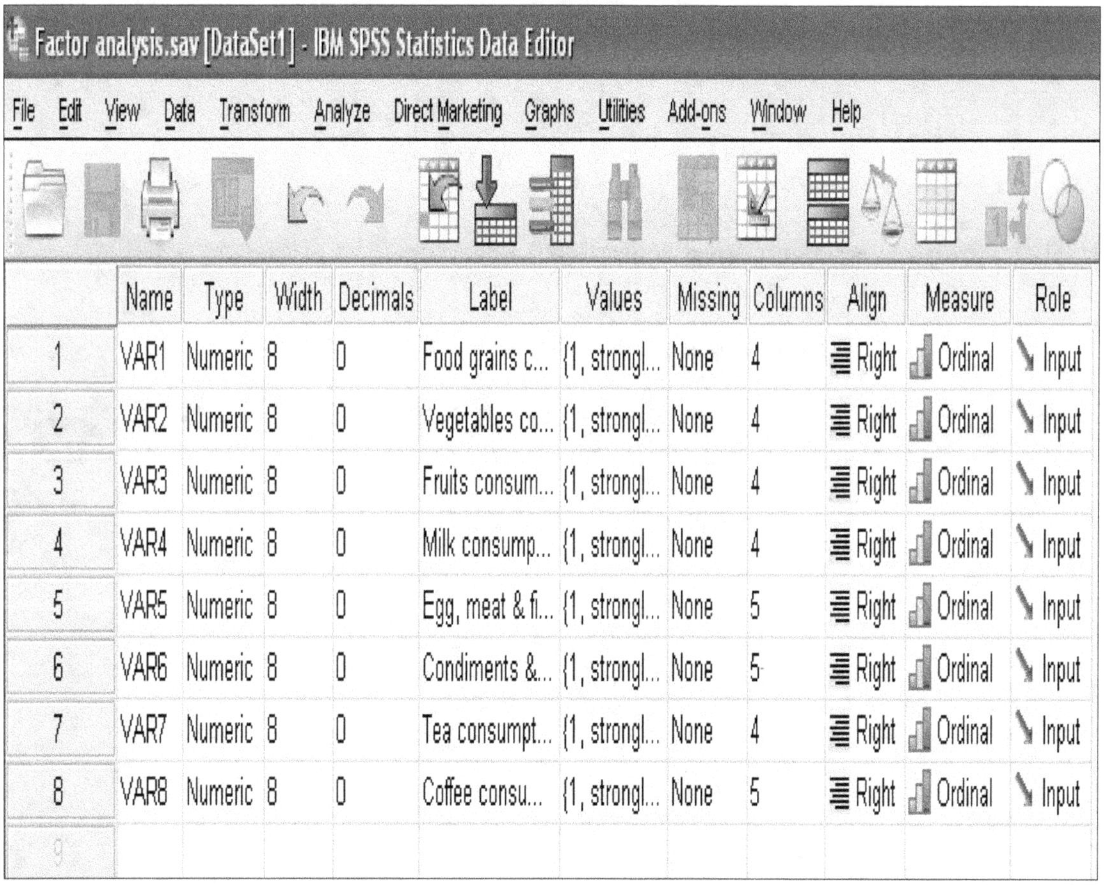

	Name	Type	Width	Decimals	Label	Values	Missing	Columns	Align	Measure	Role
1	VAR1	Numeric	8	0	Food grains c...	{1, strongl...	None	4	Right	Ordinal	Input
2	VAR2	Numeric	8	0	Vegetables co...	{1, strongl...	None	4	Right	Ordinal	Input
3	VAR3	Numeric	8	0	Fruits consum...	{1, strongl...	None	4	Right	Ordinal	Input
4	VAR4	Numeric	8	0	Milk consump...	{1, strongl...	None	4	Right	Ordinal	Input
5	VAR5	Numeric	8	0	Egg, meat & fi...	{1, strongl...	None	5	Right	Ordinal	Input
6	VAR6	Numeric	8	0	Condiments &...	{1, strongl...	None	5	Right	Ordinal	Input
7	VAR7	Numeric	8	0	Tea consumpt...	{1, strongl...	None	4	Right	Ordinal	Input
8	VAR8	Numeric	8	0	Coffee consu...	{1, strongl...	None	5	Right	Ordinal	Input
9											

2) Enter the responses from 500 respondents in the data view as shown in the figure below.

Figure 2: Factor Analysis – Data view

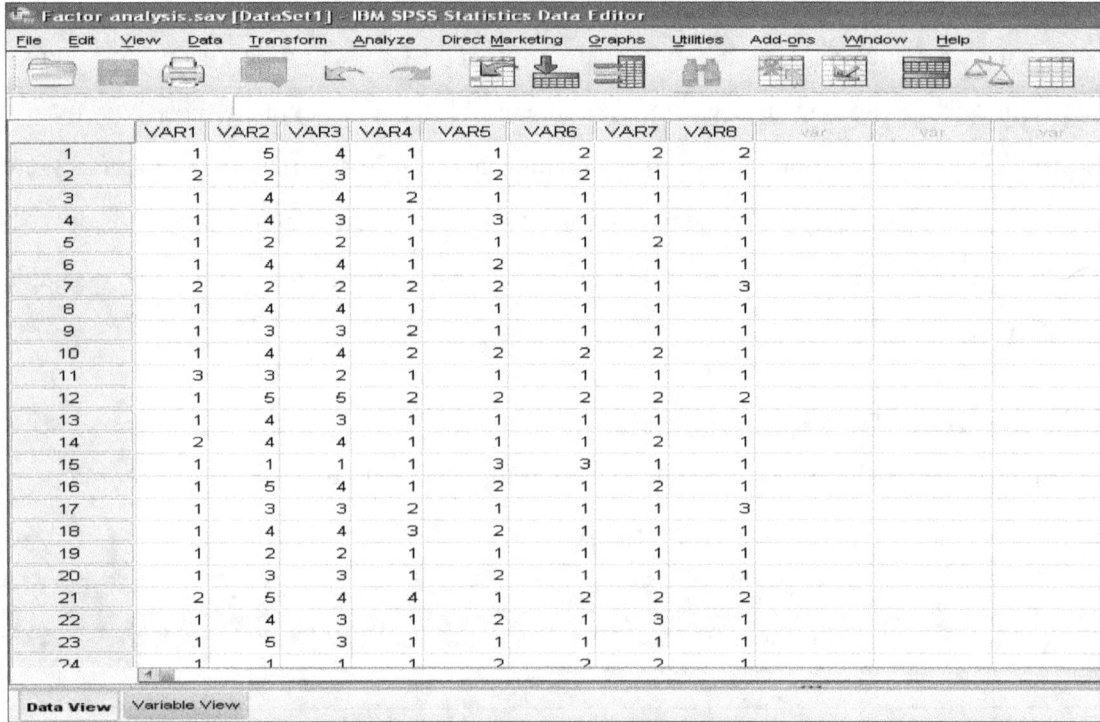

3) Click **Analyze** ➜ **Dimension reduction** ➜ **factor…..**

Figure 3: Factor Analysis – Analyze menu

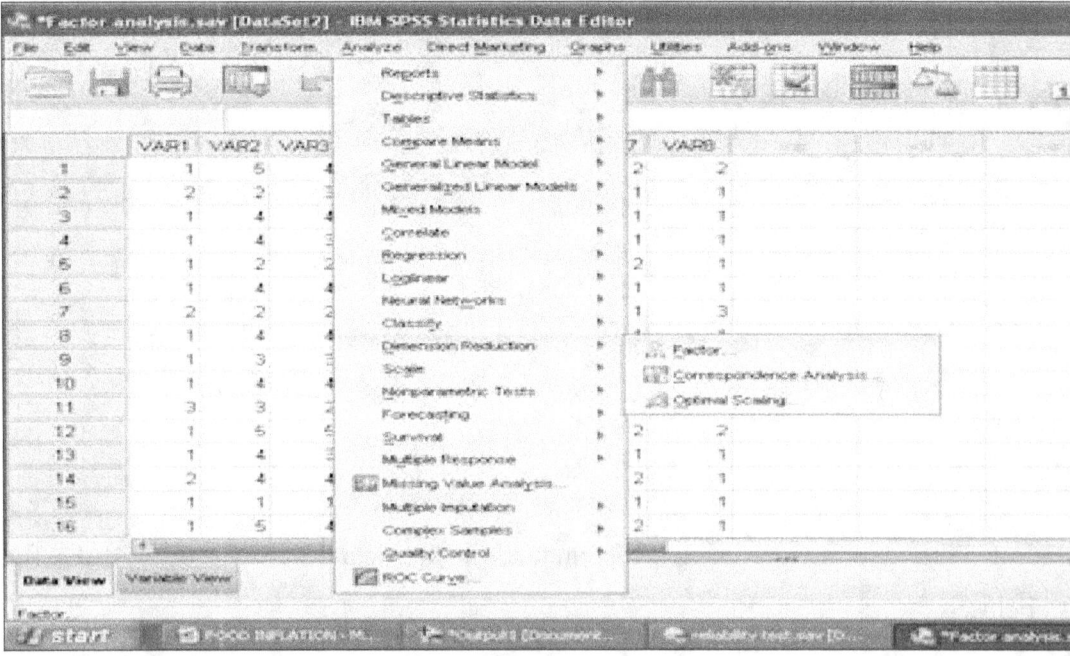

4) This will open **Factor analysis dialogue box.**

Figure 4: Factor Analysis – Factor analysis dialogue box

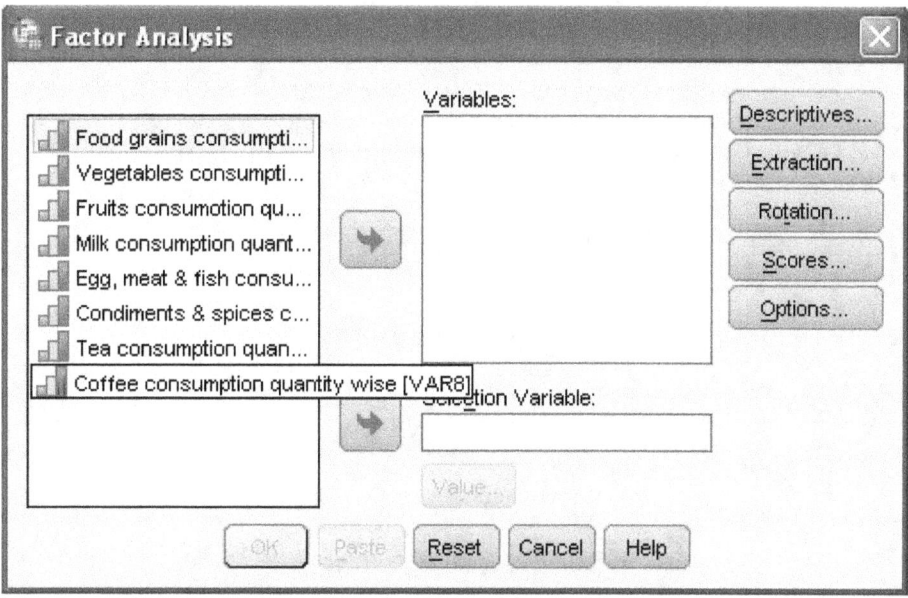

5) Click the variable in the left list box and send it in **Variables** list box by clicking upper **right arrow** button. Similarly do this for other variables.

Figure 5: Factor Analysis – Variables list box

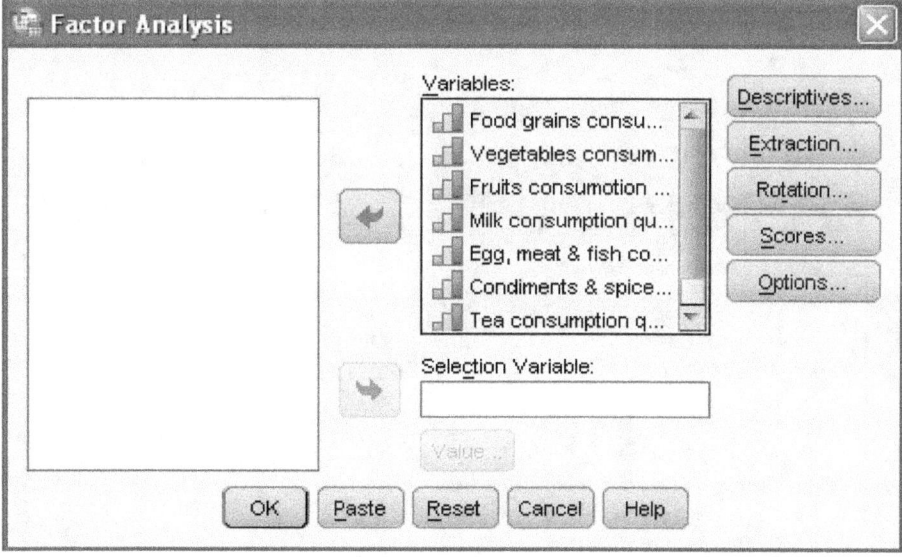

6) Click **Descriptives….** button to open its sub-dialogue box and select the desired Statistics as well as correlation matrix properties according to our need. We have selected

KMO and Bartlett's test of sphericity as well as **Anti-image** in the correlation matrix. Click **Continue** button to close the sub-dialogue box. The previous dialogue will reappear.

Figure 6: Factor Analysis – Descriptives sub-dialogue box

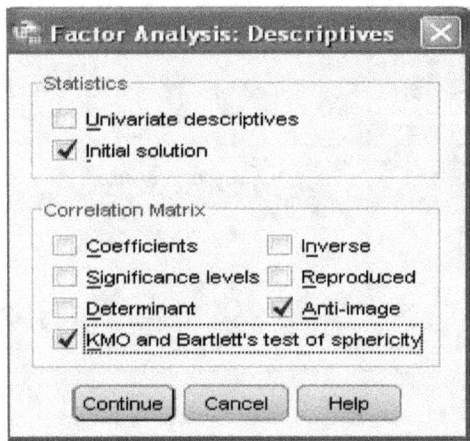

7) Click **Extraction…**.button to open its sub-dialogue box. Select the **method** as **Principal components**. We can also change other extraction methods and options as per our need. We have selected following extraction options as shown in the figure given below. Click **Continue** to close the sub-dialogue box. The previous dialogue box will reappear.

Figure 7: Factor Analysis – Extraction sub-dialogue box

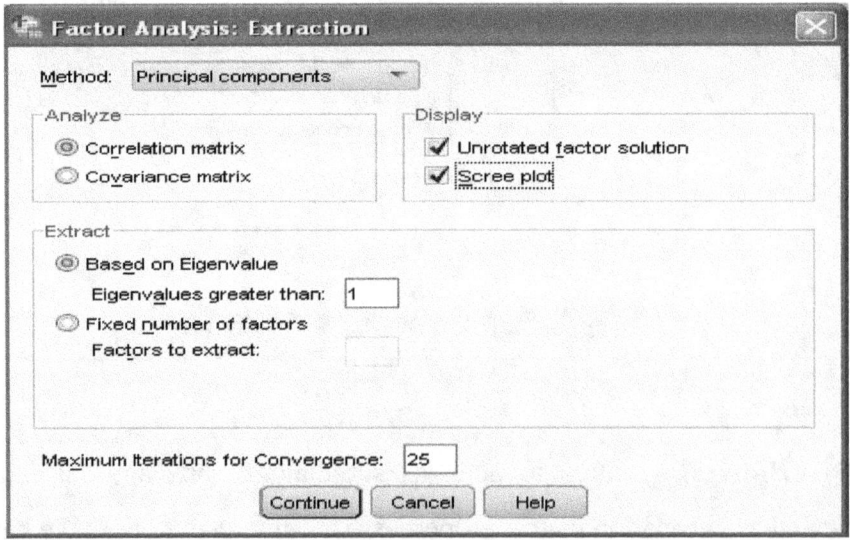

8) Click **Rotation….**button to open its sub-dialogue box. Select the **method** as **Varimax** and in **Display** select the check box of **Rotated solution**. Click **Continue** button to close the sub-dialogue box. The previous dialogue box will reappear.

Figure 8: Factor Analysis – Rotation sub-dialogue box

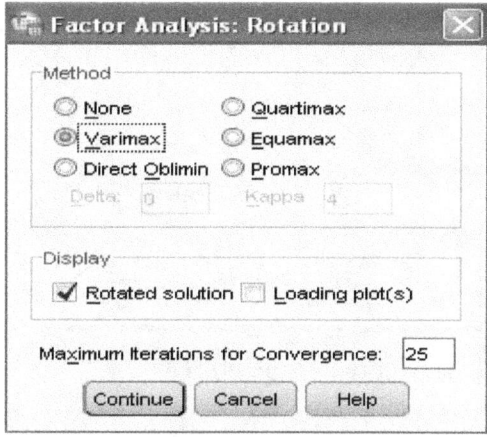

9) Click **Scores….** button to open its sub-dialogue box. Select the scores according to our need. Click **Continue** button to close the su-dialogue box. The previous dialogue box will reappear.

Figure 9: Factor Analysis – Scores sub-dialogue box

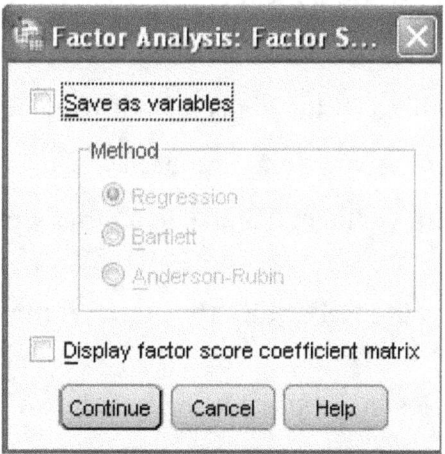

10) Click **Options….** button to open its sub-dialogue box. Select the options according to our need. Click **Continue** button to close the sub-dialogue box. The previous dialogue will reappear.

Figure 10: Factor Analysis – Options sub-dialogue box

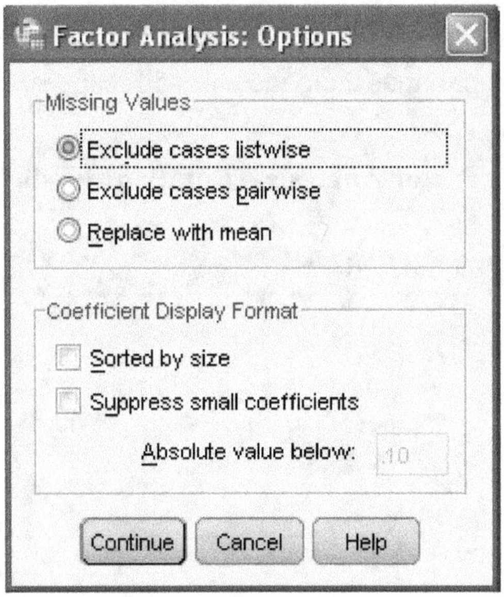

Click **OK** to see the output viewer (see page no. 187).

*Repeat the same procedure for analyzing the factors on which consumption expenditure gets affected, quality wise and frequency wise.

4.4.4 RELIABILITY ANALYSIS USING SPSS

Reliability analysis indicates the degree of accuracy of the collected data i.e. if the study is repeated, the identical results will emerge. The most commonly used reliability coefficient is Cronbach Alpha. It is based on the average correlations of items within a test if the items are standardized. If the items are not standardized, it is based on average covariance among the items. Apart from Cronbach alpha, in SPSS we can analyze the reliability based on Split half, Guttman, Parallel and Strictly parallel.

SPSS procedure for Analyzing Reliability through Cronbach alpha:

1) Enter a list of variables in the variable view as shown below:

Figure 1: Reliability Analysis – Variables view

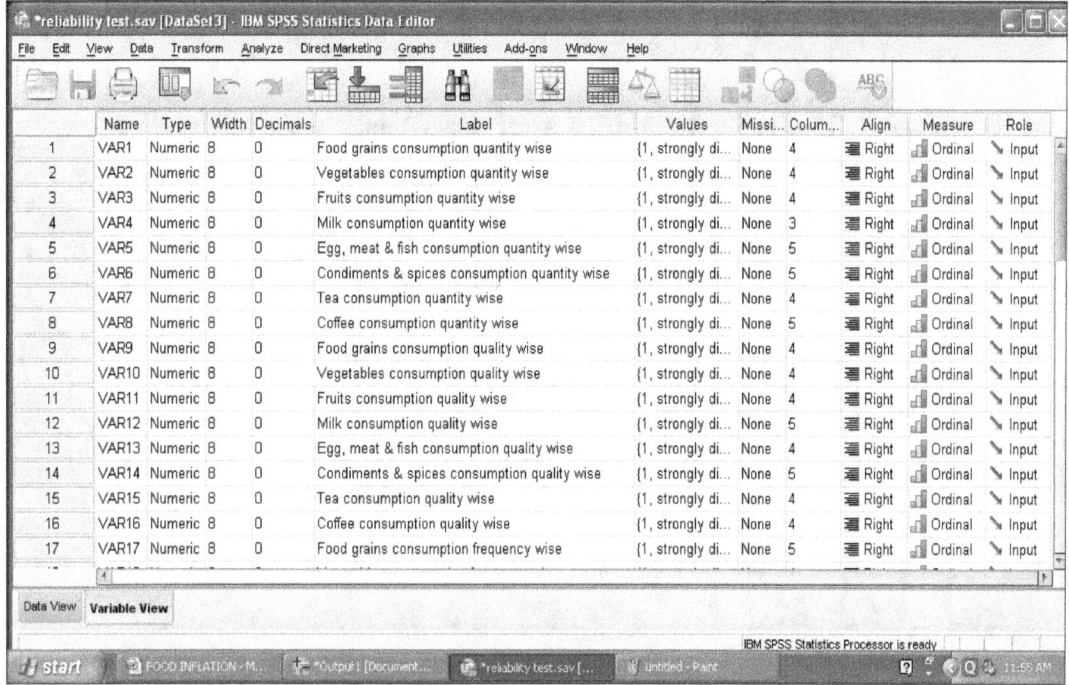

2) Enter the values of the variables in the data view as shown below. The values represented in the variables as 1- strongly disagree, 2- disagree, 3- can't say, 4- agree, 5- strongly agree.

Figure 2: Reliability Analysis –Entries under the variables in data view

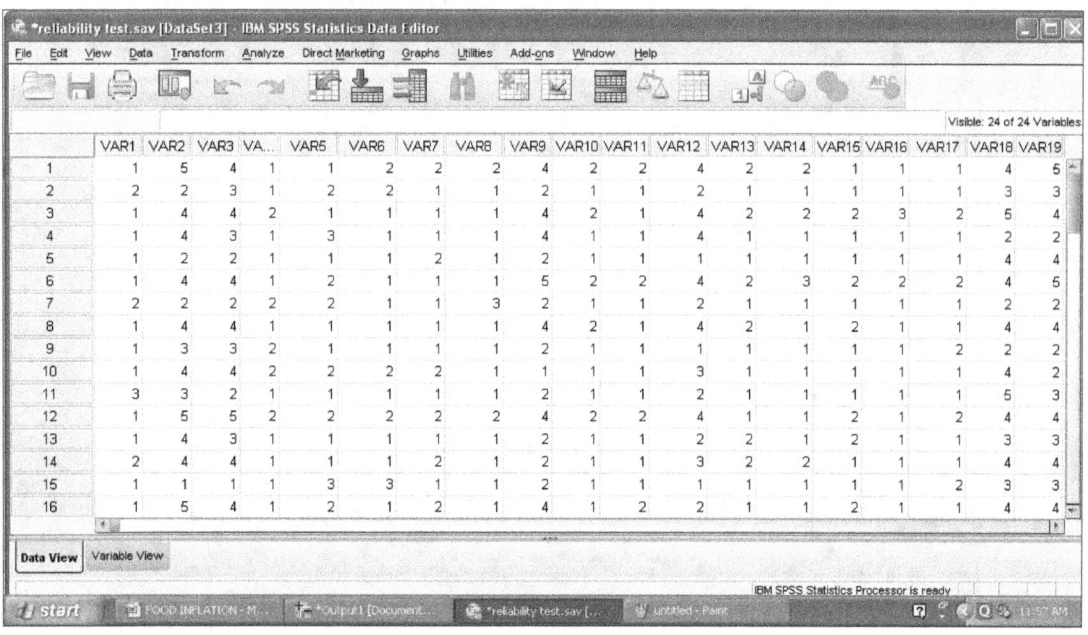

3) After entering the values click **Analyze** menu → **Scale** → **Reliability Analysis**. This will open **Reliability Analysis** dialogue box.

Figure 3: Reliability Analysis – Analyze menu

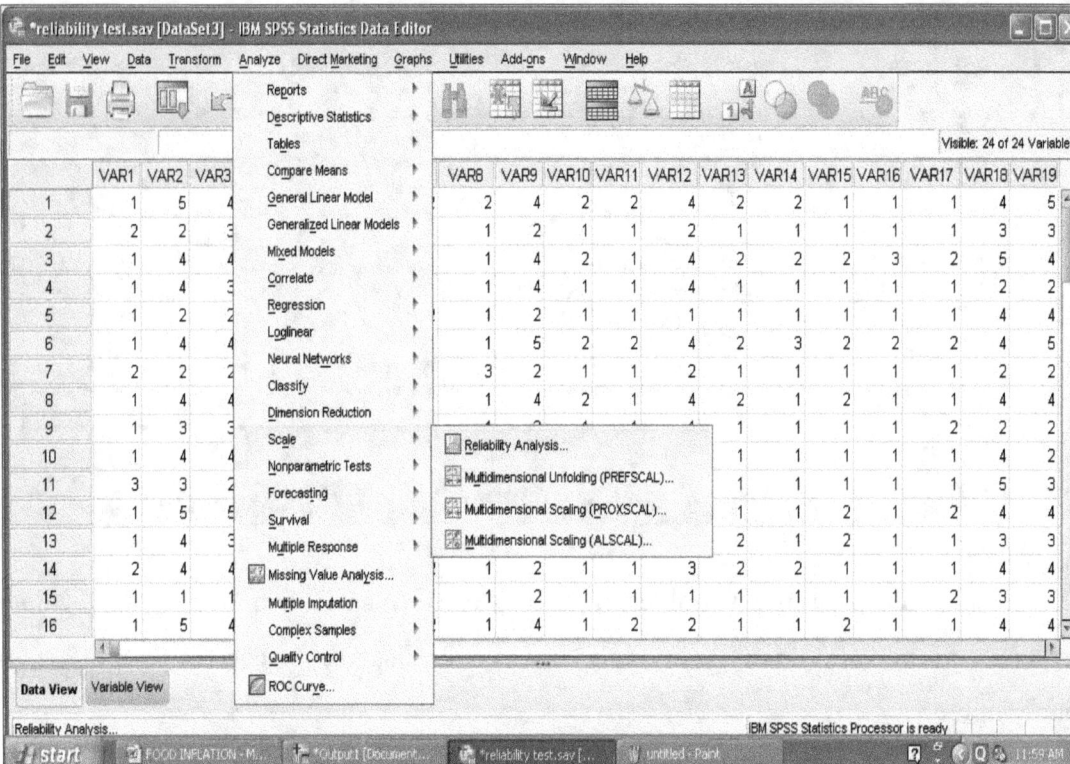

Figure 4: Reliability Analysis –Reliability analysis dialogue box

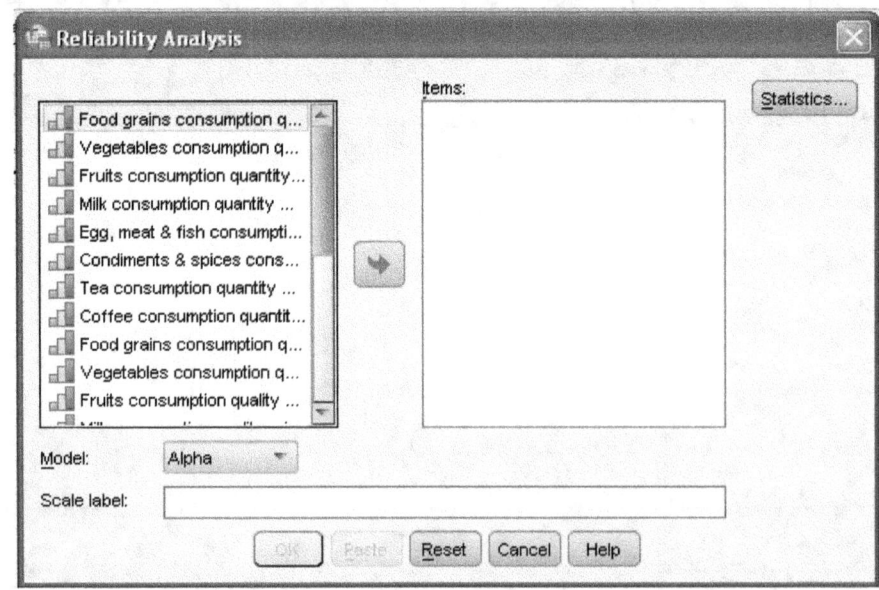

4) See that the **Model** is **Alpha.** Select the **variable** to be analyzed and click **right arrow** button to shift it in the **Items** box. Similarly move other variables, as required. In this study, we are shifting all the 24 variables as shown below.

Figure 5: Reliability Analysis –Items box

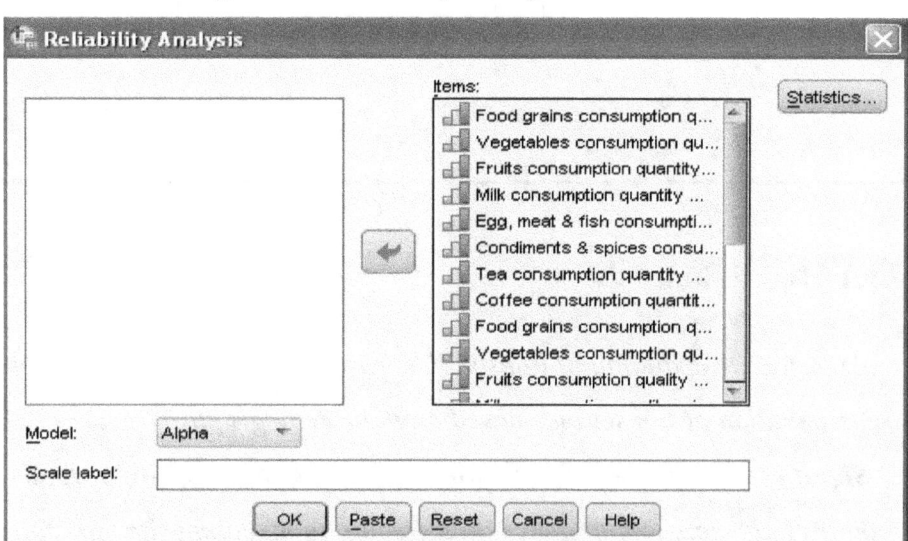

5) Click **Statistics…** button to open **Statistics** sub-dialogue box.

Select check box of **Scale** and **Scale if item deleted** in **Descriptives for.** Also select the check box of **Correlations** and **Covariances** in **Inter-Item.** Click **Continue** to close this dialogue box. The previous dialogue will re appear.

Figure 6: Reliability Analysis –Statistics sub-dialogue box

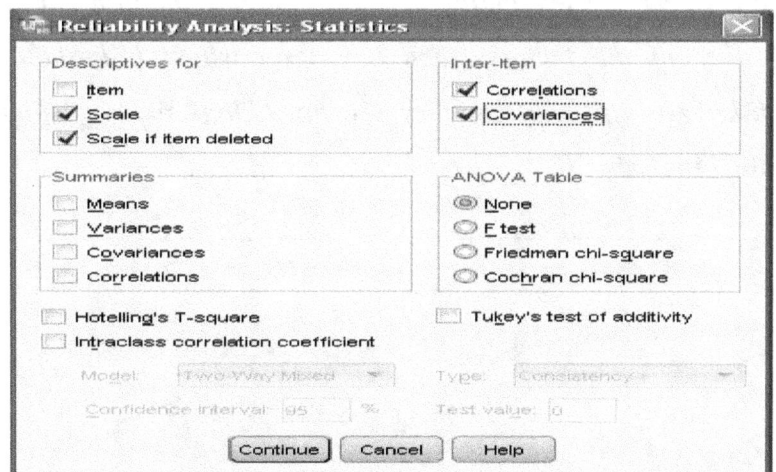

Click **OK** to see the output viewer (see page no.200).

CHAPTER 5: INTERPRETATION OF RESULTS

Chapter Highlights:

5.1   *Area-wise distribution of households who responded to the questionnaire*

5.2   *Distribution of households based on their demographic features*

5.3   *Significance of the relationship between impact of high food inflation on household consumption expenditure on food composite and individual food items*

5.4   *Significance of the extent of relationship between impact of high food inflation on household consumption expenditure on food composite and individual food items*

5.5   *Significance of the factors (food items) on which household consumption expenditure gets affected quantity wise due to high food inflation*

5.6   *Significance of the factors (food items) on which household consumption expenditure gets affected quality wise due to high food inflation*

5.7   *Significance of the factors (food items) on which household consumption expenditure gets affected frequency wise due to high food inflation*

5.8   *Reliability Analysis*

5.1 AREA-WISE DISTRIBUTION OF HOUSEHOLDS WHO RESPONDED TO THE QUESTIONNAIRE

Table 1 and figure 1 shows the area-wise distribution of respondents. The selection of respondents from a particular area is based on the population density of that area covered by TMC. From table 1, highest number of respondents were selected from Mumbra, Diva & Shilphata area (15%), Wagle Estate (15%) and Kalwa (14%), followed by moderate number of respondents were selected from Kopari (12%), Owle, Manpada & Kolshet (11%), Naupada (10%) and Vartaknagar (10%) and the least number of respondents were selected from Uthalsar (07%) and Railadevi (06%).

Table 1: Area-wise distribution of respondents

Area	No. of Respondents (Total= 500)	Percentage of respondents (%)
Uthalsar	35	07
Naupada	50	10
Kopari	60	12
Kalwa	70	14
Mumbra, Diva & Shilphata	75	15
Wagle Estate	75	15
Railadevi	30	06
Vartaknagar	50	10
Owle, Manpada & Kolshet	55	11

Source: Primary data

Figure 1: Area-wise distribution of respondents

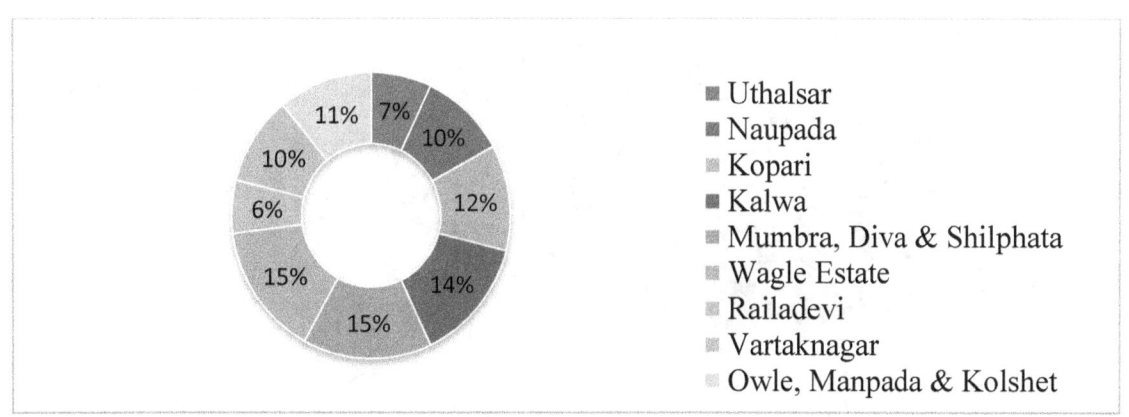

Source: Primary data

5.2 DISTRIBUTION OF HOUSEHOLDS BASED ON THEIR DEMOGRAPHIC FEATURES

5.2.1 FAMILY SIZE-WISE DISTRIBUTION OF HOUSEHOLDS

Table 1 and figure 1 shows the family size-wise distribution of households including adults and children. From table 1, the families having four members are highest in number (45%), families having five members are moderate in number (31%), families having six members are least in number (21%) and families having more than six members are negligible in numbers (3%). As per the data available from ESR 2007-08 of TMC, the average number of members in the family in Thane district was 4-5 members. So, selecting around 76% of households having four and five members is justifiable.

Table 1: Family size-wise distribution of households

No. of Members in Household	No. of Households	Percentage of respondents (%)
Four members	226	45
Five members	155	31
Six members	106	21
More than six members	13	03

Source: Primary data

Figure 1: Family size-wise distribution of Households

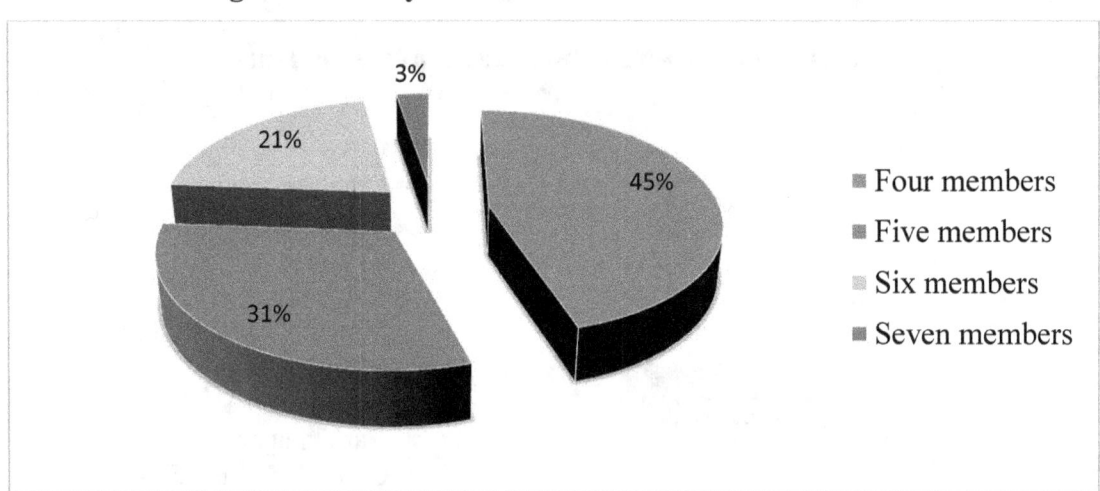

Source: Primary data

164

5.2.2 EARNING MEMBERS-WISE DISTRIBUTION OF HOUSEHOLDS

Table 2 and figure 2 shows the earning members-wise distribution of households. From table 2, the households having two earning members are highest in numbers (50%), followed by one earning member (34%), three earning member (12%) and four earning member (04%). On the basis of figures in table 2, it can be said that, in order to cope up with the high cost of living, the middle class people in Thane city are compelled to earn double income.

Table 2: Earning members-wise distribution of households

No. of members in the household	No. of earning members in the household					Total no. of households
	1	**2**	**3**	**4**	**5**	
Four members	86 (38)	121 (54)	17 (8)	02 (1)	-	226 (45)
Five members	52 (34)	78 (50)	18(12)	07 (5)	-	155 (31)
Six members	30 (28)	49 (46)	18 (17)	09 (08)	-	106 (21)
Seven members	-	04 (31)	07 (54)	02 (15)	-	13 (3)
Total no. of households	168 (34)	252 (50)	60 (12)	20 (4)	-	500 (100)
*Figures in brackets indicate percentage						

Source: Primary data

Figure 2: Earning members-wise distribution of households

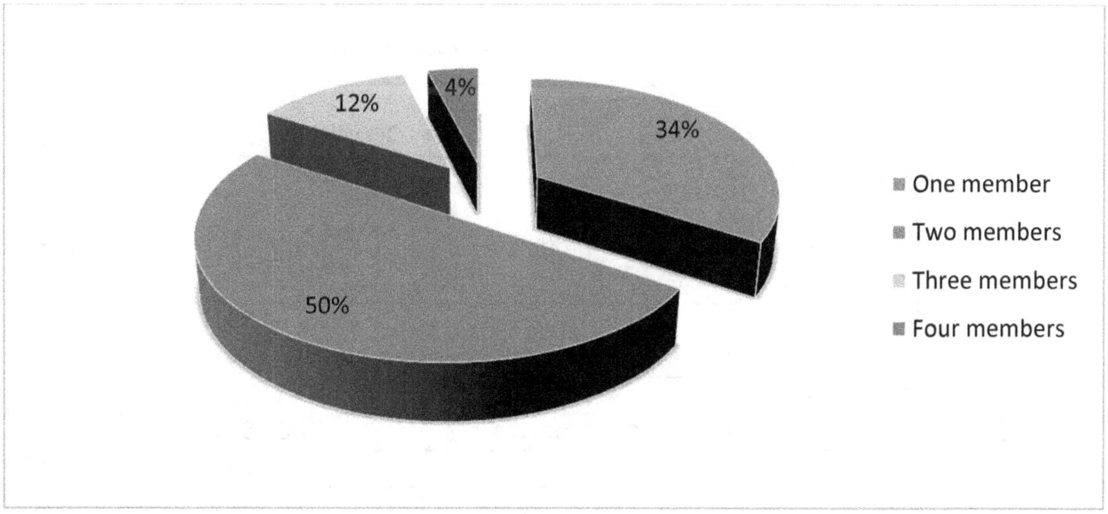

Source: Primary data

5.3 SIGNIFICANCE OF THE RELATIONSHIP BETWEEN IMPACT OF HIGH FOOD INFLATION ON HOUSEHOLD CONSUMPTION EXPENDITURE ON FOOD COMPOSITE AND INDIVIDUAL FOOD ITEMS

Table 1 shows the descriptive statistics of the responses collected for food articles composite and individual food items.

Table 1: Descriptive Statistics

	Mean	Std. Deviation	N
FOOD COMPOSITE	4.33	.687	500
FOOD GRAINS	3.17	1.247	500
VEGETABLES	3.84	1.210	500
FRUITS	3.12	1.056	500
MILK	3.96	1.128	500
EGG, MEAT AND FISH	3.46	1.120	500
CONDIMENTS & SPICES	2.70	1.334	500
TEA	3.59	.998	500
COFFEE	3.12	1.131	500

The bivariate correlation is undertaken between food composite and individual food items. It was hypothesized that there exist no significant relationship between impact of food inflation on food composite and individual food items.

Table 2 shows the correlation between impact of food inflation on food articles composite and food grains. The result shows that, there exists significantly moderate positive relationship between food composite and food grains (r=0.710, P<0.05).

Table 2: Correlation between Food composite & Food Grains

		FOOD COMPOSITE	FOOD GRAINS
FOOD COMPOSITE	Pearson Correlation	1	.710[**]
	Sig. (2-tailed)		.000
	Sum of Squares and Cross-products	235.222	303.610
	Covariance	.471	.608
	N	500	500
FOOD GRAINS	Pearson Correlation	.710[**]	1
	Sig. (2-tailed)	.000	
	Sum of Squares and Cross-products	303.610	776.550
	Covariance	.608	1.556
	N	500	500
**. Correlation is significant at the 0.01 level (2-tailed).			

Table 3 shows the correlation between impact of food inflation on food composite and vegetables. The result shows that, there exists significantly high positive relationship between food composite and vegetables (r=0.814, P<0.05).

Table 3: Correlation between Food composite & Vegetables

		FOOD COMPOSITE	VEGETABLES
FOOD COMPOSITE	Pearson Correlation	1	**.814**[**]
	Sig. (2-tailed)		.000
	Sum of Squares and Cross-products	235.222	337.388
	Covariance	.471	.676
	N	500	500
VEGETABLES	Pearson Correlation	**.814**[**]	1
	Sig. (2-tailed)	.000	
	Sum of Squares and Cross-products	337.388	730.552
	Covariance	.676	1.464
	N	500	500
**. Correlation is significant at the 0.01 level (2-tailed).			

Table 4 shows the correlation between impact of food inflation on food composite and fruits. The result shows that, there exists significantly moderate positive relationship between food composite and fruits (r=0.576, P<0.05).

Table 4: Correlation between Food composite & Fruits

		FOOD COMPOSITE	FRUITS
FOOD COMPOSITE	Pearson Correlation	1	**.576**[**]
	Sig. (2-tailed)		.000
	Sum of Squares and Cross-products	235.222	208.292
	Covariance	.471	.417
	N	500	500
FRUITS	Pearson Correlation	**.576**[**]	1
	Sig. (2-tailed)	.000	
	Sum of Squares and Cross-products	208.292	556.312
	Covariance	.417	1.115
	N	500	500
**. Correlation is significant at the 0.01 level (2-tailed).			

Table 5 shows the correlation between impact of food inflation on food composite and milk. The result shows that, there exists significantly high positive relationship between food composite and milk (r=0.817, P<0.05).

Table 5: Correlation between Food composite & Milk

		FOOD COMPOSITE	MILK
FOOD COMPOSITE	Pearson Correlation	1	.817**
	Sig. (2-tailed)		.000
	Sum of Squares and Cross-products	235.222	316.012
	Covariance	.471	.633
	N	500	500
MILK	Pearson Correlation	.817**	1
	Sig. (2-tailed)	.000	
	Sum of Squares and Cross-products	316.012	635.352
	Covariance	.633	1.273
	N	500	500
**. Correlation is significant at the 0.01 level (2-tailed).			

Table 6 shows the correlation between impact of food inflation on food composite and egg, meat & fish. The result shows that, there exists significantly moderate positive relationship between food composite and egg, meat & fish (r=0.670, P<0.05).

Table 6: Correlation between Food composite & Egg, Meat and Fish

		FOOD ARTICLES COMPOSITE	EGG, MEAT AND FISH
FOOD COMPOSITE	Pearson Correlation	1	.670**
	Sig. (2-tailed)		.000
	Sum of Squares and Cross-products	235.222	257.180
	Covariance	.471	.515
	N	500	500
EGG, MEAT AND FISH	Pearson Correlation	.670**	1
	Sig. (2-tailed)	.000	
	Sum of Squares and Cross-products	257.180	626.200
	Covariance	.515	1.255
	N	500	500
**. Correlation is significant at the 0.01 level (2-tailed).			

Table 7 shows the correlation between impact of food inflation on food composite and condiments & spices. The result shows that, there exists significantly low positive relationship between food composite and condiments & spices (r=0.419, P<0.05).

Table 7: Correlation between Food composite & Condiments and Spices

		FOOD COMPOSITE	CONDIMENTS & SPICES
FOOD COMPOSITE	Pearson Correlation	1	**.419**[**]
	Sig. (2-tailed)		.000
	Sum of Squares and Cross-products	235.222	191.432
	Covariance	.471	.384
	N	500	500
CONDIMENTS & SPICES	Pearson Correlation	**.419**[**]	1
	Sig. (2-tailed)	.000	
	Sum of Squares and Cross-products	191.432	888.192
	Covariance	.384	1.780
	N	500	500
**. Correlation is significant at the 0.01 level (2-tailed).			

Table 8 shows the correlation between impact of food inflation on food composite and tea. The result shows that, there exists significantly moderate positive relationship between food composite and tea (r=0.508, P<0.05).

Table 8: Correlation between Food composite & Tea

		FOOD COMPOSITE	TEA
FOOD COMPOSITE	Pearson Correlation	1	**.508**[**]
	Sig. (2-tailed)		.000
	Sum of Squares and Cross-products	235.222	173.804
	Covariance	.471	.348
	N	500	500
TEA	Pearson Correlation	**.508**[**]	1
	Sig. (2-tailed)	.000	
	Sum of Squares and Cross-products	173.804	497.128
	Covariance	.348	.996
	N	500	500
**. Correlation is significant at the 0.01 level (2-tailed).			

Table 9 shows the correlation between impact of food inflation on food composite and coffee. The result shows that, there exists significantly low positive relationship between food composite and coffee (r=0.429, P<0.05).

Table 9: Correlation between Food composite & Coffee

		FOOD COMPOSITE	COFFEE
FOOD COMPOSITE	Pearson Correlation	1	.429[**]
	Sig. (2-tailed)		.000
	Sum of Squares and Cross-products	235.222	166.294
	Covariance	.471	.333
	N	500	500
COFFEE	Pearson Correlation	.429[**]	1
	Sig. (2-tailed)	.000	
	Sum of Squares and Cross-products	166.294	638.038
	Covariance	.333	1.279
	N	500	500
**. Correlation is significant at the 0.01 level (2-tailed).			

5.4 SIGNIFICANCE OF THE EXTENT OF RELATIONSHIP BETWEEN IMPACT OF HIGH FOOD INFLATION ON HOUSEHOLD CONSUMPTION EXPENDITURE ON FOOD COMPOSITE AND INDIVIDUAL FOOD ITEMS

5.4.1 Between Food composite and Food Grains

Table 1 shows the variables entered or removed in the model.

Table 1: Variables Entered/Removed[a]

Model	Variables Entered	Variables Removed	Method
1	FOOD GRAINS[b]	.	Enter
a. Dependent Variable: FOOD COMPOSITE			
b. All requested variables entered.			

Table 2 shows the model summary.

Table 2: Model Summary[b]

Model	R	R Square	Adjusted R Square	Std. Error of the Estimate
1	.710[a]	.505	.504	.484
a. Predictors: (Constant), FOOD GRAINS				
b. Dependent Variable: FOOD COMPOSITE				

Table 3 shows the ANOVA values with sum of squares, degrees of freedom, mean square, F statistics and level of significance.

Table 3: ANOVA[a]

Model		Sum of Squares	Df	Mean Square	F	Sig.
1	Regression	118.703	1	118.703	507.337	.000[b]
	Residual	116.519	498	.234		
	Total	235.222	499			
a. Dependent Variable: FOOD ARTICLES COMPOSITE						
b. Predictors: (Constant), FOOD GRAINS						

Table 4 shows the regression constant and coefficient. From table 4, it can be interpreted that, one percent change in the consumption expenditure on food grains gives rise to 0.391 percent change in the consumption expenditure on food composite.

Table 4: Coefficients[a]

Model		Unstandardized Coefficients		Standardized Coefficients	t	Sig.
		B	Std. Error	Beta		
1	(Constant)	3.095	.059		52.341	.000
	FOOD GRAINS	.391	.017	.710	22.524	.000
a. Dependent Variable: FOOD COMPOSITE						

Table 5 shows the residual statistics with predicted value, residual, standard predicted values and standard residual values.

Table 5: Residuals Statistics[a]

	Minimum	Maximum	Mean	Std. Deviation	N
Predicted Value	3.49	5.05	4.33	.488	500
Residual	-1.049	.732	.000	.483	500
Std. Predicted Value	-1.740	1.467	.000	1.000	500
Std. Residual	-2.170	1.514	.000	.999	500
a. Dependent Variable: FOOD COMPOSITE					

Figure 1 shows the histogram of dependent variable food composite.

Figure 1: Histogram of dependent variable

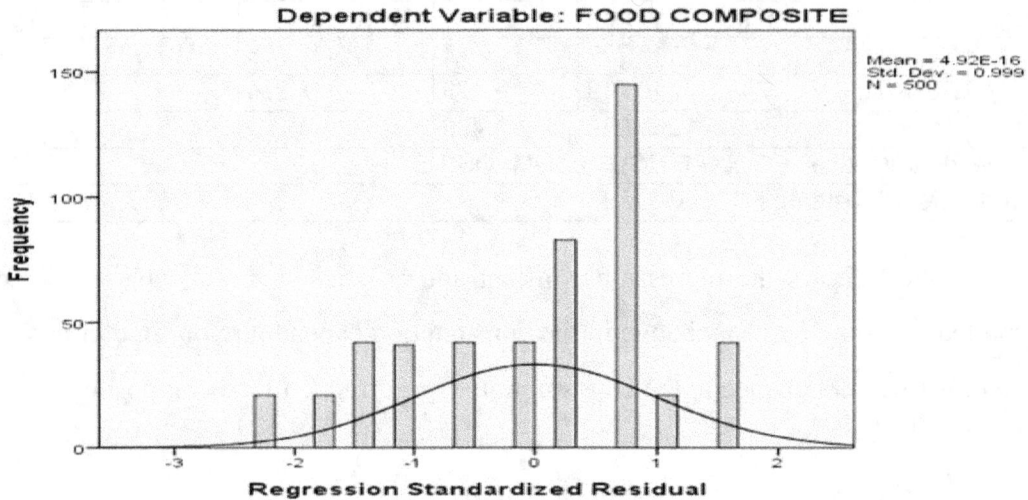

Figure 2 shows the normal P-P plot of regression standard residual values.

Figure 2: Normal P-P plot of regression standardized residual

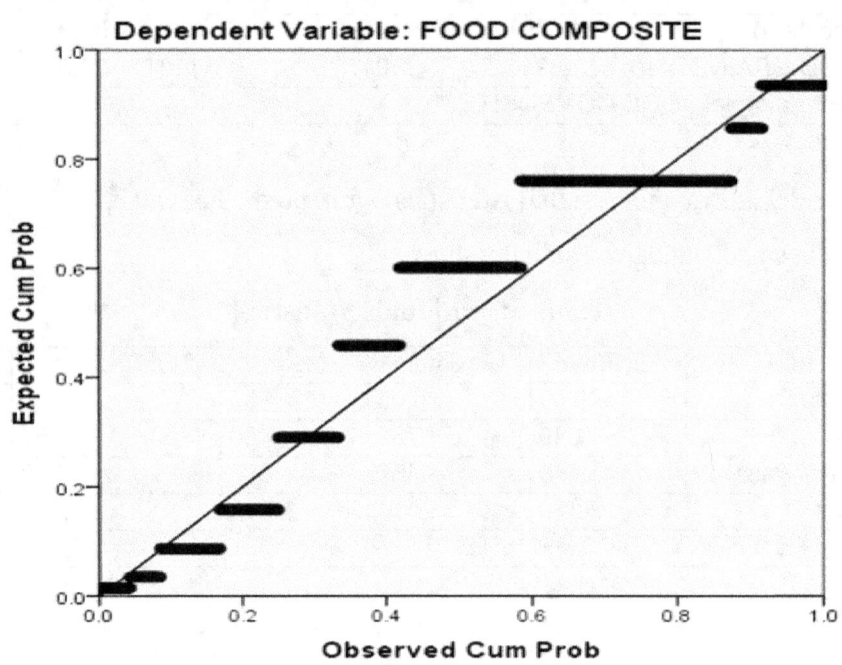

5.4.2 Between Food composite and Vegetables

Table 1 shows the variables entered or removed in the model.

Tables 1: Variables Entered/Removed[a]

Model	Variables Entered	Variables Removed	Method
1	VEGETABLES[b]	.	Enter
a. Dependent Variable: FOOD COMPOSITE			
b. All requested variables entered.			

Table 2 shows the model summary.

Table 2: Model Summary[b]

Model	R	R Square	Adjusted R Square	Std. Error of the Estimate
1	.814[a]	.662	.662	.399
a. Predictors: (Constant), VEGETABLES				
b. Dependent Variable: FOOD COMPOSITE				

Table 3 shows the ANOVA values with sum of squares, degrees of freedom, mean square, F statistics and level of significance.

Table 3: ANOVA[a]

Model		Sum of Squares	Df	Mean Square	F	Sig.
1	Regression	155.815	1	155.815	977.184	.000[b]
	Residual	79.407	498	.159		
	Total	235.222	499			
a. Dependent Variable: FOOD COMPOSITE						
b. Predictors: (Constant), VEGETABLES						

Table 4 shows the regression constant (B) and coefficient. From table 4, it can be interpreted that, one percent change in the consumption expenditure on vegetables gives rise to 0.462 percent change in the consumption expenditure on food composite.

Table 4: Coefficients[a]

Model		Unstandardized Coefficients		Standardized Coefficients	t	Sig.
		B	Std. Error	Beta		
1	(Constant)	2.562	.059		43.125	.000
	VEGETABLES	.462	.015	.814	31.260	.000
a. Dependent Variable: FOOD COMPOSITE						

Table 5 shows the residual statistics with predicted value, residual, standard predicted values and standard residual values.

Table 5: Residuals Statistics[a]

	Minimum	Maximum	Mean	Std. Deviation	N
Predicted Value	3.02	4.87	4.33	.559	500
Residual	-.948	1.052	.000	.399	500
Std. Predicted Value	-2.344	.962	.000	1.000	500
Std. Residual	-2.374	2.635	.000	.999	500
a. Dependent Variable: FOOD COMPOSITE					

Figure 1 shows the histogram of dependent variable food composite.

Figure 1: Histogram of dependent variable

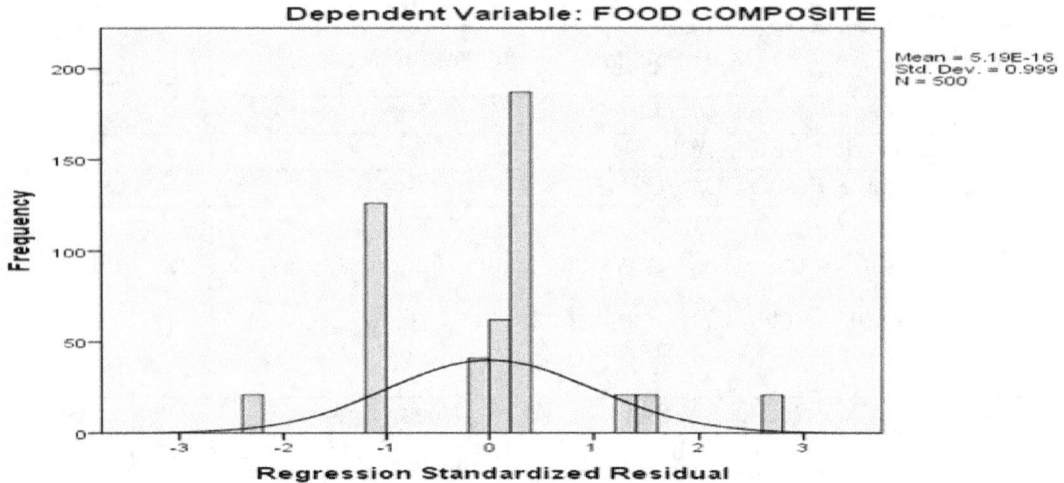

Figure 2 shows the normal P-P plot of regression standard residual values.

Figure 2: Normal P-P plot of regression standardized residual

5.4.3 Between Food composite and Fruits

Table 1 shows the variables entered or removed in the model.

Table 1: Variables Entered/Removed[a]

Model	Variables Entered	Variables Removed	Method
1	FRUITS[b]	.	Enter
a. Dependent Variable: FOOD COMPOSITE			
b. All requested variables entered.			

Table 2 shows the model summary.

Table 2:Model Summary[b]

Model	R	R Square	Adjusted R Square	Std. Error of the Estimate
1	.576[a]	.332	.330	.562
a. Predictors: (Constant), FRUITS				
b. Dependent Variable: FOOD COMPOSITE				

Table 3 shows the ANOVA values with sum of squares, degrees of freedom, mean square, F statistics and level of significance.

Table 3: ANOVA[a]

Model		Sum of Squares	Df	Mean Square	F	Sig.
1	Regression	77.988	1	77.988	247.007	.000[b]
	Residual	157.234	498	.316		
	Total	235.222	499			
a. Dependent Variable: FOOD COMPOSITE						
b. Predictors: (Constant), FRUITS						

Table 4 shows the regression constant (B) and coefficient. From table 4, it can be interpreted that, one percent change in the consumption expenditure on fruits gives rise to 0.374 percent change in the consumption expenditure on food composite.

Table 4: Coefficients[a]

Model		Unstandardized Coefficients		Standardized Coefficients	t	Sig.
		B	Std. Error	Beta		
1	(Constant)	3.164	.079		40.283	.000
	FRUITS	.374	.024	.576	15.716	.000
a. Dependent Variable: FOOD COMPOSITE						

Table 5 shows the residual statistics with predicted value, residual, standard predicted values and standard residual values.

Table 5: Residuals Statistics[a]

	Minimum	Maximum	Mean	Std. Deviation	N
Predicted Value	3.54	5.04	4.33	.395	500
Residual	-1.288	1.087	.000	.561	500
Std. Predicted Value	-2.012	1.777	.000	1.000	500
Std. Residual	-2.291	1.934	.000	.999	500
a. Dependent Variable: FOOD COMPOSITE					

Figure 1 shows the histogram of dependent variable food composite.

Figure 1: Histogram of dependent variable

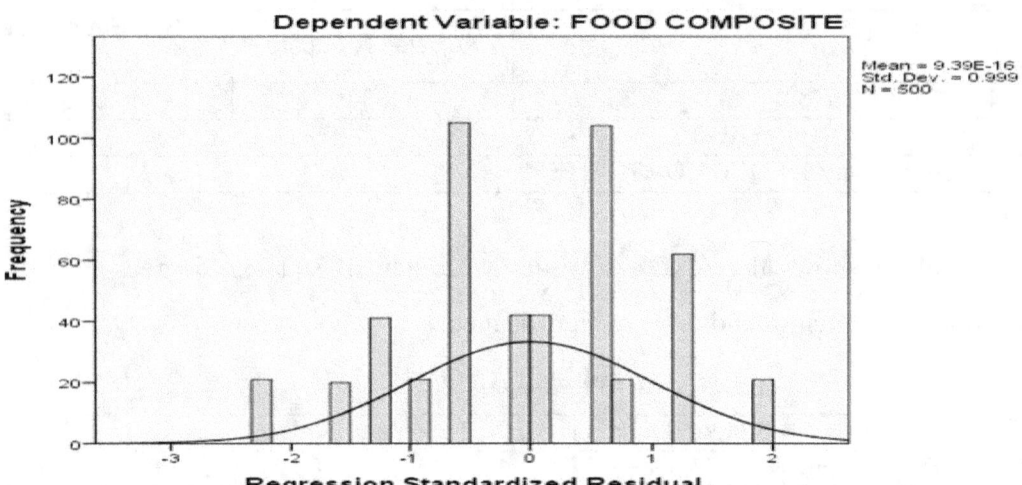

Figure 2 shows the normal P-P plot of regression standard residual values.

Figure 2: Normal P-P plot of regression standardized residual

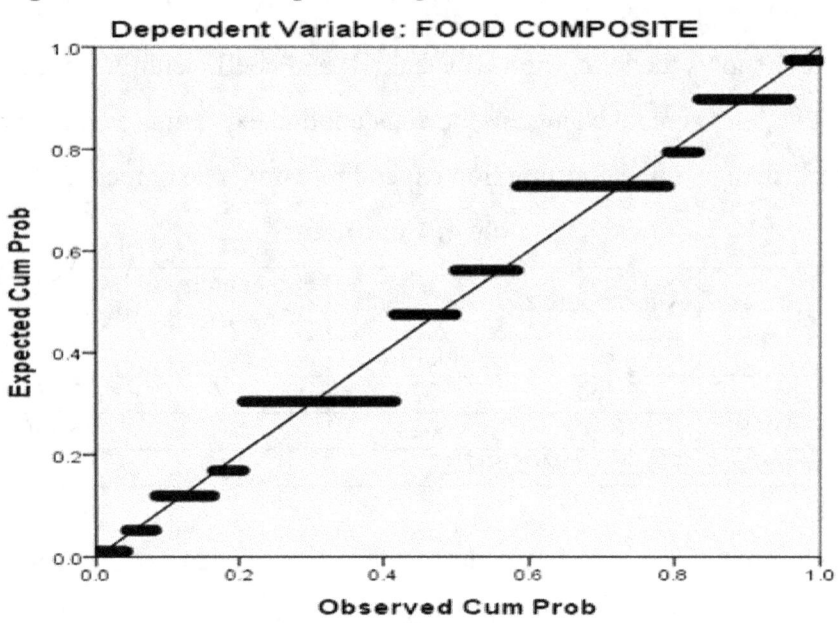

5.4.4 Between Food composite and Milk

Table 1 shows the variables entered or removed in the model.

Table 1: Variables Entered/Removed[a]

Model	Variables Entered	Variables Removed	Method
1	MILK[b]	.	Enter
a. Dependent Variable: FOOD COMPOSITE			
b. All requested variables entered.			

Table 2 shows the model summary.

Table 2:Model Summary[b]

Model	R	R Square	Adjusted R Square	Std. Error of the Estimate
1	.817[a]	.668	.668	.396
a. Predictors: (Constant), MILK				
b. Dependent Variable: FOOD COMPOSITE				

Table 3 shows the ANOVA values with sum of squares, degrees of freedom, mean square, F statistics and level of significance.

Table 3: ANOVA[a]

Model		Sum of Squares	df	Mean Square	F	Sig.
1	Regression	157.178	1	157.178	1002.962	.000[b]
	Residual	78.044	498	.157		
	Total	235.222	499			
a. Dependent Variable: FOOD COMPOSITE						
b. Predictors: (Constant), MILK						

Table 4 shows the regression constant (B) and coefficient. From table 4, it can be interpreted that, one percent change in the consumption expenditure on milk gives rise to 0.497 percent change in the consumption expenditure on food composite.

Table 4: Coefficients[a]

Model		Unstandardized Coefficients		Standardized Coefficients	t	Sig.
		B	Std. Error	Beta		
1	(Constant)	2.362	.065		36.499	.000
	MILK	.497	.016	.817	31.670	.000
a. Dependent Variable: FOOD COMPOSITE						

Table 5 shows the residual statistics with predicted value, residual, standard predicted values and standard residual values.

Table 5: Residuals Statistics[a]

	Minimum	Maximum	Mean	Std. Deviation	N
Predicted Value	2.86	4.85	4.33	.561	500
Residual	-.855	.648	.000	.395	500
Std. Predicted Value	-2.627	.918	.000	1.000	500
Std. Residual	-2.159	1.637	.000	.999	500
a. Dependent Variable: FOOD COMPOSITE					

Figure 1 shows the histogram of dependent variable food composite.

Figure 1: Histogram of dependent variable

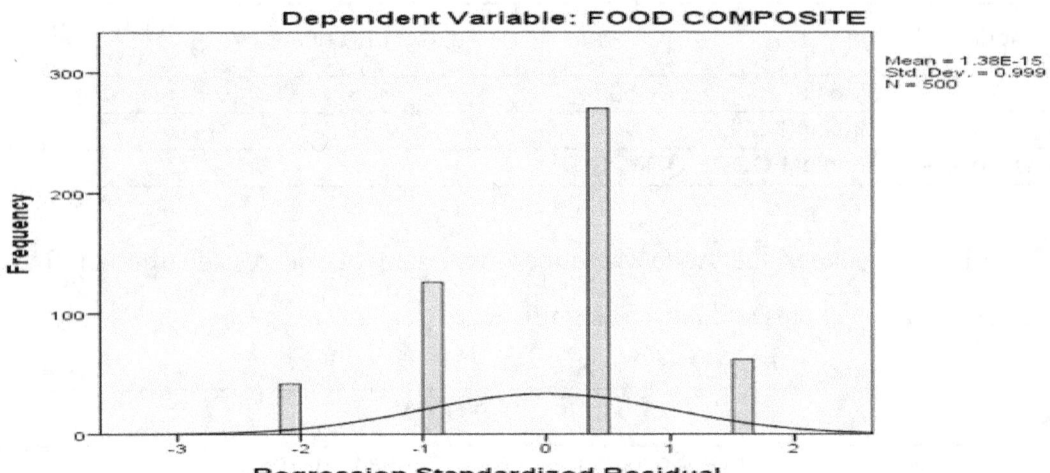

Figure 2 shows the normal P-P plot of regression standard residual values.

Figure 2: Normal P-P plot of regression standardized residual

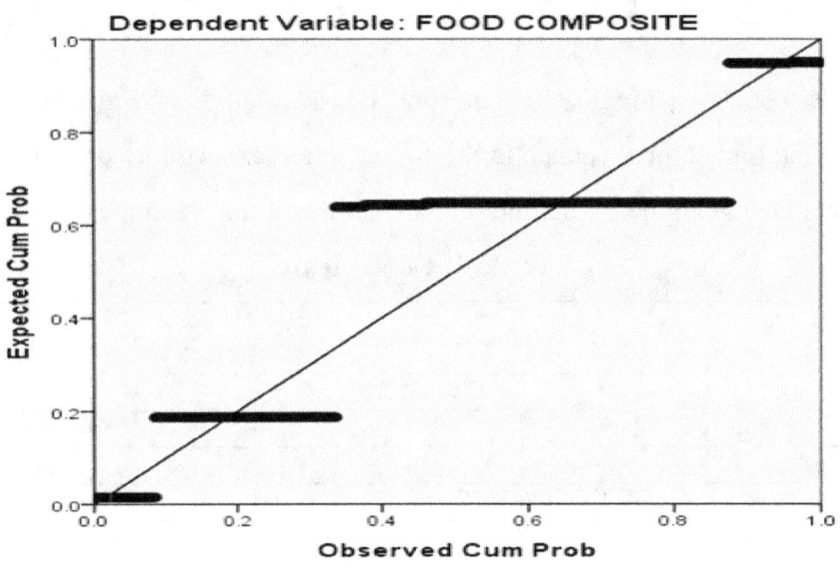

5.4.5 Between Food composite and Egg, Meat & Fish

Table 1 shows the variables entered or removed in the model.

Table 1: Variables Entered/Removed[a]

Model	Variables Entered	Variables Removed	Method
1	EGG, MEAT AND FISH[b]	.	Enter
a. Dependent Variable: FOOD COMPOSITE			
b. All requested variables entered.			

Table 2 shows the model summary.

Table 2:Model Summary^b

Model	R	R Square	Adjusted R Square	Std. Error of the Estimate
1	.670^a	.449	.448	.510
a. Predictors: (Constant), EGG, MEAT AND FISH				
b. Dependent Variable: FOOD COMPOSITE				

Table 3 shows the ANOVA values with sum of squares, degrees of freedom, mean square, F statistics and level of significance.

Table 3: ANOVA^a

Model		Sum of Squares	df	Mean Square	F	Sig.
1	Regression	105.624	1	105.624	405.874	.000^b
	Residual	129.598	498	.260		
	Total	235.222	499			
a. Dependent Variable: FOOD COMPOSITE						
b. Predictors: (Constant), EGG, MEAT AND FISH						

Table 4 shows the regression constant (B) and coefficient. From table 4, it can be interpreted that, one percent change in the consumption expenditure on egg, meat & fish gives rise to 0.411 percent change in the consumption expenditure on food composite.

Table 4: Coefficients^a

Model		Unstandardized Coefficients		Standardized Coefficients	t	Sig.
		B	Std. Error	Beta		
1	(Constant)	2.913	.074		39.294	.000
	EGG, MEAT AND FISH	.411	.020	.670	20.146	.000
a. Dependent Variable: FOOD COMPOSITE						

Table 5 shows the residual statistics with predicted value, residual, standard predicted values and standard residual values.

Table 5: Residuals Statistics^a

	Minimum	Maximum	Mean	Std. Deviation	N
Predicted Value	3.32	4.97	4.33	.460	500
Residual	-.734	1.266	.000	.510	500
Std. Predicted Value	-2.196	1.375	.000	1.000	500
Std. Residual	-1.440	2.481	.000	.999	500
a. Dependent Variable: FOOD COMPOSITE					

Figure 1 shows the histogram of dependent variable food composite.

Figure 1: Histogram of dependent variable

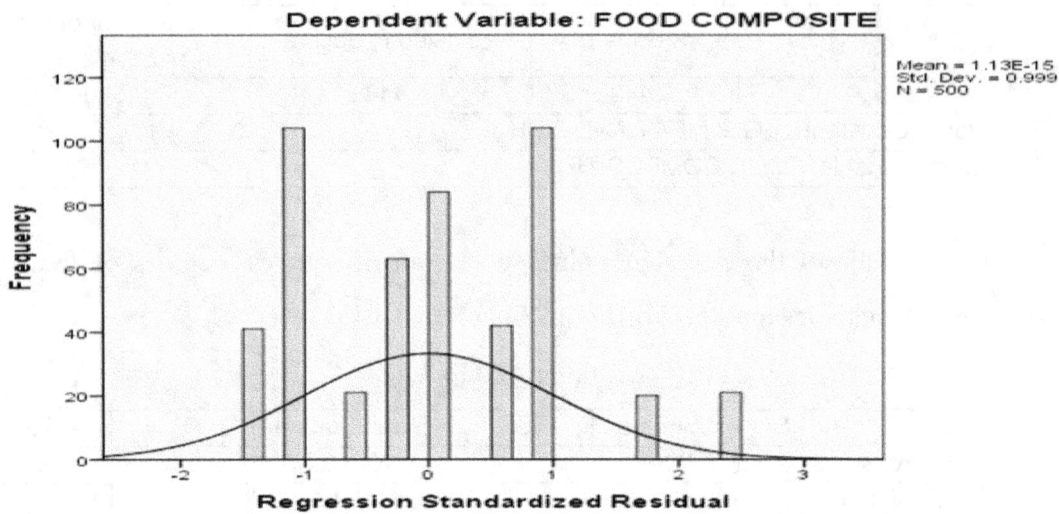

Figure 2 shows the normal P-P plot of regression standard residual values.

Figure 2: Normal P-P plot of regression standardized residual

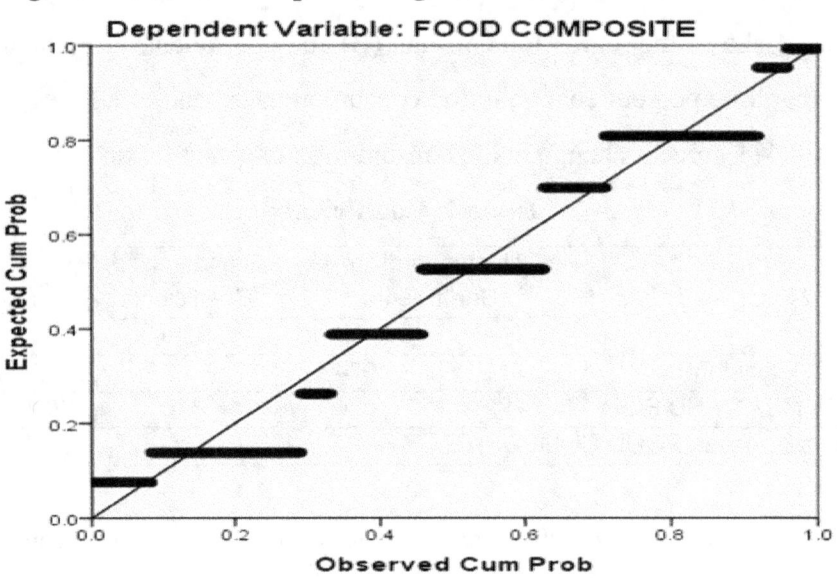

5.4.6 Between Food composite and Condiments & Spices

Table 1 shows the variables entered or removed in the model.

Table 1: Variables Entered/Removed[a]

Model	Variables Entered	Variables Removed	Method
1	CONDIMENTS & SPICES[b]	.	Enter
a. Dependent Variable: FOOD COMPOSITE			
b. All requested variables entered.			

Table 2 shows the model summary.

Table 2:Model Summary^b

Model	R	R Square	Adjusted R Square	Std. Error of the Estimate
1	.419^a	.175	.174	.624
a. Predictors: (Constant), CONDIMENTS & SPICES				
b. Dependent Variable: FOOD COMPOSITE				

Table 3 shows the ANOVA values with sum of squares, degrees of freedom, mean square, F statistics and level of significance.

Table 3: ANOVA^a

	Model	Sum of Squares	df	Mean Square	F	Sig.
1	Regression	41.259	1	41.259	105.934	.000^b
	Residual	193.963	498	.389		
	Total	235.222	499			
a. Dependent Variable: FOOD COMPOSITE						
b. Predictors: (Constant), CONDIMENTS & SPICES						

Table 4 shows the regression constant (B) and coefficient. From table 4, it can be interpreted that, one percent change in the consumption expenditure on condiments & spices gives rise to 0.216 percent change in the consumption expenditure on food composite.

Table 4: Coefficients^a

Model		Unstandardized Coefficients		Standardized Coefficients	t	Sig.
		B	Std. Error	Beta		
1	(Constant)	3.751	.063		59.422	.000
	CONDIMENTS & SPICES	.216	.021	.419	10.292	.000
a. Dependent Variable: FOOD COMPOSITE						

Table 5 shows the residual statistics with predicted value, residual, standard predicted values and standard residual values.

Table 5: Residuals Statistics[a]

	Minimum	Maximum	Mean	Std. Deviation	N
Predicted Value	3.97	4.83	4.33	.288	500
Residual	-1.398	.818	.000	.623	500
Std. Predicted Value	-1.277	1.721	.000	1.000	500
Std. Residual	-2.240	1.310	.000	.999	500
a. Dependent Variable: FOOD COMPOSITE					

Figure 1 shows the histogram of dependent variable food composite.

Figure 1: Histogram of dependent variable

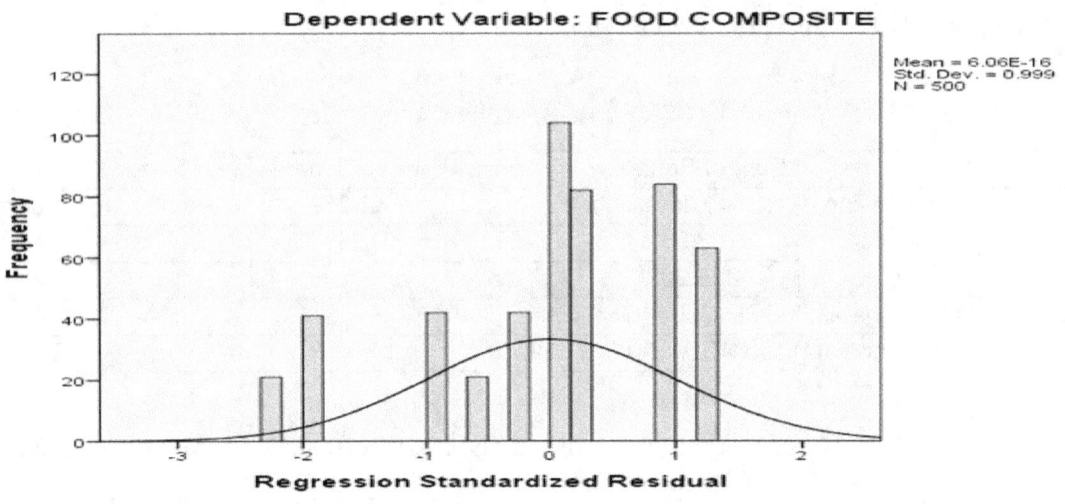

Figure 2 shows the normal P-P plot of regression standard residual values.

Figure 2: Normal P-P plot of regression standardized residual

182

5.4.7 Between Food composite and Tea

Table 1 shows the variables entered or removed in the model.

Table 1: Variables Entered/Removed[a]

Model	Variables Entered	Variables Removed	Method
1	TEA[b]	.	Enter
a. Dependent Variable: FOOD COMPOSITE			
b. All requested variables entered.			

Table 2 shows the model summary.

Table 2:Model Summary[b]

Model	R	R Square	Adjusted R Square	Std. Error of the Estimate
1	.508[a]	.258	.257	.592
a. Predictors: (Constant), TEA				
b. Dependent Variable: FOOD COMPOSITE				

Table 3 shows the ANOVA values with sum of squares, degrees of freedom, mean square, F statistics and level of significance.

Table 3: ANOVA[a]

	Model	Sum of Squares	df	Mean Square	F	Sig.
1	Regression	60.765	1	60.765	173.457	.000[b]
	Residual	174.457	498	.350		
	Total	235.222	499			
a. Dependent Variable: FOOD COMPOSITE						
b. Predictors: (Constant), TEA						

Table 4 shows the regression constant (B) and coefficient. From table 4, it can be interpreted that, one percent change in the consumption expenditure on tea gives rise to 0.350 percent change in the consumption expenditure on food composite.

Table 4: Coefficients[a]

Model		Unstandardized Coefficients		Standardized Coefficients	t	Sig.
		B	Std. Error	Beta		
1	(Constant)	3.080	.099		31.152	.000
	TEA	.350	.027	.508	13.170	.000
a. Dependent Variable: FOOD COMPOSITE						

Table 5 shows the residual statistics with predicted value, residual, standard predicted values and standard residual values.

Table 5: Residuals Statistics[a]

	Minimum	Maximum	Mean	Std. Deviation	N
Predicted Value	3.78	4.83	4.33	.349	500
Residual	-1.128	1.221	.000	.591	500
Std. Predicted Value	-1.591	1.415	.000	1.000	500
Std. Residual	-1.907	2.063	.000	.999	500
a. Dependent Variable: FOOD COMPOSITE					

Figure 1 shows the histogram of dependent variable food composite.

Figure 1: Histogram of dependent variable

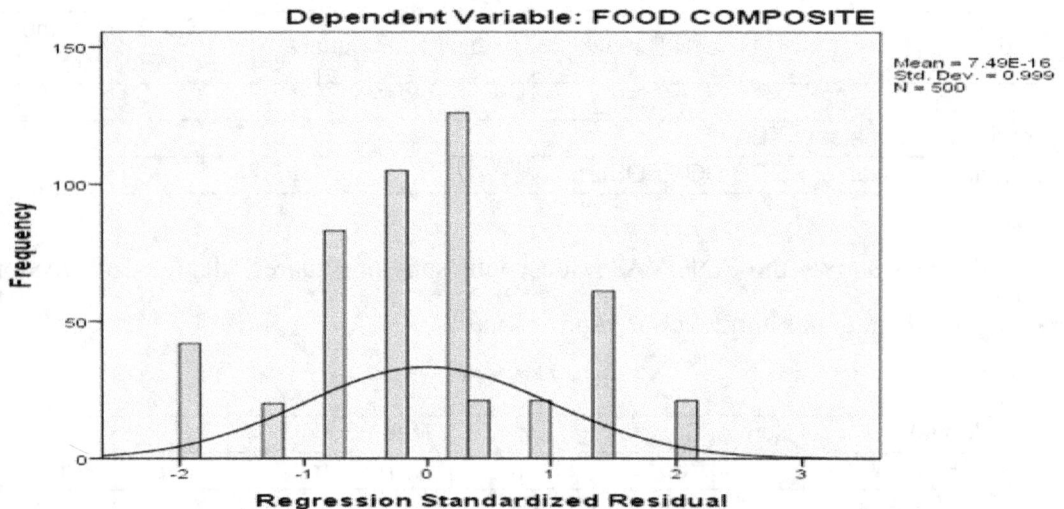

Figure 2 shows the normal P-P plot of regression standard residual values.

Figure 2: Normal P-P plot of regression standardized residual

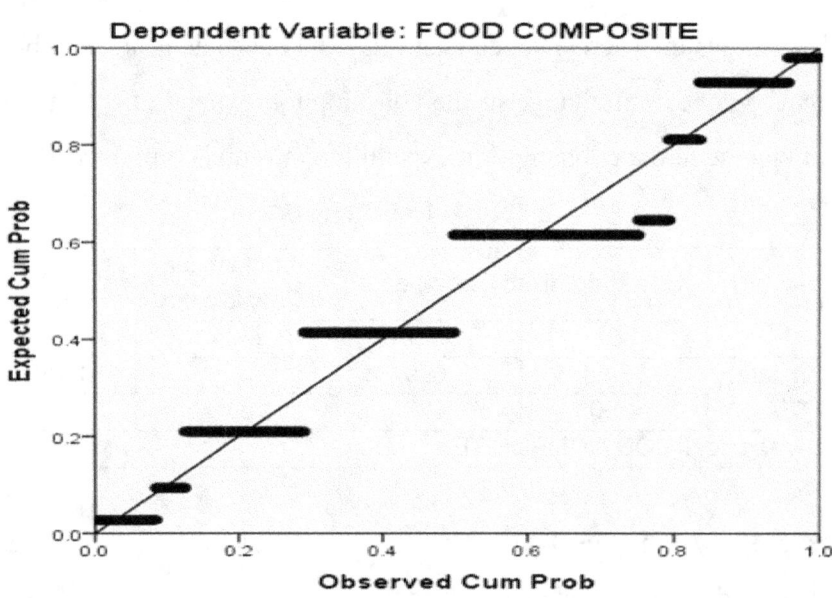

5.4.8 Between Food composite and Coffee

Table 1 shows the variables entered or removed in the model.

Table 1: Variables Entered/Removed[a]

Model	Variables Entered	Variables Removed	Method
1	COFFEE[b]	.	Enter
a. Dependent Variable: FOOD COMPOSITE			
b. All requested variables entered.			

Table 2 shows the model summary.

Table 2: Model Summary[b]

Model	R	R Square	Adjusted R Square	Std. Error of the Estimate
1	.429[a]	.184	.183	.621
a. Predictors: (Constant), COFFEE				
b. Dependent Variable: FOOD COMPOSITE				

Table 3 shows the ANOVA values with sum of squares, degrees of freedom, mean square, F statistics and level of significance.

Table 3: ANOVA[a]

Model		Sum of Squares	df	Mean Square	F	Sig.
1	Regression	43.342	1	43.342	112.488	.000[b]
	Residual	191.880	498	.385		
	Total	235.222	499			
a. Dependent Variable: FOOD COMPOSITE						
b. Predictors: (Constant), COFFEE						

Table 4 shows the regression constant (B) and coefficient. From table 4, it can be interpreted that, one percent change in the consumption expenditure on coffee gives rise to 0.261 percent change in the consumption expenditure on food composite.

Table 4: Coefficients[a]

Model		Unstandardized Coefficients		Standardized Coefficients	t	Sig.
		B	Std. Error	Beta		
1	(Constant)	3.521	.081		43.209	.000
	COFFEE	.261	.025	.429	10.606	.000
a. Dependent Variable: FOOD COMPOSITE						

Table 5 shows the residual statistics with predicted value, residual, standard predicted values and standard residual values.

Table 5: Residuals Statistics[a]

	Minimum	Maximum	Mean	Std. Deviation	N
Predicted Value	3.78	4.82	4.33	.295	500
Residual	-1.303	.957	.000	.620	500
Std. Predicted Value	-1.873	1.664	.000	1.000	500
Std. Residual	-2.100	1.542	.000	.999	500
a. Dependent Variable: FOOD COMPOSITE					

Figure 1 shows the histogram of dependent variable food composite.

Figure 1: Histogram of dependent variable

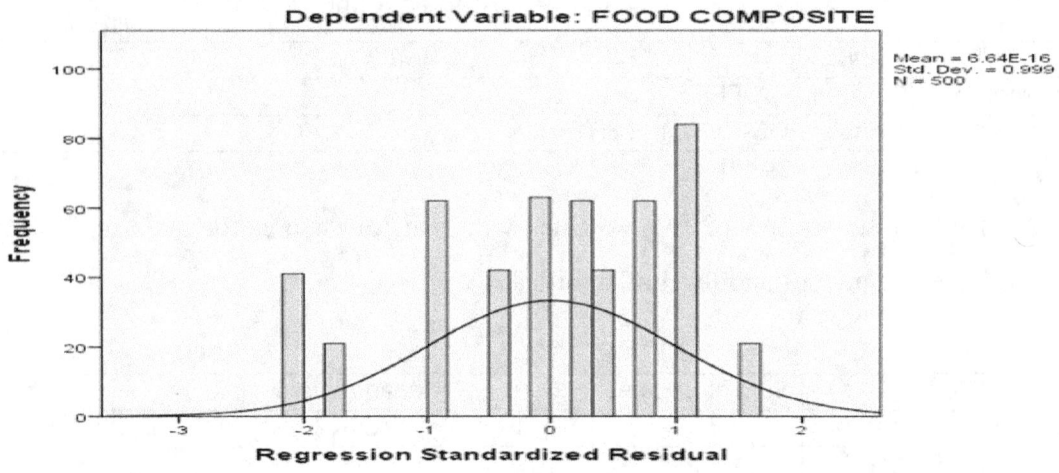

Figure 2 shows the normal P-P plot of regression standard residual values.

Figure 2: Normal P-P plot of regression standardized residual

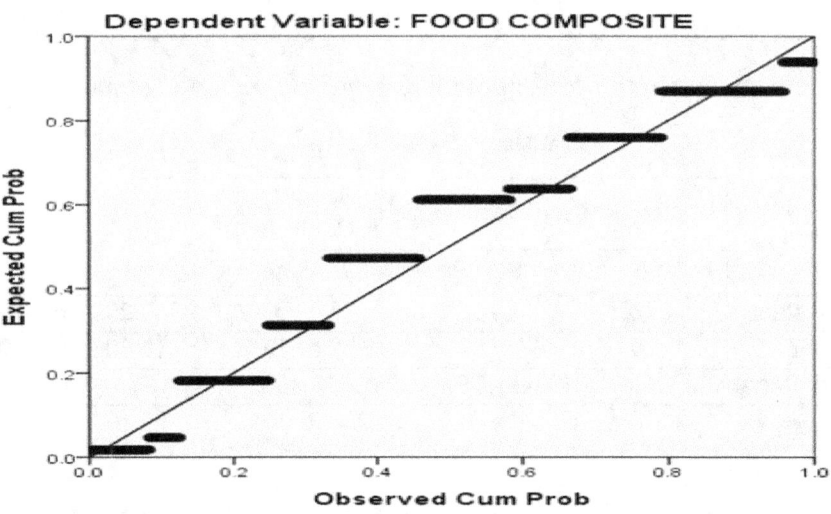

5.5 SIGNIFICANCE OF THE FACTORS (FOOD ITEMS) ON WHICH HOUSE-HOLD CONSUMPTION EXPENDITURE GETS AFFECTED QUANTITY WISE DUE TO HIGH FOOD INFLTION

Table 1 represents the descriptive statistics for all the variables under investigation. Typically 'mean', 'standard deviation' and 'number of respondents (N) who participated in the survey are given. Looking at the mean, one can conclude that household consumption expenditure on vegetables and fruits are highly affected quantity wise as they have the highest mean of 3.62 and 3.46.

Table 1: Descriptive Statistics

	N	Mean	Std. Deviation
Food grains consumption quantity wise	500	1.24	0.513
Vegetables consumption quantity wise	500	**3.62**	1.057
Fruits consumption quantity wise	500	**3.46**	0.985
Milk consumption quantity wise	500	1.32	0.615
Egg, meat & fish consumption quantity wise	500	1.54	0.574
Condiments & spices consumption quantity wise	500	1.42	0.604
Tea consumption quantity wise	500	1.38	0.526
Coffee consumption quantity wise	500	1.26	0.522
Valid N (list wise)	500		

Table 2 shows the Kaiser-Meyer-Olkin (KMO) and Bartlett's test. The KMO measures the sampling adequacy which should be greater than 0.5 for a satisfactory factor analysis to proceed. From table 2, the KMO measure is 0.537. Also, the Bartlett's test of sphericity is significant i.e. its associated probability is less than 0.05. This means that the correlation matrix is not an identity matrix.

Table 2: KMO and Bartlett's Test

Kaiser-Meyer-Olkin Measure of Sampling Adequacy.		**.537**
Bartlett's Test of Sphericity	Approx. Chi-Square	1089.931
	Df	28
	Sig.	.000

Table 3 represents anti-image covariance and correlation matrices. From table 3, in anti-image correlation matrix, all the eight concerned variables are statistically significant and collectively meet the necessary threshold of sampling adequacy with an measures of sampling adequacy (MSA) value of 0.537.

Table 3: Anti-image Matrices

		VAR1	VAR2	VAR3	VAR4	VAR5	VAR6	VAR7	VAR8
Anti-image Covariance	VAR1	.888	-.023	.065	-.186	.100	-.022	.091	-.023
	VAR2	-.023	.242	-.206	-.003	.027	.073	-.051	.036
	VAR3	.065	-.206	.240	-.066	-.030	-.051	.032	-.011
	VAR4	-.186	-.003	-.066	.793	.056	-.019	.012	-.234
	VAR5	.100	.027	-.030	.056	.773	-.288	-.020	.043
	VAR6	-.022	.073	-.051	-.019	-.288	.679	-.233	-.042
	VAR7	.091	-.051	.032	.012	-.020	-.233	.774	-.212
	VAR8	-.023	.036	-.011	-.234	.043	-.042	-.212	.812
Anti-image Correlation	VAR1	.544[a]	-.050	.142	-.221	.120	-.028	.110	-.027
	VAR2	-.050	.509[a]	-.855	-.007	.062	.181	-.117	.081
	VAR3	.142	-.855	.509[a]	-.150	-.070	-.127	.075	-.025
	VAR4	-.221	-.007	-.150	.610[a]	.071	-.026	.015	-.292
	VAR5	.120	.062	-.070	.071	.587[a]	-.398	-.026	.055
	VAR6	-.028	.181	-.127	-.026	-.398	.552[a]	-.322	-.057
	VAR7	.110	-.117	.075	.015	-.026	-.322	.581[a]	-.267
	VAR8	-.027	.081	-.025	-.292	.055	-.057	-.267	.553[a]
a. Measures of Sampling Adequacy(MSA)									

Table 4 is a 'table of communalities' which shows how much of the variance in the variables has been accounted for by the extracted factors.

Table 4: Communalities

	Initial	Extraction
Food grains consumption quantity wise	1.000	.458
Vegetables consumption quantity wise	1.000	.903
Fruits consumption quantity wise	1.000	.911
Milk consumption quantity wise	1.000	.626
Egg, meat & fish consumption quantity wise	1.000	.554
Condiments & spices consumption quantity wise	1.000	.652
Tea consumption quantity wise	1.000	.532
Coffee consumption quantity wise	1.000	.604
Extraction Method: Principal Component Analysis.		

Table 5 shows all the factors extractable from the analysis along with their Eigen values, the percent of variance attributable to each factor and the cumulative variance of the factors. The first factor accounts for 25.043% of the variance, the second factor accounts for 22.673% and the third factor accounts for 17.795%. All the remaining factors are not significant.

Table 5: Total Variance Explained

Component	Initial Eigen values			Extraction Sums of Squared Loadings			Rotation Sums of Squared Loadings		
	Total	% of Variance	Cumulative %	Total	% of Variance	Cumulative %	Total	% of Variance	Cumulative %
1	2.003	**25.043**	25.043	2.003	25.043	25.043	1.972	24.653	24.653
2	1.814	**22.673**	47.716	1.814	22.673	47.716	1.805	22.561	47.214
3	1.424	**17.795**	65.510	1.424	17.795	65.510	1.464	18.297	**65.510**
4	.896	11.198	76.708						
5	.699	8.737	85.445						
6	.558	6.981	92.427						
7	.478	5.970	98.396						
8	.128	1.604	100.000						
Extraction Method: Principal Component Analysis.									

Figure 1 shows a graph of Eigen values against all the factors. The graph is useful for determining how many factors to retain. The point of interest is where the curve starts to flatten. It can be seen that the curve begins to flatten between factor 3 and factor 4. Moreover, factor 4 has Eigen value of less than 1. So, only three factors have been retained.

Figure 1: Scree plot

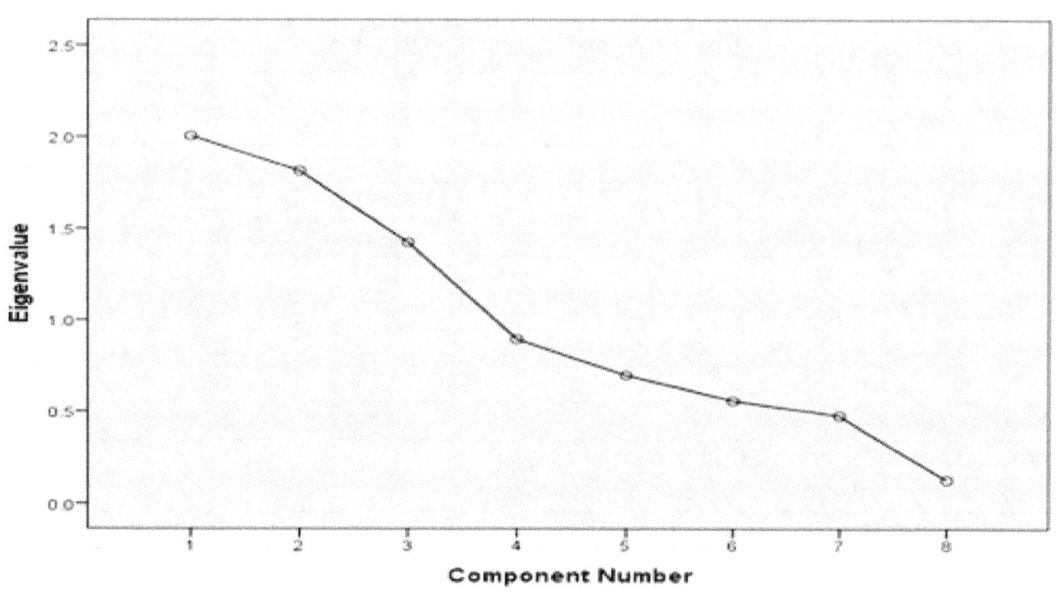

Table 6 shows the loadings of the eight variables on the three factors extracted. The higher the absolute value of the loading, the more the factor contributes to variable. As all the three factors accounts for the largest amount of variance and are the general factors, with every variable having a high loading. Based on this factor loading pattern, interpretations would be difficult and theoretically less meaningful. Therefore, the only way is to rotate the factor matrix to redistribute variance from the earlier factors to the later factors.

Table 6: Component Matrix[a]

	Component		
	1	2	3
Food grains consumption quantity wise	-.103	-.243	**.623**
Vegetables consumption quantity wise	**.930**	-.070	-.181
Fruits consumption quantity wise	**.934**	.030	-.194
Milk consumption quantity wise	.462	.082	**.637**
Egg, meat & fish consumption quantity wise	-.089	**.641**	-.368
Condiments & spices consumption quantity wise	-.108	**.799**	-.043
Tea consumption quantity wise	.100	**.712**	.123
Coffee consumption quantity wise	.109	.431	**.638**
Extraction Method: Principal Component Analysis.			
a. 3 components extracted.			

Table 7 shows the rotated component matrix. The idea of Varimax Rotation with Kaiser Normalization is to reduce the number of factors on which the variables under investigation have high loading.

Table 7: Rotated Component Matrix[a]

	Component		
	1	2	3
Food grains consumption quantity wise	-.243	-.332	**.537**
Vegetables consumption quantity wise	**.947**	-.070	.029
Fruits consumption quantity wise	**.953**	.031	.033
Milk consumption quantity wise	.301	-.031	**.731**
Egg, meat & fish consumption quantity wise	-.006	**.692**	-.274
Condiments & spices consumption quantity wise	-.100	**.799**	.058
Tea consumption quantity wise	.064	**.682**	.253
Coffee consumption quantity wise	-.044	.324	**.705**
Extraction Method: Principal Component Analysis. Rotation Method: Varimax with Kaiser Normalization.			
a. Rotation converged in 4 iterations.			

Rotation does not change anything but makes the interpretation of the analysis easier. From table 7, variables 2 and 3 load significantly on factor 1; variables 5,6 and 7 load significantly on factor 2; and variables 1,4 and 8 load significantly on factor 3.

After going through the above, we shall now be able to perform a factor analysis and interpret the result obtained. From table 7, it is interpreted that, household consumption expenditure on **vegetables and fruits is significantly affected quantity wise** followed by egg, meat & fish, condiments & spices, tea, food grains, milk and coffee.

5.6 SIGNIFICANCE OF THE FACTORS (FOOD ITEMS) ON WHICH HOUSE-HOLD CONSUMPTION EXPENDITURE GETS AFFECTED QUALITY WISE DUE TO HIGH FOOD INFLTION

Table 1 represents the descriptive statistics for all the variables under investigation. Typically 'mean', 'standard deviation' and 'number of respondents (N) who participated in the survey' are given. Looking at the mean, one can conclude that household consumption expenditure on food grains and milk are highly affected quality wise as they have the highest mean of 2.97 and 2.75.

Table 1: Descriptive Statistics

	N	Mean	Std. Deviation
Food grains consumption quality wise	500	**2.97**	1.070
Vegetables consumption quality wise	500	1.50	.638
Fruits consumption quality wise	500	1.20	.437
Milk consumption quality wise	500	**2.75**	1.049
Egg, meat & fish consumption quality wise	500	1.37	.667
Condiments & spices consumption quality wise	500	1.19	.492
Tea consumption quality wise	500	1.30	.460
Coffee consumption quality wise	500	1.19	.550
Valid N (list wise)	500		

Table 2 shows the Kaiser-Meyer-Olkin (KMO) and Bartlett's test. From table 2, the KMO measure is 0.662. Also, the Bartlett's test of sphericity is significant i.e. its associated probability is less than 0.05. This means that the correlation matrix is not an identity matrix.

Table 2: KMO and Bartlett's Test

Kaiser-Meyer-Olkin Measure of Sampling Adequacy.		**.662**
Bartlett's Test of Sphericity	Approx. Chi-Square	779.307
	Df	28
	Sig.	.000

Table 3 represents anti-image covariance and correlation matrices. From table 3, in anti-image correlation matrix, all the eight concerned variables are statistically significant and collectively meet the necessary threshold of sampling adequacy with an measures of sampling adequacy (MSA) value of 0.662.

Table 3: Anti-image Matrices

		VAR1	VAR2	VAR3	VAR4	VAR5	VAR6	VAR7	VAR8
Anti-image Covariance	VAR1	.519	-.033	-.122	-.247	-.101	-.058	-.183	.023
	VAR2	-.033	.791	-.001	-.186	-.058	.088	-.141	.123
	VAR3	-.122	-.001	.834	.073	-.115	-.112	-.088	.107
	VAR4	-.247	-.186	.073	.578	.015	-.135	.080	-.165
	VAR5	-.101	-.058	-.115	.015	.784	-.064	-.153	.109
	VAR6	-.058	.088	-.112	-.135	-.064	.830	.069	-.142
	VAR7	-.183	-.141	-.088	.080	-.153	.069	.626	-.238
	VAR8	.023	.123	.107	-.165	.109	-.142	-.238	.743
Anti-image Correlation	VAR1	.711[a]	-.052	-.185	-.450	-.158	-.089	-.320	.037
	VAR2	-.052	.682[a]	-.001	-.275	-.073	.109	-.201	.161
	VAR3	-.185	-.001	.692[a]	.104	-.142	-.135	-.121	.135
	VAR4	-.450	-.275	.104	.623[a]	.023	-.194	.133	-.251
	VAR5	-.158	-.073	-.142	.023	.761[a]	-.079	-.218	.143
	VAR6	-.089	.109	-.135	-.194	-.079	.684[a]	.095	-.181
	VAR7	-.320	-.201	-.121	.133	-.218	.095	.644[a]	-.349
	VAR8	.037	.161	.135	-.251	.143	-.181	-.349	.518[a]
a. Measures of Sampling Adequacy(MSA)									

Table 4 is a 'table of communalities' which shows how much of the variance in the variables has been accounted for by the extracted factors.

Table 4: Communalities

	Initial	Extraction
Food grains consumption quality wise	1.000	.668
Vegetables consumption quality wise	1.000	.684
Fruits consumption quality wise	1.000	.676
Milk consumption quality wise	1.000	.647
Egg, meat & fish consumption quality wise	1.000	.550
Condiments & spices consumption quality wise	1.000	.675
Tea consumption quality wise	1.000	.500
Coffee consumption quality wise	1.000	.616
Extraction Method: Principal Component Analysis.		

Table 5 shows all the factors extractable from the analysis along with their Eigen values, the percent of variance attributable to each factor and the cumulative variance of the factors. The first factor accounts for 33.061% of the variance, the second factor accounts for 16.648% and the third factor accounts for 12.986%. All the remaining factors are not significant.

Table 5: Total Variance Explained

Compo nent	Initial Eigen values			Extraction Sums of Squared Loadings			Rotation Sums of Squared Loadings		
	Total	% of Varian ce	Cumul ative %	Total	% of Varian ce	Cumul ative %	Total	% of Varian ce	Cumulati ve %
1	2.645	**33.061**	33.061	2.645	33.061	33.061	1.826	22.830	22.830
2	1.332	**16.648**	49.708	1.332	16.648	49.708	1.658	20.722	43.552
3	1.039	**12.986**	62.694	1.039	12.986	62.694	1.531	19.142	62.694
4	.898	11.225	73.919						
5	.695	8.685	82.604						
6	.592	7.397	90.001						
7	.480	6.001	96.001						
8	.320	3.999	100.000						
Extraction Method: Principal Component Analysis.									

Figure 1 shows a graph of Eigen values against all the factors. The graph is useful for determining how many factors to retain. The point of interest is where the curve starts to flatten. It can be seen that the curve begins to flatten between factor 3and factor 4. Moreover, factor 4 has Eigen value of less than 1. So, only three factors have been retained.

Figure 1: Scree plot

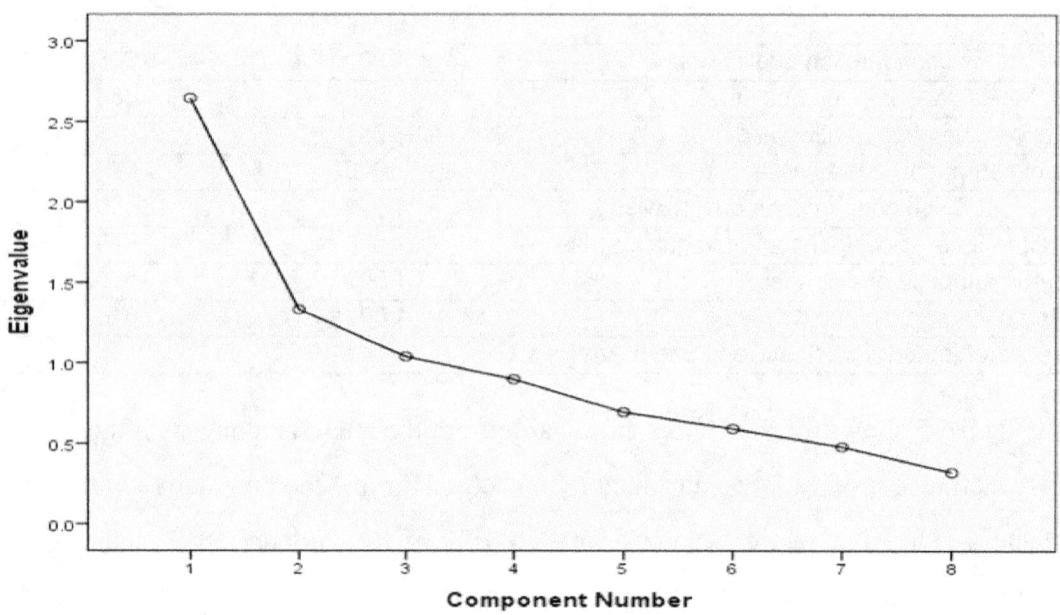

Table 6 shows the loadings of the eight variables on the three factors extracted. The higher the absolute value of the loading, the more the factor contributes to variable. As all the three factors accounts for the largest amount of variance and are the general factors, with every variable having a high loading. Based on this factor loading pattern, interpretations would be difficult and theoretically less meaningful. Therefore, the only way is to rotate the factor matrix to redistribute variance from the earlier factors to the later factors.

Table 6: Component Matrix[a]

	Component		
	1	2	3
Food grains consumption quality wise	**.817**	-.023	-.024
Vegetables consumption quality wise	.505	-.244	**-.607**
Fruits consumption quality wise	.411	-.500	**.507**
Milk consumption quality wise	**.679**	.382	-.200
Egg, meat & fish consumption quality wise	**.534**	-.490	.157
Condiments & spices consumption quality wise	.427	.399	**.577**
Tea consumption quality wise	**.685**	-.129	-.121
Coffee consumption quality wise	.396	**.678**	.017
Extraction Method: Principal Component Analysis.			
a. 3 components extracted.			

Table 7 shows the rotated component matrix. The idea of Varimax Rotation with Kaiser Normalization is to reduce the number of factors on which the variables under investigation have high loading. Rotation does not change anything but makes the interpretation of the analysis easier. From table 7, variables 1, 2 and 7 load significantly on factor 1; variables 4, 6 and 8 load significantly on factor 2; and variables 3 and 5 load significantly on factor 3.

Table 7: Rotated Component Matrix[a]

	Component		
	1	2	3
Food grains consumption quality wise	**.590**	.404	.396
Vegetables consumption quality wise	**.814**	-.142	.025
Fruits consumption quality wise	.005	.016	**.822**
Milk consumption quality wise	.557	**.579**	-.031
Egg, meat & fish consumption quality wise	.335	-.039	**.661**
Condiments & spices consumption quality wise	-.166	**.741**	.313
Tea consumption quality wise	**.581**	.218	.339
Coffee consumption quality wise	.164	**.736**	-.219
Extraction Method: Principal Component Analysis. Rotation Method: Varimax with Kaiser Normalization.			
a. Rotation converged in 6 iterations.			

After going through the above, we shall now be able to perform a factor analysis and interpret the result obtained. From table 7, it is interpreted that, household consumption expenditure on **food grains, vegetables and tea is significantly affected** quality wise followed by milk, condiments & spices, coffee, fruits and egg, meat & fish.

5.7 SIGNIFICANCE OF THE FACTORS (FOOD ITEMS) ON WHICH HOUSEHOLD CONSUMPTION EXPENDITURE GETS AFFECTED FREQUENCY WISE DUE TO HIGH FOOD INFLTION

Table 1 represents the descriptive statistics for all the variables under investigation. Typically 'mean', 'standard deviation' and 'number of respondents (N) who participated in the survey' are given. Looking at the mean, one can conclude that household consumption expenditure on food grains and milk are highly affected frequency wise as they have the highest mean of 3.22, 3.16, 2.98 and 2.40.

Table 1: Descriptive Statistics

	N	Mean	Std. Deviation
Food grains consumption frequency wise	500	1.22	.460
Vegetables consumption frequency wise	500	**3.16**	1.028
Fruits consumption frequency wise	500	**2.98**	1.011
Milk consumption frequency wise	500	1.28	.531
Egg, meat & fish consumption frequency wise	500	**3.22**	1.083
Condiments & spices consumption frequency wise	500	1.52	.782
Tea consumption frequency wise	500	**2.40**	1.040
Coffee consumption frequency wise	500	1.34	.682
Valid N (list wise)	500		

Table 2 shows the Kaiser-Meyer-Olkin (KMO) and Bartlett's test. From table 2, the KMO measure is 0.698. Also, the Bartlett's test of sphericity is significant i.e. its associated probability is less than 0.05. This means that the correlation matrix is not an identity matrix.

Table 2: KMO and Bartlett's Test

Kaiser-Meyer-Olkin Measure of Sampling Adequacy.		**.698**
Bartlett's Test of Sphericity	Approx. Chi-Square	1136.084
	df	28
	Sig.	.000

Table 3 represents anti-image covariance and correlation matrices. From table 3, in anti-image correlation matrix, all the seven concerned variables are statistically significant except variable 22 and collectively meet the necessary threshold of sampling adequacy with an measures of sampling adequacy (MSA) value of 0.698.

Table 3: Anti-image Matrices

		VAR1	VAR 2	VAR 3	VAR 4	VAR 5	VAR 6	VAR 7	VAR 8
Anti-image Covariance	VAR1	.898	-.029	-.007	-.221	-.063	.080	.013	.056
	VAR2	-.029	.326	-.217	.003	-.091	-.128	-.127	.047
	VAR3	-.007	-.217	.352	-.043	-.077	.109	-.027	-.101
	VAR4	-.221	.003	-.043	.902	.012	-.085	.060	-.044
	VAR5	-.063	-.091	-.077	.012	.614	.040	-.098	-.101
	VAR6	.080	-.128	.109	-.085	.040	.710	.088	-.320
	VAR7	.013	-.127	-.027	.060	-.098	.088	.683	-.027
	VAR8	.056	.047	-.101	-.044	-.101	-.320	-.027	.685
Anti-image Correlation	VAR1	.605[a]	-.054	-.012	-.246	-.085	.101	.016	.071
	VAR2	-.054	.684[a]	-.639	.005	-.204	-.266	-.270	.100
	VAR3	-.012	-.639	.700[a]	-.076	-.166	.218	-.055	-.207
	VAR4	-.246	.005	-.076	.580[a]	.016	-.107	.077	-.056
	VAR5	-.085	-.204	-.166	.016	.876[a]	.061	-.151	-.156
	VAR6	.101	-.266	.218	-.107	.061	.422[a]	.126	-.459
	VAR7	.016	-.270	-.055	.077	-.151	.126	.850[a]	-.040
	VAR8	.071	.100	-.207	-.056	-.156	-.459	-.040	.620[a]
a. Measures of Sampling Adequacy(MSA)									

Table 4 is a 'table of communalities' which shows how much of the variance in the variables has been accounted for by the extracted factors.

Table 4: Communalities

	Initial	Extraction
Food grains consumption frequency wise	1.000	.675
Vegetables consumption frequency wise	1.000	.779
Fruits consumption frequency wise	1.000	.755
Milk consumption frequency wise	1.000	.691
Egg, meat & fish consumption frequency wise	1.000	.597
Condiments & spices consumption frequency wise	1.000	.746
Tea consumption frequency wise	1.000	.579
Coffee consumption frequency wise	1.000	.685
Extraction Method: Principal Component Analysis.		

Table 5 shows all the factors extractable from the analysis along with their Eigen values, the percent of variance attributable to each factor and the cumulative variance of the factors. The first factor accounts for 36.071% of the variance, the second factor accounts for 17.691% and the third factor accounts for 15.075%. All the remaining factors are not significant.

Table 5: Total Variance Explained

Component	Initial Eigen values			Extraction Sums of Squared Loadings			Rotation Sums of Squared Loadings		
	Total	% of Variance	Cumulative %	Total	% of Variance	Cumulative %	Total	% of Variance	Cumulative %
1	2.886	**36.071**	36.071	2.886	36.071	36.071	2.700	33.755	33.755
2	1.415	**17.691**	53.761	1.415	17.691	53.761	1.545	19.314	53.069
3	1.206	**15.075**	68.836	1.206	15.075	68.836	1.261	15.768	**68.836**
4	.695	8.686	77.522						
5	.578	7.228	84.750						
6	.547	6.839	91.590						
7	.478	5.969	97.559						
8	.195	2.441	100.000						
Extraction Method: Principal Component Analysis.									

Figure 1 shows a graph of Eigen values against all the factors. The graph is useful for determining how many factors to retain. The point of interest is where the curve starts to flatten. It can be seen that the curve begins to flatten between factor 3 and factor 4. Moreover, factor 4 has Eigen value of less than 1. So, only three factors have been retained.

Figure 1: Scree plot

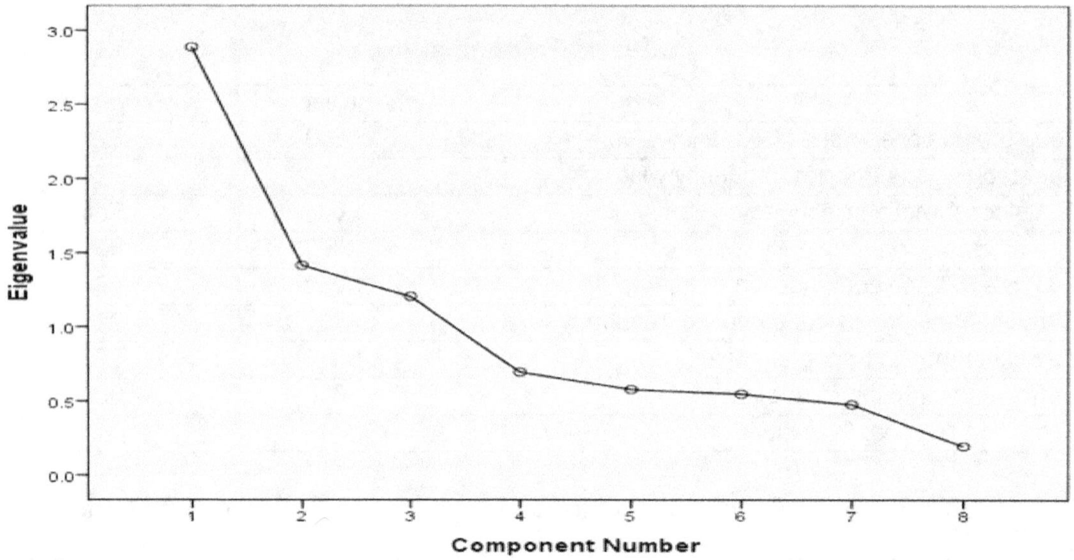

Table 6 shows the loadings of the eight variables on the three factors extracted. The higher the absolute value of the loading, the more the factor contributes to variable.

As all the three factors accounts for the largest amount of variance and are the general factors, with every variable having a high loading. Based on this factor loading pattern, interpretations would be difficult and theoretically less meaningful. Therefore, the only way is to rotate the factor matrix to redistribute variance from the earlier factors to the later factors.

Table 6: Component Matrix[a]

	Component		
	1	2	3
Food grains consumption frequency wise	.209	-.313	**.730**
Vegetables consumption frequency wise	**.876**	-.089	-.064
Fruits consumption frequency wise	**.856**	-.143	-.036
Milk consumption frequency wise	.196	.214	**.779**
Egg, meat & fish consumption frequency wise	**.760**	-.126	-.054
Condiments & spices consumption frequency wise	.227	**.833**	.011
Tea consumption frequency wise	**.661**	-.294	-.236
Coffee consumption frequency wise	.486	**.668**	-.050
Extraction Method: Principal Component Analysis.			
a. 3 components extracted.			

Table 7 shows the rotated component matrix. The idea of Varimax Rotation with Kaiser Normalization is to reduce the number of factors on which the variables under investigation have high loading. Rotation does not change anything but makes the interpretation of the analysis easier. From table 7, variables 2, 3, 5 and 7 load significantly on factor 1; variables 6 and 8 load significantly on factor 2; and variables 1 and 4 load significantly on factor 3.

Table 7: Rotated Component Matrix[a]

	Component		
	1	2	3
Food grains consumption frequency wise	.152	-.243	**.770**
Vegetables consumption frequency wise	**.859**	.176	.099
Fruits consumption frequency wise	**.851**	.118	.127
Milk consumption frequency wise	-.024	.255	**.791**
Egg, meat & fish consumption frequency wise	**.760**	.106	.090
Condiments & spices consumption frequency wise	-.034	**.863**	.012
Tea consumption frequency wise	**.750**	-.082	-.098
Coffee consumption frequency wise	.269	**.783**	.007
Extraction Method: Principal Component Analysis. Rotation Method: Varimax with Kaiser Normalization.			
a. Rotation converged in 3 iterations.			

After going through the above, we shall now be able to perform a factor analysis and interpret the result obtained. From table 7, it is interpreted that, household consumption expenditure on **vegetables, fruits, egg, meat & fish and tea is significantly affected** in terms of frequency of consumption followed by condiments & spices, coffee, food grains and milk.

5.8 RELIABILITY ANALYSIS

Table 1: Case Processing Summary

		N	%
Cases	Valid	500	100.0
	Excluded[a]	0	.0
	Total	500	100.0
a. List wise deletion based on all variables in the procedure.			

Table 2: Reliability Statistics

Cronbach's Alpha	Cronbach's Alpha Based on Standardized Items	N of Items
.743	.707	24

According to the table 2, the Cronbach alpha value for overall scale is equal to **0.743** and Cronbach alpha based on standardized items is **0.707**. Hence, we can say that the data collected from the respondents and the scale used to collect the responses is reliable. Table 3 and table 4 shows inter-item correlation matrix and inter-item covariance matrix.

Table 3: Inter-item correlation matrix

Inter-item Correlation Matrix

	VAR1	VAR2	VAR3	VAR4	VAR5	VAR6	VAR7	VAR8	VAR9	VAR10	VAR11	VAR12	VAR13	VAR14	VAR15	VAR16	VAR17	VAR18	VAR19	VAR20	VAR21	VAR22	VAR23	VAR24
VAR1	1.000	-.090	-.140	.201	-.169	-.067	-.116	.066	-.156	-.188	-.025	-.013	-.146	-.094	-.087	.193	-.135	.049	-.170	-.097	-.015	-.161	.083	-.100
VAR2	-.090	1.000	.861	.218	-.057	-.126	.044	-.038	.302	.014	.271	.272	.098	.074	.311	.131	-.056	.284	.314	.295	.119	-.058	.324	-.048
VAR3	-.140	.861	1.000	.253	.021	-.022	.049	.001	.246	.056	.118	.185	-.022	.092	.246	.156	-.028	.253	.298	.148	.161	-.028	.330	-.046
VAR4	.201	.218	.253	1.000	-.093	.015	.057	.302	-.029	-.177	-.132	.076	-.183	.017	.125	.460	.452	.300	.023	.232	.287	-.110	.205	-.004
VAR5	-.169	-.057	.021	-.093	1.000	.443	.182	-.001	-.142	-.046	.052	-.225	-.261	-.137	-.232	-.218	.210	-.117	.009	-.221	.027	-.049	.006	-.014
VAR6	-.067	-.126	-.022	.015	.443	1.000	.380	.296	-.038	-.071	.147	-.264	-.039	-.154	-.155	-.096	.162	.002	-.024	-.112	.058	-.022	.125	.051
VAR7	-.116	.044	.049	.057	.182	.380	1.000	.296	.171	.146	.038	-.114	-.049	-.070	.030	.027	-.014	.249	.207	-.161	.204	.127	.181	.254
VAR8	.066	-.038	.001	.302	-.001	.296	.296	1.000	.171	.122	-.006	.106	.025	.143	.098	.086	-.066	.009	.001	.018	.158	.073	.007	-.049
VAR9	-.156	.302	.246	-.029	-.142	-.038	.171	.171	1.000	.311	.290	.542	.348	.257	.474	.200	.025	.171	.271	.283	.007	.006	.057	-.097
VAR10	-.188	.014	.056	-.177	-.046	-.071	.146	.122	.311	1.000	.106	.330	.211	-.002	.293	-.007	-.044	.066	.177	-.050	-.039	.115	.137	-.068
VAR11	-.025	.271	.118	-.132	.052	.147	.038	-.006	.290	.106	1.000	.050	.280	.151	.240	-.065	.089	.041	.195	.236	-.054	-.078	-.059	.066
VAR12	-.013	.272	.185	.076	-.225	-.264	-.114	.106	.542	.330	.050	1.000	.140	.312	.221	.321	-.066	.147	.181	.193	.068	-.048	.066	-.146
VAR13	-.146	.098	-.022	-.183	-.261	-.039	-.049	.025	.348	.211	.280	.140	1.000	.123	.345	-.032	-.094	.048	.100	.184	-.176	.122	-.088	.073
VAR14	-.094	.074	.092	.017	-.137	-.154	-.070	.143	.257	-.002	.151	.312	.123	1.000	.082	.244	.087	.105	.213	.187	.135	-.115	-.065	-.006
VAR15	-.087	.311	.246	.125	-.232	-.155	.030	.098	.474	.293	.240	.221	.345	.082	1.000	.312	.074	.318	.258	.223	-.047	.198	.148	-.011
VAR16	.193	.131	.156	.460	-.218	-.096	.027	.086	.200	-.007	-.065	.321	-.032	.244	.312	1.000	.191	.341	.137	.217	.131	-.006	.137	-.043
VAR17	-.135	-.056	-.028	.452	.210	.162	-.014	-.066	.025	-.044	.089	-.066	-.094	.087	.074	.191	1.000	.137	.146	.261	.145	-.088	.065	-.032
VAR18	.049	.284	.253	.300	-.117	.002	.249	.009	.171	.066	.041	.147	.048	.105	.318	.341	.137	1.000	.777	.106	.577	.172	.531	.274
VAR19	-.170	.314	.298	.023	.009	-.024	.207	.001	.271	.177	.195	.181	.100	.213	.258	.137	.146	.777	1.000	.119	.566	.034	.487	.310
VAR20	-.097	.295	.148	.232	-.221	-.112	-.161	.018	.283	-.050	.236	.193	.184	.187	.223	.217	.261	.106	.119	1.000	.075	.119	-.018	.119
VAR21	-.015	.119	.161	.287	.027	.058	.204	.158	.007	-.039	-.054	.068	-.176	.135	-.047	.131	.145	.577	.566	.075	1.000	.076	.431	.304
VAR22	-.161	-.058	-.028	-.110	-.049	-.022	.127	.073	.006	.115	-.078	-.048	.122	-.115	.198	-.006	-.088	.172	.034	.119	.076	1.000	-.032	.448
VAR23	.083	.324	.330	.205	.006	.125	.181	.007	.057	.137	-.059	.066	-.088	-.065	.148	.137	.065	.531	.487	-.018	.431	-.032	1.000	.160
VAR24	-.100	-.048	-.046	-.004	-.014	.051	.254	-.049	-.097	-.068	.066	-.146	.073	-.006	-.011	-.043	-.032	.274	.310	.119	.304	.448	.160	1.000

Table 4: Inter-item covariance matrix

Inter-Item Covariance Matrix

	VAR1	VAR2	VAR3	VAR4	VAR5	VAR6	VAR7	VAR8	VAR9	VAR10	VAR11	VAR12	VAR13	VAR14	VAR15	VAR16	VAR17	VAR18	VAR19	VAR20	VAR21	VAR22	VAR23	VAR24
VAR1	.263	-.049	-.071	.063	-.050	-.021	-.031	.018	-.085	-.062	-.006	-.007	-.050	-.024	-.021	.055	-.031	.026	-.088	-.026	-.008	-.065	.044	-.035
VAR2	-.049	1.118	.897	.142	-.035	-.081	.024	-.021	.342	.009	.125	.301	.069	.038	.151	.076	-.027	.310	.337	.162	.136	-.049	.358	-.034
VAR3	-.071	.897	.970	.153	.012	-.013	.025	.000	.259	.035	.051	.192	-.014	.045	.111	.085	-.012	.258	.297	.076	.172	-.022	.339	-.031
VAR4	.063	.142	.153	.378	-.033	.006	.018	.097	-.019	-.069	.018	.049	-.075	.005	.035	-.069	.126	.190	.014	.074	.191	-.054	.132	-.002
VAR5	-.050	-.035	.012	-.033	.329	.154	.055	.000	-.087	-.017	-.001	-.135	-.100	-.039	-.061	-.069	.055	-.069	.005	-.066	.017	-.022	.004	-.005
VAR6	-.021	-.081	-.013	.006	.154	.364	.121	.081	-.021	.049	.039	-.167	-.016	-.046	-.043	-.032	.044	.001	-.015	-.035	.038	-.011	.079	.021
VAR7	-.031	.024	.025	.018	.055	.121	.276	.081	-.021	-.027	-.001	-.063	-.017	-.018	.007	.008	-.003	.135	.110	-.044	.116	.053	.099	.091
VAR8	.018	-.021	.000	.097	.000	.081	.081	.273	.095	.041	-.001	.058	.009	.037	.024	.025	-.016	.005	.000	.005	.090	.030	.004	-.017
VAR9	-.085	.342	.259	-.019	-.087	-.021	-.021	.095	1.146	.212	.136	.608	.249	.136	.233	.118	.012	.189	.294	.158	.118	.005	.064	-.071
VAR10	-.062	.009	.035	-.069	-.017	.049	-.027	.041	.212	.407	.029	.221	.090	-.001	.086	-.003	-.013	.043	.114	-.016	-.027	.058	.091	-.029
VAR11	-.006	.125	.051	.018	-.001	.039	-.001	-.001	.136	.029	.191	.023	.098	.032	.019	.048	.018	.018	.087	.054	-.026	-.027	-.027	.020
VAR12	-.007	.301	.192	.049	-.135	-.167	-.063	.058	.608	.221	.023	1.100	.098	.161	.107	.185	-.031	.159	.193	.106	.078	-.040	.073	-.104
VAR13	-.050	.069	-.014	-.075	-.100	-.016	-.017	.009	.249	.090	.098	.098	.445	.041	.106	-.012	-.028	.033	.068	.064	-.127	.064	-.061	.033
VAR14	-.024	.038	.045	.005	-.039	-.046	-.018	.037	.136	-.001	.032	.161	.041	.242	.019	.066	.019	.054	.106	.048	.072	-.045	-.034	-.002
VAR15	-.021	.151	.111	.035	-.061	-.043	.007	.024	.233	.086	.019	.107	.106	.019	.211	.079	.015	.151	.120	.053	-.023	.072	.071	-.003
VAR16	.055	.076	.085	-.069	-.069	-.032	.008	.025	.118	-.003	.048	.185	-.012	.066	.079	.303	.047	.064	.076	.062	.078	-.003	.079	-.016
VAR17	-.031	-.027	-.012	.126	.055	.044	-.003	-.016	.012	-.013	.018	-.031	-.028	.019	.015	.047	.205	.064	.067	.061	.071	-.031	.031	-.010
VAR18	.026	.310	.258	.190	-.069	.001	.135	.005	.189	.043	.018	.159	.033	.054	.151	.064	.064	1.066	.812	.057	.646	.141	.572	.192
VAR19	-.088	.337	.297	.014	.005	-.015	.110	.000	.294	.114	.087	.193	.068	.106	.120	.076	.067	.812	1.025	.063	.622	.027	.514	.213
VAR20	-.026	.162	.076	.074	-.066	-.035	-.044	.005	.158	-.016	.054	.106	.064	.048	.053	.062	.061	.057	.063	.271	.043	.049	-.010	.042
VAR21	-.008	.136	.172	.191	.017	.038	.116	.090	.118	-.027	-.026	.078	-.127	.072	-.023	.078	.071	.646	.622	.043	1.176	.065	.487	.224
VAR22	-.065	-.049	-.022	-.054	-.022	-.011	.053	.030	.005	.058	-.027	-.040	.064	-.045	.072	-.003	-.031	.141	.027	.049	.065	.626	-.026	.240
VAR23	.044	.358	.339	.132	.004	.079	.099	.004	.064	.091	-.027	.073	-.061	-.034	.071	.079	.031	.572	.514	-.010	.487	-.026	1.088	.113
VAR24	-.035	-.034	-.031	-.002	-.005	.021	.091	-.017	-.071	-.029	.020	-.104	.033	-.002	-.003	-.016	-.010	.192	.213	.042	.224	.240	.113	.460

Table 5: Item-Total Statistics

	Scale Mean if Item Deleted	Scale Variance if Item Deleted	Corrected Item-Total Correlation	Squared Multiple Correlation	Cronbach's Alpha if Item Deleted
Food grains consumption quantity wise	44.56	49.161	-.146		.755
Vegetables consumption quantity wise	42.18	40.893	.471		.718
Fruits consumption quantity wise	42.34	41.720	.447		.721
Milk consumption quantity wise	44.48	45.669	.280		.735
Egg, meat & fish consumption quantity wise	44.26	48.998	-.118		.755
Condiments & spices consumption quantity wise	44.38	48.040	-.003		.750
Tea consumption quantity wise	44.42	46.493	.224		.738
Coffee consumption quantity wise	44.54	46.878	.171		.741
Food grains consumption quality wise	42.83	41.686	.401		.725
Vegetables consumption quality wise	44.30	46.339	.188		.740
Fruits consumption quality wise	44.60	46.893	.216		.739
Milk consumption quality wise	43.05	43.150	.300		.735
Egg, meat & fish consumption quality wise	44.43	46.923	.110		.745
Condiments & spices consumption quality wise	44.61	46.791	.199		.740
Tea consumption quality wise	44.50	45.493	.431		.730
Coffee consumption quality wise	44.61	45.597	.333		.733
Food grains consumption frequency wise	44.59	47.317	.137		.742
Vegetables consumption frequency wise	42.65	38.949	.649		.700
Fruits consumption frequency wise	42.83	39.278	.636		.702
Milk consumption frequency wise	44.53	46.146	.277		.736
Egg, meat & fish consumption frequency wise	42.59	41.317	.422		.723
Condiments & spices consumption frequency wise	44.27	46.931	.076		.749
Tea consumption frequency wise	43.39	41.301	.447		.720
Coffee consumption frequency wise	44.46	46.257	.180		.741

Table 5 can be interpreted based on the following column explanations.

Scale Mean if item deleted: Tells average score for the scale if item were excluded from the scale.

Scale Variance if item deleted: Tells scale variance if items were excluded from the scale.

Corrected Item-Total Correlation: Gives Pearson correlation coefficient between score on the individual item and the sum of the scores on the remaining items.

Squared Multiple Correlation: Gives result of a multiple regression equation with item of interest as the dependent variable and all others as independent ones.

Cronbach's Alpha if item Deleted: Provides alpha coefficient that would result if the item is removed from the scale.

The analysis of the table 5 shows that variable 1, 5, 6, 8, 13, 17, 22 and 24 have lowest corrected item-total correlations. The Cronbach alpha value for the overall scale is equal to 0.743. If these variables are removed from the scale, the "Cronbach's Alpha if Item Deleted", column shows that overall reliability would increase slightly.

Table 6 shows the mean, variance, standard deviation of the computed data variables.

Table 6: Scale Statistics

Mean	Variance	Std. Deviation	N of Items
45.80	48.377	6.955	24

CHAPTER 6: FINDINGS OF THE STUDY

Chapter Highlights:

6.1   Findings of the Primary Data Analysis

6.2   Findings of the Secondary Data Analysis

6. FINDINGS OF THE STUDY

The findings of the study are divided in to: 1) Findings of the primary data analysis and 2) Findings of the secondary data analysis.

6.1 FINDINGS OF THE PRIMARY DATA ANALYSIS

Following are the findings of the primary data analysis:

From the area-wise distribution of respondents, it is found that, the concentration of the respondents in Thane city is more in Wagle Estate, Mumbra, Diva & Shilphata and Kalwa.

From the family size-wise distribution of households, it is clear that, majority of households in Thane city are having four members (45%) followed by five members (31%), which is justifiable from Environmental Status Report of Thane Municipal Corporation 2007-08.

From the earning members-wise distribution of households, it is clear that, majority of the households are having two earning members (50%) followed by one working member (34%), which is justifiable from the fact that, **double income is a key to cope up with the high cost of living.**

From the relationship (correlation analysis) between the impact of high food inflation on food composite and individual food items, it is found that, there exists significantly moderate positive relationship between food composite and food grains (r=0.701); there exists significantly high positive relationship between food composite and vegetables (r=0.814); there exists significantly moderate positive relationship between food composite and fruits (r=0.576); there exists significantly high positive relationship between food composite and milk (r=0.817); there exists significantly moderate positive relationship between food composite and egg, meat & fish (r=0.670); there exists significantly low positive relationship between food composite and condiments & spices (r=0.419); there exists significantly moderate positive relationship between food composite and tea (r=0.508); there exists significantly low positive relationship between food composite and coffee (r=0.429). It can be said that, in Thane city, except all food items, vegetables, milk and food grains showing significantly high degree of positive relationship with the food composite i.e. **rising consumption expenditure on food composite has significant positive impact on the consumption expenditure of individual food items.**

From the extent of relationship (regression analysis) between the impact of high food inflation on food composite and individual food items, it is found that, one percent change in the consumption expenditure on food grains gives rise to 0.391 percent change in the consumption expenditure on food composite; one percent change in the consumption expenditure on vegetables gives rise to 0.462 percent change in the consumption expenditure on food composite; one percent change in the consumption expenditure on fruits gives rise to 0.374 percent change in the consumption expenditure on food composite; one percent change in the consumption expenditure on milk gives rise to 0.497 percent change in the consumption expenditure on food composite; one percent change in the consumption expenditure on meat & fish gives rise to 0.411 percent change in the consumption expenditure on food composite; one percent change in the consumption expenditure on condiments & spices gives rise to 0.216 percent change in the consumption expenditure on food composite; one percent change in the consumption expenditure on tea gives rise to 0.350 percent change in the consumption expenditure on food composite; one percent change in the consumption expenditure on coffee gives rise to 0.261 percent change in the consumption expenditure on food composite. **It can be said that, in Thane city, the relative importance of vegetables, milk and egg, meat & fish is significantly high in food inflation followed by food grains and fruits.**

From the significance of the factors (factor analysis) on which household consumption expenditure gets affected quantity wise due to high food inflation, **it is found that, in Thane city, household consumption expenditure on vegetables and fruits is significantly affected quantity wise followed by egg, meat & fish, condiments & spices, tea, food grains, milk and coffee.**

From the significance of the factors (factor analysis) on which household consumption expenditure gets affected quality wise due to high food inflation, **it is found that, in Thane city, household consumption expenditure on food grains, vegetables and tea is significantly affected quality wise followed by milk, condiments & spices, coffee, fruits and egg, meat & fish.**

From the significance of the factors (factor analysis) on which household consumption expenditure gets affected frequency wise due to high food inflation, **it is found that, in Thane city, household consumption expenditure on vegetables, fruits, egg, meat & fish and tea is significantly affected in terms of frequency of consumption followed by condiments & spices, coffee, food grains and milk.**

From the rel1iability test conducted on the data the Cronbach alpha value of 0.743 shows that, the data collected is fairly accurate.

6.2 FINDINGS OF THE SECONDARY DATA ANALYSIS

From the study, it has been found that, over the years there has been persistent rise in inflation in India, particularly food inflation and it was severe since 2006, the long-term monthly average trend shows structural break contributed by primary food articles in WPI.

In recent years India's inflation rate has been higher than the world's average. During the period 2008-2010, the world inflation was in the negative territory, but India was facing high inflation which was primarily due to domestic supply side constraints.

The contribution of the agriculture and allied sector in the country's GDP shows a gradual fall from the Eight plan period (1992-97) to Eleventh plan period (2007-12).

One popular reason for the spurt in the prices of the food items in recent years is the rising demand for high value food items like, pulses, milk, livestock, fishery, vegetables and fruits which is attributed by the rise in per capita income and structural shift in the dietary pattern. As the supply response to growing demand for these high value food items is weak, their prices continued to remain high.

India, being net exporter of agricultural produce, the handling of exports and imports of food stocks by the central government has contributed to domestic price rise in food grains.

Over the last two decades, since 1993-94, the share of food in the total consumption basket has gone down from a level of 54.7 percent to 38.5 percent in 2011-12.Subsequently, the share of non-food in the consumption basket has risen from 45.3 percent in 1993-94 to 61.5 percent in 2011-12.

As per the household consumption expenditure survey carried out by National Sample Survey Office (NSSO) between 2004-05 and 2009-10, the per capita consumption of cereals and pulses declined in urban households which indicate food grains consumption in urban India is below the availability.

A study reveals that, the per capita requirement of food grains in India is 140 kg to 160 kg per annum which is in the range of per capita availability of food grains.

A distinct feature of recent food price inflation has been the sustained price pressure in protein rich items (milk, pulses, fish, meat and eggs). Inflation in protein rich items has generally exceeded both headline (WPI) inflation and inflation in primary food articles.

WPI inflation measure is preferred over CPI as a headline measure of inflation and it has broader coverage in terms of commodities. On the contrary, CPI covers services which are not accounted for in WPI.

The main factors causing food inflation and high food prices are low growth of production of agricultural output, growing population and per capita income, changing dietary patterns, inadequate storage facility, constraints in importing, nature of the market, hoardings and speculations, etc. Apart from these factors, some of the factors are shift in dietary habits towards protein foods, pressure stemming from inclusive growth policies, large increases in MSPs of food grains, shocks from global food inflation and financialization of commodities.

Government measures to curb inflation comprises of fiscal and administrative measures, budgetary measures, monetary measures, etc.

High inflation leads to decline in GDP, investors invests in bank's fixed deposits, second round of food inflation and cascading effect on food prices, exacerbation of inflation in food importing countries.

The measures to tame food inflation are increasing supply, deflating the stimulus package, setting up commercial intelligence agency, reform of the Mandi system, encourage farm-firm linkages, enhancing investments in agriculture, etc.

The rising prices of the food causing decline in the per capita calorie consumption which is an indicator of pervasive hunger.

The sustained level of high inflation is bad for economy as it imposes real cost which is borne disproportionately by different segments of the economy.

The government inefficiency in food management also leads to higher food inflation. For example, higher procurement of food stock at higher MSP and inability to release the stock in open market at cheaper rate due to costly purchase.

There is a huge gap between the average yield of food production between India and most of the countries worldwide.

According to NSS data, the average calorie consumption in rural area was about 10 percent lower in 2004-05 than in 1983. The proportionate decline was larger in better off sections of the population, and close to zero for the bottom quartile of the per capita consumption expenditure scale. In urban area, there was little change in average calorie consumption over this period.

Food inflation neutralizes the positive effects of inclusive growth and the major challenge is how to insulate the beneficiaries of these programmes from the effects of food inflation.

The long term inflation exhibits a U-shaped pattern with a structural break in 2000 and inflection point in 2002. There is an evidence for a moderate correlation between international and domestic food price inflation with significant variation across commodities. Moreover, the correlation is low when the world prices are high than when they are low.

Many economists and business groups have criticized the RBI's decision to policy rate hike in the past, as they assert that inflation is related to supply-side factors and therefore tighter monetary policy will have little effect on it and hurt growth without helping control inflation. These differences of opinion persist unless we get the better understanding of the causes of inflation.

India's share in total global exports of agri-products has increased from 0.8 percent in 1990 to 2.1 percent in 2011. This share is more than India's share in global merchandise exports i.e. 1.7 percent in 2011 (0.6 percent in 1990). Thus, from this point of view, Indian agriculture likely to have a greater comparative trade advantage than manufactured goods.

The domestic and international food prices have moved in the same direction in the current decade, the Indian food prices have remained lower than international prices, in absolute terms, growth rate and volatility. This indicates that, the rise in international prices have had limited effect on domestic food prices in India. The main reason is that, in India the prices are generally determined by domestic supply conditions in relation to demand with dependence on imports only at the margin for most of the food articles.

The state intervention in food grain marketing in India especially in rice and wheat aims at protecting producers against sharp reductions in prices and ensuring adequate availability and access of low income households to food grains. However, the subsidies have grown rapidly and contributed to large fiscal deficit in recent years. Moreover, the benefits of the subsidies have accrued mostly to large farmers in a few of the major wheat and rice producing states.

The sharp fall in the total investment, more so in the public sector investment in agriculture has been the main cause for the deceleration of agricultural growth and development.

During the last four decades, at the global level, export of inflation from oil exporting countries is significantly higher than that of industrial and non-oil developing countries including Asia. At the same time, despite low domestic inflation, export of inflation from industrial countries is significantly higher than that of non-oil developing countries.

The changing scenario demands a much different role for government in the future than it has exercised in the past. Food security is more important than food grains availability.

The cropping pattern in India has undergone significant changes with a significant shift from the cultivation of food grains to commercial crops.

The impact of monetary policy on aggregate demand in India on the basis of quarterly data from 2000 Q1 to 2011 Q1 finds that, an interest rate hike has a significant negative impact on the growth of aggregate demand.

The Reserve Bank's household expectations surveys suggest that, inflation expectations are formed adaptively with learning, but there is a dominance of food inflation in shaping overall household inflation expectations.

The poor and vulnerable were significantly lagging behind in terms of human development, and social and financial security even before the onset of the food and global economic crises, which have further undermined their food security and livelihoods.

As the level of income increases, the share of food in total household expenditure declines, while the absolute expenditure on food has gone up.

Food inflation in many cases is more persistent than non-food inflation, and shocks in many countries are propagated strongly into non-food inflation. Under these conditions, and particularly given high global commodity price inflation in recent years, a policy focus on measures of core inflation that exclude food prices can mis-specify inflation, leading to higher inflationary expectations, a downward bias to forecasts of future inflation and lags in policy responses.

Higher farm commodity prices and energy costs are the leading factors behind higher food prices.

Income elasticity of demand for cereals, pulses and spices found to be much lower than those of non-staple high value products.

Most Indian studies on food inflation suggest that there is a need, to increase the public and private investment in the supply and distribution infrastructure, strong institutional mechanism, dissemination of advance farming technologies, higher yield and productivity, food market regulator to look after the activity of hoarders and speculators, etc.

Increased interest on the part of global investors in holdings of commodity futures contracts and mutual funds focused on commodities has contributed to the rise in the level of food prices and it may change inventory behavior, because this trading does not reduce the quantity of food available for consumption.

Fruit and vegetable consumption is particularly low, and the perceived high cost of these foods has been suggested to be a barrier to food stamp participants purchasing and consuming them. This raises the question of food purchasing power as a barrier to making more healthful food choices.

A more efficient Public Food Distribution System (PFDS) can play a central role in government's food policy and make a significant contribution to the food security of households who receive transfers.

The successful resolution of the food crisis should be measured not primarily by declines in food prices, but by significant declines in the number of food-insecure people.

CHAPTER 7: CONCLUSIONS & POLICY IMPLICATIONS

Chapter Highlights:

7.1   Conclusions

7.2   Policy Implications

---

7. CONCLUSIONS & POLICY IMPLICATIONS

Following conclusions are drawn from the study and suggests for suitable policy implications.

7.1 CONCLUSIONS

It is concluded that, the food items from the basket of primary food articles in wholesale price index have relative importance in the food inflation based on consumption. In Thane city, the consumption expenditure on cereals, vegetables, milk and egg, meat & fish is affected significantly very high in lower middle class segment of the population due to high food inflation. It will be difficult to draw any conclusion based on the consumption expenditure on food items in absolute terms. To understand it better, the consumption expenditure on food items is disaggregated in to consumption expenditure quantity wise, quality wise and frequency wise. From the analysis, it can be concluded that, in Thane city, the lower middle class households (LMCHs) consume food grains with lower quality. However, over the years people have been shifted from coarse cereals to refined cereals as their income increases and it applies to lower middle class also, but within refined cereals they hardly afford to maintain the quality. This is supported by the findings that, the MSP offered by the government to the farmers, the inefficient management of buffer stock and export and import policy causing the surge in food grains prices and hence food inflation. The prices of the high quality of food grains have gone up well above the affordable limits of lower middle class people.

On several occasions, the LMCHs consume lesser quantity of vegetables or cheaper vegetables or even postponed the purchase of consumption of vegetables due to high prices of vegetables. Also, vegetables are substitutable with pulses or non-veg. This is justified from the fact that, in recent past, the rise in fuel prices, lack of infrastructure for the storage of perishables and hoardings were causing the rise in the prices of vegetables.

Fruit is a nutritional diet, the consumption expenditure on it increases with the increase in real income of the households. The LMCHs consume lesser quantity of fruits or postponed the purchase as fruits do not take major share of their consumption basket.

However, the consumption expenditure on milk is being affected severely; the LMCHs are reluctant to compromise on milk as it is the only source of protein diet which they can afford even at higher prices.

Non-veg (egg, meat & fish) are the food items which are preferred only by the non-vegetarians and the source of protein diet. The LMCHs consume non-veg with lesser frequency of consumption as the prices of non-veg rose drastically in recent years.

Condiments and spices are the food items basically used in the preparation of food; consumption expenditure on it is highly influenced by the tastes and preferences of the households. Moreover, in LMCHs, the consumption expenditure on condiments & spices is not affected too much as the share of these items in consumption basket is low compared to other food items.

Tea is an important food item; consumption expenditure on it gets affected quality wise as well as frequency wise. This means that, the LMCHs consume tea with lower quality or even postponed the consumption.

The consumption expenditure on coffee increases with the increase in income and highly influenced by the status of the households. In Thane city, LMCHs do not consider coffee as their essential food item and hence, rising prices of coffee does not affect their consumption expenditure too much.

7.2 POLICY IMPLICATIONS

Following policy decisions have to be taken in order to keep inflation, particularly food inflation within comfortable levels:

Increasing policy rates or monetary tightening does not make any sense as the problem actually lies in the domestic supply of commodities. Moreover, excessive rate hike could affect the growth rate of GDP of the country. Attention has to be paid to the growing demand for high value food items like, pulses, milk, livestock, fishery, vegetables and fruits as their prices continued to remain high. Exports should be banned for a short period of time on the food items like rice, onions, etc. in order to fulfill the domestic demand. Duty free import for specific food items like wheat, onions, pulses etc. to maintain the availability in the domestic markets. Making availability of food items is not sufficient but more reliance has to be given to assure food security to the most vulnerable sections of the society. A public and private investment in agriculture needs to be encouraged to develop agriculture infrastructure, strengthen the supply chain, research and development, dissemation of advance farming techniques. Yield and productivity of crops should be increased as India is lagging in yield compared to world's average. The procurement of stock should be done at the average MSP and up to the requirement of the minimum buffer stock norms. The government stock of food should be timely released in the situation of high food price inflation. Essential commodities should be removed from the future trading. A food market regulator should be in place to look after the activity of hoarders. Farm-firm linkage should be encouraged to reduce the role of middle men in the wholesale market. Finally, a more efficient Public Food Distribution System (PFDS) should be implemented which makes a significant contribution to the food security of households who receive transfers.

CHAPTER 8: BIBLIOGRAPHY

Chapter Highlights:

8. BIBLIOGRAPHY

8.1 BOOKS

(1) C.R.Kothari. (2009). *Research Methodology: Methods and Techniques, Second Revised Edition.* India: New Age International Publishers.

(2) Chakravrty, P. (2009). *Quantitative Methods for Management and Economics.* Mumbai: Himalaya Publishing House.

(3) Donald Cooper, P. S. (2012). *Business Research Methods, 11th Edition.* New Delhi: Tata McGRaw Hill Eductaion Pvt. Ltd.

(4) S.L.Gupta, H. G. (2011). *SPSS 17.0 for Researchers.* New Delhi: International Book House Pvt. Ltd.

(5) J.K.Sachdeva. (2011). *Business Research Methodology.* Mumbai: Himalaya Publishing House.

(6) J.K.Sharma. (2009). *Quantitative Techniques for Managerial Decisions.* New Delhi: Macmillan Publishers India Ltd.

(7) Kumar, R. (2005). *Research Methodology, Second Edition.* London: Sage Publications India Pvt. Ltd.

(8) Mishra, A. K. (2011). *A Hand Book on SPSS for Research work.* Mumbai: Himalaya Publishing House.

(9) O.R.Krishnaswami, M. R. (2009). *Methodology of Research in Social Sciences.* Mumbai: Himlaya Publishing House.

(10) P.C.Tripathi. (2008). *Research Methodology in Social Sciences.* Sultan Chand & Sons.

(11) Pannerselvam, R. (2009). *Research Methodology.* New Delhi: PHI Learning Pvt. Ltd.

(12) S.K.Puri, V. (2008). *Economic Environment of Business.* Mumbai: Himalaya Publishing House.

(13) S.K.Ray. (2007). *The Indian Economy.* New Delhi: PHI Learning Pvt. Ltd.

(14) Zikmund, W. G. (2010). *Business Research Methods.* New Delhi: Cengage Learning.

(15) De Amitabha, B. (1996). *Inflation Theory and Policy*. New Delhi: Macmilan India Ltd.

8.2 NEWSPAPERS

(1) The Hindu Business Line

(2) The Indian Express

(3) The Economic Times

(4) The Times of India

(5) Business Standard

8.3 MAGAZINES

(1) Economic & Political Weekly

(2) India Outlook

(3) India Today

(4) Outlook Business

(5) Business World

8.4 JOURNALS

(1) Arthshastra: Indian Journal of Economics & Research-ISSN: 2278-1811

(2) The IUP Journal of Applied Economics-ISSN: 0972-6861

(3) Asian Economic Papers-ISSN: 1535-3516

(4) Indian Journal of Agricultural Economics-ISSN: 0019-5014

(5) Agricultural Economics Research Review-ISSN: 0971-3441

(6) J-Gate (E-Journal)

(7) EBSCO (E-Journal)

8.5 REPORTS

(1) GoI, Economic Survey (Various Issues).

(2) RBI, Annual Report (Various Issues).

(3) Thane Municipal Corporation, Environment Status Report (2007-08, 2012-13).

(4) MOSPI, National Sample Survey Organization (55th, 61th, 66th & 68th Round).

(5) RBI, Handbook of Statistics on Indian Economy (2009-10, 2010-11 & 2011-12).

(6) RBI, Handbook of Monetary Statistics on India (2006-07).

(7) GoI, Ministry of Agriculture, State of Indian Agriculture (2011-12 & 2012-13).

(8) GoI, Ministry of Agriculture, Department of Animal Husbandry, Dairying and Fisheries, Handbook on Fisheries Statistics, 2011.

(9) GoI, Ministry of Agriculture, Department of Animal Husbandry, Dairying and Fisheries, Basic Animal Husbandry Statistics, 2012.

(10) Indian Horticulture Database (Various issues).

(11) GoI, Ministry of Agriculture, Department of Agriculture & Cooperation, Agriculture Statistics at a glance (Various Issues).

(12) GoI, Ministry of Agriculture, Department of Agriculture & Cooperation, Annual Report (Various Issues).

8.6 MANUALS

1) WPI Manual, MOSPI, GoI.
2) CPI Manual, Ministry of labour Statistics, Labour Bureau, GoI.
3) Manual on Horticulture Statistics.

8.7 WEBSITES

(1) http://indiabudget.nic.in
(2) http://www.tradingeconomics.com
(3) http://www.economywatch.com
(4) http://www.rbi.org.in
(5) http://www.eaindustry.nic.in
(6) http://www.iegindia.org
(7) http://www.fao.org
(8) http://www.economicshelp.org
(9) http://www.atulvaid.com
(10) http://www.nddb.org

(11) http://www.iari.res.in/index.php

(12) http://mofpi.nic.in/Index1.aspx

(13) http://dare.nic.in/

(14) http://cacp.dacnet.nic.in/

(15) http://censusindia.gov.in/default.aspx

(16) http://labourbureau.nic.in/indexes.htm

(17) http://data.gov.in/category/keywords/production

(18) http://agricoop.nic.in/Agristatistics.htm

(19) http://fciweb.nic.in/upload/Stock/6.pdf

(20) http://stats.oecd.org/glossary/search.asp

(21) http://planningcommission.nic.in/

(22) http://dahd.nic.in/dahd/default.aspx

(23) http://www.indiastat.com

(24) http://www.igidr.ac.in/pdf/publication/WP-2010-012.pdf

8.8 REFERENCES

(1)   A. Ganesh-Kumar, A. G. (2007, March). Food grains Policy and Management in India. *International Food Policy Research Institute (IFPRI), New Delhi* , pp. 1-140.

(2)   Abebe Shimeles, A. D. (2013, September). Rising Food Prices and Household Welfare in Ethiopia: Evidence from Micro Data. *African Development Bank Group, Office of the Chief Economist, Working Paper Series No. 182* , pp. 1-41.

(3)   Agrawal, A. (2011, January 11). Why food inflation is likely to remain persistent in India. *STCI primary dealer ltd.* , pp. 1-10.

(4)   Anand Patil, S. H. (2012, April). Food inflation: An exploratory study. *Zenith, International journal of multidisciplinary research,* , pp. 170-181.

(5)   Angus Deaton, J. D. (2009, February 14). Food and nutition in India: Facts and interpretations. *Economic & Political Weekly, Vol XLIV No. 7*, pp. 42-65.

(6)   Anwarul Hoda, A. G. (2007). *WTO Negotiations on Agriculture and Developing Countries.* New Delhi: Oxford University Press.

(7)   Ashima Goyal, S. T. (2010, August). Extracting information on inflation from consumer and wholesale prices and the NKE aggregate supply curve. *Indira Gandhi institute of development research, Mumbai* , pp. 1-29.

(8)   Ashok Gulati, K. G. (2011, January 13). Agri-reform to tame food inflation. *The Economic Times, New Delhi* .

(9)   Ashok Gulati, S. J. (2013, February). Farm trade: tapping the hidden potential. *Commission for Agricultural Costs & Prices, Discussion Paper No. 3, Department of Agriculture and Cooperation, Ministry of Agriculture, GoI, New Delhi GOI,* , pp. 1-29.

(10)   Ashok Gulati, S. S. (2013, April). Taming food inflation in India, Discuyssion paper No. 04. *Commisssion fore agricultural cost and prices, Department of agriculture and cooperation, Ministry of agriculture, GoI, New Delhi* , pp. 1-32.

(11)   Ashok Gulati, T. K. (1999). Trade Liberalization and Indian Agriculture. New Delhi: Oxford University Press.

(12)   Basu, K. (2011, January 20). India's Food grain Policy: An Economic Theory Perspective. *Economic & Political Weekly, vol. XLVI No 5* , pp. 37-46.

(13)   Bathla, S. (2012, February 23-24). Volatility in Agriculture Commodity Prices in India:Impact and Macroeconomic and Sector-Specific Policy. *123rd EAAE Seminar, Dublin* , pp. 1-16.

(14)   Beinhocker, D. F. (2007, May 19). Next big spenders: India's middle class. *Mckinsey Global Institute* .

(15)   Braun, J. v. (2008, December). Food and Financial Crises: Implications for Agriculture and the Poor. *International Food Policy Research Institute* , pp. 1-17.

(16)   Bullard, J. (2011, July-August). Measuring Inflation: The Core Is Rotten. *Federal Reserve Bank of St. Louis Review, 93(4)* , pp. 223-33.

(17)   C.R.Kothari. (2009). Research Methodology (Methods & Techniques). *New Age International Publishers* , pp. 122-123.

(18)   Chand, R. (2010, February 27). Understanding the nature & causes of food inflation. *Economic & Political weekly,Vol. XLV No. 9* , pp. 10-13.

(19)   Chand, R. (2005). Whither India's Food Policy. *Economic & Political Weekly 40(11): 1055-62* .

(20) Chhibber, A. (2013, October 5). *India's inflation puzzle: Not just a matter of supply but also of demand.* Retrieved from http://www.business-standard.com/article/opinion/ajay-chhibber-india-s-inflation-puzzle-not-just-a-matter-of-supply-but-also-of-demand-113100500622_1.html.

(21) Christopher Adam, D. K. (2012, December). Food Prices and Inflation in Tanzania. *African Development Bank Group, Office of the Chief Economist, Working Paper No. 163* , pp. 1-30.

(22) DBResearch. (2010, February). The middle class in India: Issues and opportunities. *Deutsche Bank Research* , pp. 1-8.

(23) Dev, S. M. (2010). Rising Food Prices and Financial Crises in India: Impact on Women and Children and Ways of Tackling the Problem. *Institute for Human Development- UNICEF Working Paper Series No. 3* , pp. 1-55.

(24) Elizabeth Frazao, M. A. (2007, September). Food Spending Patterns of Low-Income Households. *United States Department of Agriculture, Economic Research Service, Economic Information Bulletin No. 29-4* , pp. 1-8.

(25) Elumalai Kannan, S. S. (2011). Analysis of Trends in India's Agricultural Growth. *The Institute for Social and Economic Change,Bangalore, Working Paper 276* , pp. 1-25.

(26) ESCAP. (2011, March). Rising food prices and inflation in the Asia-Pacific region: causes, impact and policy response. *Macroecomic Policy and Development Division, Policy Briefs No. 7,* , pp. 1-8.

(27) Francisco H. G. Ferreira, A. F. (2011, May). Rising Food Prices and Household Welfare: Evidence from Brazil in 2008. *The World Bank, Policy Research Working Paper Series 5652* , pp. 1-43.

(28) Gabriel A. Huppe, S. S. (2013, January). Food Price Inflation and Food Security: A Morocco case study. *The International Institute for Sustainable Development (IISD)* , pp. 1-80.

(29) GoI. (2011-12). *Economic survey 2011-12.* Retrieved from Ministry of Finance, Governemnt of India: http://indiabudget.nic.in/es2011-12/estat1.pdf

(30) Gokarn, S. (2011, August). Striking the Balance between Growth and Inflation in India. *RBI Monthly Bulletin* , pp. 1253-1262.

(31) Gosh, J. (2011, March 16). Retrieved from eastasiaforum: http://www.eastasiaforum.org/2011/03/16/food-inflation-in-india/

(32) Idrees. M., A. M. (2012, April). Welfare impacts of food price inflation in Pakistan. *International Food Research Journal 19(4)* , pp. 1517-1531.

(33) IFPRI. (2008, May). High Food Prices: The What, Who, and How of Proposed Policy Actions. *International Food Policy Research Institute* , pp. 1-12.

(34) Ila Patnaik, A. S. (2011, April 16). How Should Inflation Be Measured in India? *Economic & Political Weekly, Vol XLVI No. 16* , pp. 55-64.

(35) *Indian Express.* (2012, March 25). Retrieved from http://www.indian express.com/news/daily-foodgrains-availability-rises-by-over-25-g-in-2011/928186/.

(36) J.K.Sachdeva. (2011). Business Research Methodology. *Himalaya Publishing House* , pp. 154-155.

(37) J.K.Sachdeva. (2011). Business Research Methodology. *Himalya Publishing House* , pp. 156-175.

(38) Janak Raj, S. D. (2008). Imported Inflation: The Evidence from India. *Reserve Bank of India Occasional Papers, Vol. 29, No. 3* , pp. 69-117.

(39) Janak Raj, S. M. (2011, September). Measures of Core Inflation in India: An Empirical Evaluation. *Department of Economic and Policy Research, RBI working paper series* , pp. 1-31.

(40) Jha, R. (2006, September). Inflation Targeting in India: Issues and Prospects. *Political Economy Research Institute,* , pp. 1-38.

(41) John M. Ulimwengu, R. R. (2009, July). How Does Food Price Increase Affect Ugandan Households? *International Food Policy Research Institute, Discussion Paper 00884* , pp. 1-28.

(42) Johnson, K. H. (2008, July 7). Food Price Inflation. *A Maurice R. Greenberg Center for Geoeconomic Studies Working Paper* , pp. 1-28.

(43) Josef L. Loening, D. D. (2009, February). Inflation Dynamics and Food Prices in an Agricultural Economy: The case of Ethiopia. *Gotheborgs Universitet, Working Paper in Economics No. 347* , pp. 1-58.

(44) Khalid, A. Y. (2011). Food inflation in India. *International Conference on Information and Finance, IPEDR Vol. 21* (pp. 42-46). Singapore: LACSET press.

(45) Khundrakpam, J. K. (2012, December). Estimating Impacts of Monetary Policy on Aggregate Demand in India. *RBI Working Paper Series, Department of Economic & Policy Research : 18/12* , pp. 1-20.

(46) Kumar, P. (2001). Agricultural performance and productivity. In S. A. Chaudhri, *Indian Agricultural Policy at the Crossroads.* New Delhi: Rawat Publications.

(47) Kumari, R. (2013, February). Food inflation in India: Present scenario. *International Journal of Social Science & Interdisciplinary Research, ISSN 2277- 3630, Vol.2 (2)* , pp. 49-58.

(48) Lahiri, H. (2012). Food inflation in India and role of middlemen: The case of speculative buffering and governemnt intervention. *Developing country studies, ISSN 2224-607X, Vol. 2, No. 01* , pp. 53-62.

(49) Luis A.V. Catao, R. C. (2010, June). World Food Prices and Monetary Policy. *IMF, Research Department, Working Paper No. 161* , pp. 1-66.

(50) Mahabub Hossain, F. N. (2005). Food Security and Nutrition in Bangladesh: Progress and Determinants. *Journal of Agricultural and Development Economics, Agricultural and Development Economics Division (ESA) FAO, Vol. 2, No. 2* , pp. 103-132.

(51) Michael Debabrata Patra, J. K. (2013, July 16-17). Post-Global Crisis Inflation Dynamics in India: What has changed? *India Policy Forum, NCAER, India International Centre, New Delhi* , pp. 1-69.

(52) Min Bahadur Shrestha, S. K. (2012). The Impact of Food Inflation on Poverty in Nepal. *Nepal Rashtra Bank Economic Review* , pp. 1-14.

(53) Mittal, S. (2010, January). Application of the quaids model to th e food sector in India. *Journal of quantitative economics, Vol. 08 No. 1* , pp. 42-54.

(54) Mittal, S. (2008, March 14). Demand-Supply trends and projection of food in India. *Indian council for economic research on international, Working paper No. 209* , pp. 1-20.

(55) Mittal, S. (2006, August 30). Structural shift in demand for food: Projections for 2020, Working paper No. 184. *Indian council for research on International economic relations (ICRIER),* , pp. 1-35.

(56) MoF. (2012-13). Mid-Year Economic Review 2012-13. *Ministry of Finance, Government of India* .

(57) Mohanty, D. (2011, August 13). Changing inflation dynamics in India. *Speech delivered at the Motilal Nehru National Institute of Technology (MNNIT), Allahabad, Reserve Bank of India* , pp. 3-4.

(58) Mohanty, D. (2013, January 31). India Inflation Puzzle. *Speech delivered in the function of Late Dr. Ramchandra Parnerkar Outstanding Economics Award 2013 at Mumbai* .

(59) Mohanty, D. (2012, November 9). The importance of inflation expectations. *delivered a speech at S.P. Jain Institute of Management & Research, Mumbai* , pp. 1-11.

(60) Naveed Ahamad Lone, D. (2013). Inclusive Growth and Food Inflation: An Analysis of their Nullification Effect. *Global journal of management and business studies, ISSN 2248-9878 Volume 3, Number 6* , pp. 633-638.

(61) Niimi, Y. (2005, May). An Analysis of Household Responses to Price Shocks in Vietnam: Can Unit Values Substitute for Market Prices? *Poverty Research Unit at Sussex (PRUS), Department of Economics, University of Sussex, Working Paper No. 30* , pp. 1-60.

(62) P&BD. (2010, December 31). Focus: Food inflation in India. *Corporate Planning and Economic Studies, Ecconomy Mirror, Vol. 17* .

(63) Paul R. Masson, M. A. (1997, October). The scope for Inflation Targeting in Developing Countries. *IMF, Research Department, Working Paper No. 130* , pp. 1-53.

(64) Pons, N. (2011, September 23). Food and prices in India: Impact of rising food prices on welfare. *Centre de Sciences Humaines, Delhi* , pp. 1-33.

(65) Prachi Mishra, D. R. (2011, October 31). Explaining inflation in India: The Role of Food Prices. *NCAER* , pp. 1-83.

(66) Pradeep Agrawal, D. K. (2012). Food price inflation in India: Causes and cures. *Institute of Economic Growth, Working paper no. 318,* , pp. 1-27.

(67) Praduman Kumar, P. P. (2009, July-December). Demand Projections for food grains in India. *Agricultural Economics Research Review, Vol. 22* , pp. 237-243.

(68) Praduman Kumar, S. M. (2006). Agricultural Productivity Trends in India: Sustainability Issues. *Agricultural Economics Research Review, Vol. 19,* , pp. 71-88.

(69) Raghav Gaiha, V. S. (2005, November). Foodgrain Surpluses, Yields and Prices in India. *Global Forum on Agriculture: Policy Coherence for Development* , pp. 1-23.

(70) Rahman, A. (2012, September). Characterizing Food Prices in India. *Indira Gandhi Institute of Development Research, Mumbai* , pp. 1-30.

(71) Rajmal, S. M. (2009, August). Transmission from International Food Prices to Domestic Food Prices- The Indian Evidence. *Department of Economic Analysis & Poicy, RBI Staff Studies,* , pp. 1-38.

(72) Rakshit, M. (2009). India admist the global crisis. *Economic & Political Weekly, 44(13)* , pp. 94-106.

(73) Ramesh Chand, P. S. (2011, February). Managing food inflation in India: Reforms and policy options, Policy brief 35. *National Centre for Agricultural Economics and Policy Research, New Delhi* .

(74) Ramya. (2011, January 24). DBS Group Research. *India- Food inflation demand driven* , pp. 1-2.

(75) RBI. (2010-11). Annual Report 2010-11. *Governement of India* , p. 2.

(76) RBI. (2011-12). Annual Report 2011-12. pp. 32-33.

(77) RBI. (2006-07). *Handbook of Statistics on Indian Economy 2006-07.* Retrieved from http://rbidocs.rbi.org.in/rdocs/publication/PDFS/690.

(78) RBI. (2011-12). *Handbook of Statistics on Indian Economy 2011-12.* Retrieved from http://rbidocs.rbi.org.in/rdocs/publication/PDFS/232 .

(79) Reiko Miskelly, S. C.-K. (2011, March). Food Price Increase in the Pacific Islands. *UNICEF Pacific Working Paper* , pp. 1-25.

(80) S.K.Goyal, J. (2001, July 8-13). Demand versus supply of food grains in India: Implications to food security, . *13th International IFMA congress of farm mangement on "Feed the world-please the consumer-maintain the environment" held at Wageningen, The Netherlands* , pp. 1-20.

(81) S.L.Gupta, H. G. (2011). SPSS 17.0 for researchers. *International book house pvt. ltd., New Delhi* , p. 142.

(82) Shukla, R. (2011, September 26). Changing Consumption Basket. *The Economic Times* .

(83) Shukla, R. (2011). *National Council of Advance Economic Research (NCAER).* PTI Interviewer.

(84) Singh, P. (2011, May 10). Inflation in India: An Empirical Analysis. *ISAS Working Paper No. 121* , pp. 1-13.

(85) Sitikantha Pattanaik, G. N. (2011, Sepetember). Why Persistent High Inflation Impedes Growth? An Emperical Assessment of Threshold Level of Inflation for India. *RBI Working Paper Series, Department of Economic and Policy Research* , pp. 1-17.

(86) Soumyatanu Mukherjee, P. C. (2012, August). Reasons and Impact of Soaring Food Prices in India. *GRP International Journal of Business and Economics, Vol. 1 No.2* , pp. 64-86.

(87) Steindel, R. R. (2007, December). A Comparison of Measures of Core Inflation. *Federal Reserve Bank of NewYork, Economic Policy Review* , pp. 19-38.

(88) Stephen G Cecchetti, R. M. (2008, December). Commodity prices and inflation dynamics. *BIS Quarterly Review* , pp. 55-66.

(89) Sthanu Nair, L. M. (2012, May 19). Food price inflation in India (2008-2010), A commodity-wise analysis of the causal factors. pp. 46-54.

(90) Sthanu R Nair, L. M. (2011, September 3). Wheat price inflation in recent times: Causes, lessons and new perspectives. *Economic & Political Weekly, XLVI No. 36* , pp. 58-65.

(91) Subbarao, D. (2011, November 22). The Challenge of Food Inflation. *At the 25th Annual Conference of the Indian Society of Agricultural Marketing at Hyderabad* , pp. 1-26.

(92) Tom Capehart, J. R. (2008, April 10). Food Price Inflation: Causes and Impacts. *CRS Report for Congress* , pp. 1-6.

(93) Torres, M. J. (2013, August 4-6). The Impact of Food Price Shocks on the Consumption and Nutritional Patterns of Mexican Households. *Agricultural & Applied Economics Association's 2013 AAEA & CAES Joint Annual Meeting, Washington, DC* , pp. 1-22.

(94) Vagias, W. M. (2006). Likert-type scale response anchors. *Clemson International Institute for Tourism & Research Development, Department of Parks, Recreation and Tourism Management, Clemson University* .

(95)   Vaid, A. (2006). *India Profiles: Consumer Incomes & Spending Patterns.* Retrieved from www.atulvaid.com.

(96)   Venkitaramanan, S. (2009, December 28). *How not to tackle food inflation.* Retrieved from http://www.thehindubusinessline.com/todays-paper/tp-opinion/how-not-to-tackle-food-inflation/article1072627.ece.

(97)   Vishwakarma, R. k. (2012, Feruary-March). Future Scenario of Foodgrains: A Case Study for Gap between Demand and Supply. *indiastat.com* , pp. 1-8.

(98)   Vivek Moorthy, S. K. (2011, January). Rising Food Prices and India's Monetary Policy. *Indian Institute of Management, Bangalore, Working Paper No. 325* , pp. 1-30.

(99)   Walsh, J. P. (2011, April). Reconsidering the Role of Food Prices in Inflation. *IMF working Paper/11/17* , pp. 1-22.

(100) Worako, T. K. (2009, June). Analysis of Changes in Food Consumption pattern in Urban. *7th International Conference on the Ethiopian Economy* , pp. 1-28.

(101) Zikmund, W. G. (2010). Business Research Methods. *Cengage Learning, New Delhi* , p. 65.

CHAPTER 9: ANNEXURE

Chapter Highlights:

9.1   Glossary of Terms

9.2   Questionnaire

9.1 GLOSSARY OF TERMS

1) **Inflation:** It is the persistent rise in the general price level of goods and services in an economy.

2) **Food inflation:** It is the persistent rise in the price of food articles included in the Wholesale Price Index over time.

3) **Reference Period:** The consumption of any good by a household or person and consumption expenditure on it occurs in the form of flow over time. Since, the research is based on the analysis of the data from various secondary sources, the period between 2006-2011 is considered as reference period.

4) **Household consumption expenditure:** The expenditure incurred by a household on domestic consumption is the household's consumer expenditure.

5) **Household:** A group of person normally living together and taking food from a common kitchen constitutes a household.

6) **Household size:** The size of a household is the total number of persons in the household including adults and children.

7) **Middle class household:** A family having an annual household income in the range of Rs 3.4 Lakh to Rs 17 Lakh (at 2009-10 price levels) is termed as middle class household.

8) **Lower middle class household:** A family having an annual household income in the range of Rs 3.4 Lakh to Rs 10 Lakh (at 2009-10 price levels) is considered as lower middle class household.

9) **Food composite:** It refers to the combined primary food articles and food products contributing to food inflation.

10) **Seekers:** It refers to the section of the population which belongs to lower middle class.

11) **Strivers:** It refers to the section of the population which belongs to upper middle class.

12) **Deflation:** Deflation is a condition of falling prices. It is just opposite of inflation. In deflation, the value of money goes up and prices fall down. Deflation brings a depression phase of business in the economy.

13) **Disinflation:** Disinflation refers to lowering of prices through anti-inflationary measures without causing unemployment and reduction in output.

14) **Reflation:** Reflation is a situation of rising prices intentionally adopted to ease the depression phase of the economy. In reflation along with rising prices, the employment, output and income also increase until the economy reaches the stage of full employment.

15) **Stagflation:** Paul Samuelson describes Stagflation as the paradox of rising prices with increasing rate of unemployment.

16) **Stagflation:** Paul Samuelson describes Stagflation as the paradox of rising prices with increasing rate of unemployment.

17) **Stagnation:** Stagnation is the rate of economic growth which may be a slow or no economic growth at all.

18) **Statflation:** The term' Statflation' was coined by Dr. P. R. Brahmananda to describe the inflationary situation of India. According to Brahmananda, rising prices in the middle of recession is known as Statflation.

9.2 QUESTIONNAIRE

Date: _____

Dear Respondents,

As a part of **PhD research**, we are conducting a survey of middle class households in Thane city to understand the impact of high food inflation on their consumption expenditure on food articles and how they manage their consumption expenditure on food articles alongside high food inflation. You are kindly requested to answer the questions in Part I, Part II and Part III of Questionnaire.

Name of the Respondent: _____

Address: _____

_____**City:** _____

Disclosure: The identity of the respondent will not be disclosed to anybody and the information gathered from him/her will be used for research purpose only.

Instructions: The respondent has to **tick mark (✓)** in the box given below the questions to select the option of his/her choice.

PART I: PERSONAL DETAILS

1) **How many members are there in your family including adults and children?**

Number of Adults						Number of children						Total no. of members									
1	2	3	4	5	6	1	2	3	4	5	6	1	2	3	4	5	6	7	8	9	10

2) **What is your present average annual household income (in Lakh)?**
   Below 3.4 Lakh ☐   Above 3.4 Lakh & below 10 Lakh ☐
   Above 10 Lakh & below 17 Lakh ☐   Above 17 Lakh ☐

3) **What is the source of income in your family?**
   Only Service ☐   Only Business ☐   Both Service & Business ☐

4) How many earning members are there in your family?

One ☐ Two ☐ Three ☐ Four ☐

Conditions applied: If the members in the family are **4 or more**; the average annual income of the household is between **3.4 Lakh to 10 LaKh** (lower middle class); the source of income is **service**, then the respondent need to proceed to answer the questions in **PART II & PART III.**

PART-II: QUESTIONS RELATED TO IMPACT OF HIGH FOOD INFLATION ON CONSUMPTION EXPENDITURE

Sr. No.	Research Questions	Impact on Consumption Expenditure					Options
		1	2	3	4	5	
1)	To what extent your household consumption expenditure on food articles gets affected?						
2)	To what extent your household consumption expenditure on food grains gets affected?						1-Not at all affected
3)	To what extent your household consumption expenditure on vegetables gets affected?						
4)	To what extent your household consumption expenditure on fruits gets affected?						2- Somewhat affected
5)	To what extent your household consumption expenditure on milk gets affected?						3- Neutral
6)	To what extent your household consumption expenditure on non-veg. gets affected?						4- Moderately affected
7)	To what extent your household consumption expenditure on condiment & spices gets affected?						5- Highly affected
8)	To what extent your household consumption expenditure on Tea gets affected?						
9)	To what extent your household consumption expenditure on coffee gets affected?						

PART-III (A): QUESTIONS RELATED TO MANAGING THE IMPACT OF HIGH FOOD INFLATION ON CONSUMPTION EXPENDITURE IN TERMS OF QUANTITY

Sr. No.	Research Questions	Impact on Consumption Expenditure Quantity-wise					Options
		1	2	3	4	5	
1)	Do you feel that your household consumption expenditure on Food grains gets affected in terms of quantity alongside high food inflation?						**1**-Strongly Disagree **2**- Disagree **3**- Can't say (Neither agree Nor disagree) **4**- Agree **5**- Strongly Agree
2)	Do you feel that your household consumption expenditure on Vegetables gets affected in terms of quantity alongside high food inflation?						
3)	Do you feel that your household consumption expenditure on Fruits gets affected in terms of quantity alongside high food inflation?						
4)	Do you feel that your household consumption expenditure on Milk gets affected in terms of quantity alongside high food inflation?						
5)	Do you feel that your household consumption expenditure on Non-veg. gets affected in terms of quantity alongside high food inflation?						
6)	Do you feel that your household consumption expenditure on Condiment & spices gets affected in terms of quantity alongside high food inflation?						
7)	Do you feel that your household consumption expenditure on Tea gets affected in terms of quantity alongside high food inflation?						
8)	Do you feel that your household consumption expenditure on Coffee gets affected in terms of quantity alongside high food inflation?						

PART-III (B): QUESTIONS RELATED TO MANAGING THE IMPACT OF HIGH FOOD INFLATION ON CONSUMPTION EXPENDITURE IN TERMS OF QUALITY

Sr. No.	Research Questions	Impact on Consumption Expenditure Quality-wise					Options
		1	2	3	4	5	
1)	Do you feel that your household consumption expenditure on Food grains gets affected in terms of quality alongside high food inflation?						1-Strongly Disagree 2- Disagree 3- Can't say (Neither agree Nor disagree) 4- Agree 5- Strongly Agree
2)	Do you feel that your household consumption expenditure on Vegetables gets affected in terms of quality alongside high food inflation?						
3)	Do you feel that your household consumption expenditure on Fruits gets affected in terms of quality alongside high food inflation?						
4)	Do you feel that your household consumption expenditure on Milk gets affected in terms of quality alongside high food inflation?						
5)	Do you feel that your household consumption expenditure on Non-veg. gets affected in terms of quality alongside high food inflation?						
6)	Do you feel that your household consumption expenditure on Condiment & spices gets affected in terms of quality alongside high food inflation?						
7)	Do you feel that your household consumption expenditure on Tea gets affected in terms of quality alongside high food inflation?						
8)	Do you feel that your household consumption expenditure on Coffee gets affected in terms of quality alongside high food inflation?						

PART-III (C): QUESTIONS RELATED TO MANAGING THE IMPACT OF HIGH FOOD INFLATION ON CONSUMPTION EXPENDITURE IN TERMS OF FREQUENCY OF CONSUMPTION

Sr. No.	Research Questions	Impact on Consumption Expenditure Frequency-wise					Options
		1	2	3	4	5	
1)	Do you feel that your household consumption expenditure on Food grains gets affected in terms of frequency alongside high food inflation?						
2)	Do you feel that your household consumption expenditure on Vegetables gets affected in terms of frequency alongside high food inflation?						1- Strongly Disagree
3)	Do you feel that your household consumption expenditure on Fruits gets affected in terms of frequency alongside high food inflation?						2- Disagree
4)	Do you feel that your household consumption expenditure on Milk gets affected in terms of frequency alongside high food inflation?						3- Can't say (Neither agree Nor disagree)
5)	Do you feel that your household consumption expenditure on Non-veg. gets affected in terms of frequency alongside high food inflation?						
6)	Do you feel that your household consumption expenditure on Condiment & spices gets affected in terms of frequency alongside high food inflation?						4- Agree
7)	Do you feel that your household consumption expenditure on Tea gets affected in terms of frequency alongside high food inflation?						5- Strongly Agree
8)	Do you feel that your household consumption expenditure on Coffee gets affected in terms of frequency alongside high food inflation?						

www.ingramcontent.com/pod-product-compliance
Lightning Source LLC
Chambersburg PA
CBHW080244290526
45790CB00005B/1698